CARING
FOR
ELDERLY PARENTS

CARING
FOR
ELDERLY PARENTS

Juggling Work, Family, and Caregiving in
Middle and Working Class Families

Deborah M. Merrill

AUBURN HOUSE
Westport, Connecticut • London

Library of Congress Cataloging-in-Publication Data

Merrill, Deborah M., 1962–
    Caring for elderly parents : juggling work, family, and caregiving
in middle and working class families / Deborah M. Merrill.
        p.   cm.
    Includes bibliographical references and index.
    ISBN 0–86569–269–6 (alk. paper)
    1. Aging parents—Care. I. Title.
HQ1063.6.M47   1997
306.874—dc21   96–45347

British Library Cataloguing in Publication Data is available.

Library of Congress Catalog Card Number: 96–45347
ISBN: 0–86569–269–6

First published in 1997

Auburn House, 88 Post Road West, Westport, CT 06881
An imprint of Greenwood Publishing Group, Inc.

Printed in the United States of America

∞™

The paper used in this book complies with the
Permanent Paper Standard issued by the National
Information Standards Organization (Z39.48–1984).

10 9 8 7 6 5 4 3 2

Copyright Acknowledgments

The author and publisher gratefully acknowledge permission to reprint the following as chapter 4:

Merrill, Deborah M. (1996). "Conflict and Cooperation among Adult Siblings during the Transition to the Role of Filial Caregiver." *Journal of Social and Personal Relationships* 13 (3): 399–413.

*This book is dedicated to
the caregivers who have so generously
shared their lives with me.*

Contents

Contents

Acknowledgments

The completion of this manuscript would not have been possible without the assistance of many individuals. I would first like to thank my colleagues in the Sociology Department at Clark University who have provided unwavering support over the years. Chairpersons Bruce London and Robert Ross have always been there when I needed their assistance. Marc Steinberg and Patricia Ewick have lent advice and friendship to a novice faculty member, while Shelly Tenenbaum was even willing to read earlier drafts of several of the chapters. Joseph Roidt picked up much of the slack during his first year of teaching while I took a semester sabbatical to complete this book. I have been very fortunate to work in an atmosphere of such camaraderie and good will. Finally, Sarah Barry has expertly taken care of administrative work for me over the years.

I am also indebted to Clark University for granting me a pre-tenure sabbatical of one semester to work on this manuscript without interruption. Ensconced in a library carrel for the winter and spring of 1996, I worked without distraction (except for that of my own creation). As a result, the members of my department taught larger courses and advised my students. I am grateful for their assistance.

Two of my students, Zoe-Maja Engvall and Jennifer Berner, also provided valuable research assistance. Zoe and Jen were always very professional and dependable, and I am thankful for their help.

I am most indebted, however, to my family. My husband, Ken Basye, and I have gone through graduate school and our pre-tenure years at Clark together. Without his love and encouragement, I am not sure I would have endured. Often picking up more than his fair share of the household maintenance and dog care and standing by with encouragement during even the worst of moments, I could not ask for a better partner. I am also grateful to my mother, Nancy Merrill, for her encouragement and to Gracie for her unconditional friendship. Friends, old and new, Liliane Floge and Laurie Porter, have also been there to listen during the high and low points of my career.

My thanks also go to the many students at Clark who make me feel fortunate to be a professor and, of course, to the caregivers who were willing to tell me their stories. Without them, this book would not be possible.

CHAPTER 1

Introduction

I have to be to work at 8:30. I get to my mother's house in the morning and there is shit everywhere. She is soaked. The bed is soaked. Sometimes I yell at her, "Look what you have done! Look what you have done." But I get her cleaned up and dressed, and I throw a load of clothes in. . . . I am thinking about them all day at work. Sometimes I call to check on them. . . . When I get a minute, I try to do their paperwork. But I have to take a day off just to renew my father's license. This is one and a half jobs, and I can't work any less. I can't be tired. . . . Still, I leave work early to go over and make their dinner. I dry the clothes. . . . I don't get home until 6:30 and I am still thinking about work and about them. Then there is my family. . . .

Adult children who care for frail, elderly parents are pressured daily trying to juggle the responsibilities of work, family, and caregiving. The statistics inform us of the number of hours of care they provide, the degrees of stress they are under, and how frequently caregivers have to quit their jobs or give up caregiving. Yet these statistics do not tell the story from the caregiver's perspective. They cannot adequately explain how caregivers manage to work and care for their parents simultaneously or why they provide care despite all of their competing obligations. The purpose of this book is to go beyond the statistics to describe the caregiving experience for "just plain folk" (as one woman called herself), middle and working class caregivers, using the caregivers' own words. I will begin with an overview of the literature.

THE NATURE OF FAMILY CAREGIVING

Despite the popular misconception that formal institutions have replaced the family as the main source of care for the elderly, substantial evidence suggests that families provide multiple forms of support and assistance across and within generations, including care for the elderly (Connidis, 1994; Gallagher, 1994; Lee, Netzer, and Coward, 1994; Rossi and Rossi, 1990; Stone, Cafferata, and Sangl, 1987; Walker and Pratt, 1991). In fact, families provide between 80 and 90 percent of the overall care of elders living in the community, including for example, medically related care, personal care, household maintenance, transportation, and shopping (Day, 1985; Kane and Penrod, 1995). It has been estimated that as many as 5.1 million noninstitutionalized older persons receive at least one form of such aid from family and friends (Toseland, Smith, and McCallion, 1995).

Providing care for an elderly family member is usually done for an extensive period. In a national survey of family caregivers, researchers found that while nearly half (44 percent) of the caregivers assisted between one and four years, 20 percent provided care for five years or more. Similarly, two-thirds (67 percent) contributed one to four hours of care per day, while fully one-quarter (25 percent) furnished five or more hours on an average day. Consistent with such lengthy caregiving, 75 percent of caregivers shared living arrangements with the elderly relative. In addition, family caregivers were predominantly female (72 percent). Wives provided the bulk of care to their husbands, while daughters provided care to widowed mothers (Stone, Cafferata, and Sangl, 1987).

Caregivers assist with a wide array of tasks (Kaye and Applegate, 1990; Koch, 1990). In the earlier stages of caregiving, the caregiver may help with shopping/transportation or household tasks (referred to as instrumental activities of daily living), while more advanced impairment requires assistance with personal care, such as feeding, bathing, dressing, or toileting (referred to as activities of daily living). Two-thirds of caregivers assist with at least one of these tasks (Stone, Cafferata, and Sangl, 1987). Most primary caregivers have at least one helper; the majority of these helpers also provide hands-on assistance (Penrod, Kane, Kane, and Finch, 1995).

Despite the extensive commitment that caregiving entails, many adult children will become caregivers. Brody (1985) was one of the first to note that caregiving was a "normative family stress," suggesting that caregiving was a typical role in the life course. Himes (1994) also found that parental caregiving was common. According to her estimates, over half of middle-aged women (45 to 49 years of age) with a surviving parent could expect to provide care to their parent at some point in the future.

Caregiving is also common among those who work outside of the home. According to results of employee surveys, between 23 and 32 percent of the workforce has elder care responsibilities (Neal, Chapman, Ingersoll-Dayton, and Emlen, 1993; Scharlach and Boyd, 1989; Wagner, Creedon, Sasala, and Neal, 1989). Such estimates, however, do not take into account those caregivers who must quit their jobs in order to provide care and thus may underestimate the extent of employees who provide care. In contrast to these findings, Rosenthal, Matthews, and Marshall (1991) found in a study of Hamilton, Ontario residents that only a minority of adult children provided parent care and that it was not typical or normative.

Caring for an elderly family member is likely to become more common in the future. As the members of the baby boom enter older age and as life expectancy increases, the need for elder care will also increase. Currently, those 85 years of age and older are the fastest growing segment of the population (*Aging in America*, 1991; Kinsella, 1995). Similarly, the anticipated increase in life expectancy will mean that elders will require care over a longer period of time (increases varying depending on the rates of morbidity and mortality decline) (Himes, 1994). At the same time, lower levels of fertility will mean that adult children will have fewer siblings to depend on when their parents become elderly, thus increasing the chance that they themselves will provide the bulk of care alone (Aldous, 1994). In addition, the noted trend toward deinstitutionalization of all but the most medically needy (Gaumer and Stavins, 1992; Mor et al., 1988; Shaughnessy and Kramer, 1990) also means that there will be more elderly people left in the community who require care. Finally, increases in women's labor force participation, high levels of divorce, and increases in geographical mobility will all result in an increased difficulty in providing elder home care as adult children become less available (Aldous, 1994; Cantor, 1993; Maugans, 1994). Thus, just as the need for caregiving increases, barriers to providing care will also increase. This emphasizes the importance of considering a caregiver's policy (based on an examination of the needs of caregivers) in order to plan for the future.

WHO WILL BE THE CAREGIVER?

Certain characteristics increase the likelihood that one family member will become the primary caregiver or the person with the main responsibility for care. While married elders tend to receive care from their spouses, nonmarried elders are more likely to name their children as their primary caregivers (Chappell, 1991). Primary caregivers are more likely to be female members of the family versus male members (e.g., daughters versus sons), geographically proximate, and only children. In like manner, the caregiver role tends to fall to the person with the fewest competing responsibilities, including obligations to one's own spouse or children, employment, or being a caregiver for another family member (Brody, 1990; Stern, 1996; prior research: Horowitz and Dobrof, 1982; Ikles, 1983; Lang and Brody, 1983; Stoller, 1983; Stueve and O'Donnell, 1989).

Prior family history also affects the likelihood of becoming a caregiver. According to earlier research, an interruption in the parent-child relationship had a significant effect on later caregiving arrangements. Being separated from one's mother before the age of 18 decreased the likelihood of providing care for her. In contrast, being separated from one's father in the same time frame increased the likelihood of caring for one's elderly *mother* (Dwyer and Henretta, 1994). This implies that separation from one's father increases one's ties and later obligations to one's mother but not vice versa. This is consistent with findings that although adult children of divorce perceived relationships with both mothers and fathers to be of lower quality, the effect was generally two to three times greater for fathers (Webster and Herzog, 1995).

Researchers have extensively explored the characteristics that increase the likelihood of becoming a caregiver, but less is known about *how* one becomes a caregiver or the changes throughout the caregiving career. We do know that for some caregivers, severe impairment in the elder precedes the start of caregiving (Albert, Moss, and Lawton, 1993). This would suggest that caregiving often begins quite suddenly. In contrast, others have found that a period of sporadic assistance or aid-giving preceded entry into the self-defined career of caregiving (Dwyer, Henretta, Coward, and Barton, 1992; Walker and Pratt, 1991). But under what conditions does either prevail? In addition, many aspects of the self-defined entry of the caregiving career have not been explored, such as whether or not caregivers nominate themselves for caregiving or whether they are selected by other family members and under what conditions. In this book, I examine the different pathways caregivers take in becoming a caregiver so that we can better understand the inception of the role as part of the overall caregiving career. It is important to investigate how a caregiving career begins since it is likely to have important implications for how the career course develops.

Once caregiving begins, it is not static, although definitive stages can be differentiated along the caregiving career. Pearlin (1992) found that at least three stages constituted the careers of many caregivers: residential caregiving, institutional placement, and bereavement. Within each stage, there are particular patterns and courses of events. In this book, I explore these changes in much greater detail, within the stage of residential or community care, in order to see how being a caregiver evolves over time.

ADULT CHILDREN AS CAREGIVERS

Most studies of caregiving differentiate spousal from filial care, focusing on one group or the other (Abel, 1991; Brody, Kleban, Johnsen, Hoffman, and Schoonover, 1987; Coward and Dwyer, 1990; Matthews, Werkner, and Delaney, 1989; Spitze and Logan, 1990b; Stueve and O'Donnell, 1989). This is due to the differences in the caregiving roles and experiences between the two groups, including, for example, the greater likelihood of competing obligations for children such as their own nuclear families and job responsibilities. Such obstacles to caregiving not only decrease the likelihood of being a caregiver but also substantially alter the nature of caregiving. Thus, not separating the populations would likely obliterate any observable patterns one might find for either group.

The prevalence of adult children as providers of assistance, ranging from emotional support to medical and personal care, has been widely documented over the last decade (Brody, 1985, 1990; Dwyer and Coward, 1991; Montgomery and Kamo, 1989; Mui, 1995; Stoller, 1983, 1990; Stone, Cafferata, and Sangl, 1987). More than one-third of older people who need help carrying out at least one activity of daily living (i.e., eating, bathing, dressing, toileting, getting in and out of bed, and indoor mobility) depend on a child for this assistance (Aldous, 1994). According to the National Long Term Care Survey, 37 percent of family caregivers were adult children compared to 36 percent who were spouses (Stone, Cafferata, and Sangl, 1987). In fact, adult children are the main providers of care for widowed mothers, while wives are the main providers of care for their husbands (Coward, Horne, and Dwyer, 1992).

GENDER DIFFERENCES

Over the last decade, researchers have extensively explored potential gender differences in the provision of care to elderly parents (Montgomery, 1992). Among the more well-known findings is the greater likelihood that daughters serve as primary caregivers in comparison to sons (Coward and Dwyer, 1990; Spitze and Logan, 1990; Stoller and Pugliesi, 1989; Stone, Cafferata, and Sangl, 1987). The key to an older, unmarried person receiving help is having at least one daughter. (Having additional children of either gender does not increase the probability of receiving assistance, although it may increase the total amount of assistance; see Spitze and Logan, 1990.) In contrast, sons tend to be caregivers only in the absence of an available female sibling (Horowitz, 1985b). In addition, daughters spend more hours per week providing care than do sons (Montgomery and Kamo, 1989). As a result, daughters experience a higher level of emotional strain from caregiving (Mui, 1995).

Daughters also perform different caregiving tasks. For example, daughters are more likely to assist with household chores and personal care tasks (Cantor, 1983; Horowitz, 1985b; Kramer and Kipnis, 1995; Matthews and Rosner, 1988; Montgomery and Kamo, 1989; Noelker and Townsend, 1987; Stoller, 1983, 1990). More specifically, daughters are 3.22 times more likely than sons to provide assistance with activities of daily living (i.e., eating, bathing, getting in and out of bed, indoor mobility, dressing, and toileting) and 2.56 times more likely to provide assistance with instrumental activities of daily living (e.g., household chores, transportation, running errands, and managing finances) (Dwyer and Coward, 1991). In comparison, sons are more likely to perform home repair and maintenance (Coward, 1987; Stoller, 1990). More generally, daughters provide routine care over long periods of time, while sons assume supportive roles that require shorter time commitments and that result in their being peripheral helpers (Matthews and Rosner, 1988; Montgomery and Kamo, 1989; Stoller, 1990).

In addition to providing less overall care, sons receive more assistance (both formal and informal) with their caregiving efforts. According to prior research, male caregivers were more likely to utilize formal services (Wright, 1983), for one of several reasons: sons may feel less capable of assuming certain tasks, such as household chores and personal care, and thus are more likely to ask for help; or they may more often be referred for assistance by medical and social services as well as by family. As for informal assistance, sons are more likely to rely on the support of their own spouses when providing care (Horowitz, 1985b). Sons do not necessarily receive more help from sisters since they are more often secondary helpers when sisters are available.

Lee, Dwyer, and Coward (1993) explained the greater tendency for daughters to be caregivers, in part, by taking into consideration the gender of the care receiver. They found that adult children were more likely to provide care to a parent of the same gender and that infirm elders were more likely to receive care from a child of the same gender. Thus, because a substantial majority of parents requiring care from children are mothers, there is a greater tendency for daughters to be caregivers. Related to this finding, Lawton, Silverstein, and Bengtson (1994) found that while sons and daughters provided assistance to mothers equally, sons were more likely than daughters to provide help to fathers. Although the authors referred to the assistance as being "hands on," they included activities such as running errands and helping with repairs. They stated that the gender difference in providing assistance to fathers may have been due to the fact that some activities divided along gender lines, such as home and car repair. It is not clear, however, why fathers would need more assistance with home repair than mothers.

It is expected that gender differences are also in part due to different gender role expectations within the family. Matthews (1995) found that in families in which there was only one sister, family members assumed that the sisters were the family caregivers based on cultural assumptions of gender-appropriate roles. Even when brothers and sisters divided responsibilities evenly, both siblings viewed the sister as being in charge. The services that brothers provided were seen as being less important. Walker (1996) concurred that the high prevalence of daughters as caregivers is normatively based on stereotyped beliefs about the debts children owe to their parents and the expectations regarding appropriate gender roles.

Although researchers have extensively explored gender differences in the likelihood of becoming a caregiver and in the types and amounts of care that sons versus daughters provide, additional gender differences in the course of the caregiving career are likely. It is important to understand gender differences since they may have important implications for the probability of institutionalizing a parent prematurely, experiencing strain, and needing formal assistance as the caregiving career progresses. As such, this study considers gender differences in how children become caregivers (i.e., the pathways to becoming a caregiver), how they accommodate their work to caregiving, and how their caregiving careers change over time. Given prior differences, it is expected that sons will become caregivers as a last resort, while daughters will pursue additional pathways. Daughters are expected to be more willing to accommodate their work to caregiving and to continue to provide care even if it interferes with their work.

I also examine differences in how sons versus daughters attempt to involve their siblings in caregiving and how they perceive their siblings' lack of assistance. It is important to understand these differences in the general study of sibling interaction in later life. Given our cultural assumptions that women are the main providers of care, it is expected that daughters will be less likely to receive assistance from siblings, especially brothers, while being more likely to accept the situation as normative. It is expected that sons will be more insistent that their siblings, especially sisters, help out and more likely to express their annoyance if they do not. Implications for sibling relationships are discussed.

CHILDREN-IN-LAW

Less is known about daughters-in-law and sons-in-law as caregivers to the elderly. We do know, however, that the integral role of daughters-in-law is not matched by the involvement of sons-in-law (Brody and Schoonover, 1986; Kleban, Brody, Schoonover, and Hoffman, 1989). In comparison to daughters, daughters-in-law are less likely to become caregivers and provide less overall care, although they assist with as many tasks and are as likely to designate themselves as the primary caregiver (Merrill, 1993). In addition, daughters-in-law do not expect to be involved in the care of in-laws as long as a daughter is available, although they are willing to provide backup care (Cotterill, 1994).

We also know little about affinal relations (related through marriage rather than blood ties) in later life families. Although in-law relationships have been characterized as both strangers and family simultaneously (Cotterill, 1994), we do not know whether or how this might change as the history of the relationship lengthens. The implications of the role of daughters-in-law as caregivers will help to shed new light on the meaning of affinal kinship.

In this study, I continue to investigate the role of daughters-in-law as caregivers. In particular, I document how they become caregivers, how they share caregiving tasks with their spouses and their spouses' families, and the meaning caregiving has for them. The differences between daughters and daughters-in-law are emphasized to more fully explore the role of the daughter-in-law and the implications of the in-law relationship for family roles and obligations.

SIBLING NETWORKS

In investigating the role of the caregiver, researchers too frequently consider the contributions of each caregiver in isolation (Kahana, Kahana, Johnson, Hammond, and Kercher, 1994). However, caregiving is often done by several family members. At least some of the research reveals that adult children often mobilize to form a caregiving network, taking into account one another's constraints and potential contributions in organizing to provide all of the elder's needs (Coward, 1987; Coward and Dwyer, 1990; Matthews and Rosner, 1988).

It is important for those who work with caregiving families to understand how siblings can successfully share care and for siblings who are trying to share care to see how other families do so. Researchers have not considered, however, how siblings manage to form these networks when they do exist. Therefore, in this study, the following questions are asked. Do siblings have to be pushed into sharing caregiving responsibilities, or do network members volunteer for the role? In families in which one person does assume the bulk of care, does that caregiver try to engage available siblings in participating? If so, what measures does the caregiver take? How do siblings respond? And finally, how does this conflict affect one's relationships with siblings?

There is some evidence that primary caregivers are reluctant to give up control of their caregiving responsibilities. In examining the division of labor between primary and other providers, researchers found that the pattern of cooperation was one of supplementation rather than cooperation. Other helpers assisted in the same care tasks as the primary caregivers, particularly when the burden of care was greater (Stommel, Given, Given, and Collins, 1995). This research, however, included spousal caregivers among the primary caregivers and both formal and informal helpers. It is expected that when receiving assistance from siblings, adult children providing care will not only be more likely to share care, but will also want assistance from siblings. This is because as adult children, the caregivers will feel less obligated to provide care totally by themselves than perhaps spousal caregivers. In addition, children will feel more comfortable sharing care with other family members of equal status than with formal helpers or more distant relatives.

COMPETING RESPONSIBILITIES

Although significant numbers of adult children do become caregivers and provide extensive care, they often do so at great sacrifice and against enormous odds. Between 1950 and 1989, the percentage of all women in the labor force (working for pay or looking for work) increased from about 34 percent to 57 percent. And just prior to this study, more than 70 percent of all women between the ages of 18 and 50 (the ages of adult children) were in the labor force (Ferber and O'Farrell, 1991). As the main providers of family care, the increasing number of women working has meant that more caregivers are also employed outside of the home. Current estimates suggest that anywhere between one-quarter and one-third of the workforce also takes care of an elderly parent outside of work (Neal, Chapman, Ingersoll-Dayton, and Emlen, 1993). Not surprisingly, employment outside of the home has often been cited as one of the inhibitors of caregiving (of both the likelihood of caregiving and the extent of care provided), as well as being negatively affected by the caregiver role (i.e., caregiving resulting in people accommodating work) (Lang and Brody, 1983; Olson, 1989; Stone and Short, 1990; Stueve and O'Donnell, 1989).

While we know the numbers of caregivers who are employed and vice versa, to date no one has asked just how caregivers manage to fulfill both roles simultaneously. Therefore, this study focuses on the strategies that caregivers employ to work outside of the home while also caring for frail elderly parents. I also examine the caregivers' perceptions of important accommodations that employers make so that work and caregiving are compatible and the accommodations possible in different types of jobs. Understanding these issues is central in constructing policy initiatives in the workplace.

Obligations to one's own family also compete with the caregiver role. Married daughters provide less overall care themselves (Brody, Litvin, Albert, and Hoffman, 1994). Some evidence also exists that the presence of minor children imposes a significant burden for "women in the middle," resulting in daughters feeling pulled in separate directions by elderly parents versus children (Brody, 1990). As for the reciprocal effect, it appears that caregiving has a negative effect on marital satisfaction, but primarily when husbands do not offer emotional support (Suitor and Pillemer, 1994). In this study, I examine in greater detail how caregiving affects the caregiver's own family, investigating both spouses' and children's reactions. I also examine how caregivers involve their families in caregiving, if at all. Such topics have received little attention.

CLASS STATUS

In any investigation of elder care, it is important to consider the context of the family system and its characteristics, including class status. Class, as defined by the occupational statuses of the heads of family, family income, and education (Kerbo, 1991; see also Appendix), significantly determines relationships within the family and the focus of family life. Since this study examines middle and working class families, I begin with a general discussion of the known differences between these two groups.

Working Class

Working class, or blue collar families, never seem to have enough money (Rubin, 1976, 1994). Tracked into unskilled and semiskilled positions (including service workers, factory operatives, and construction workers), opportunities for career mobility are limited (Langman, 1987). While some positions are better remunerated than others (such as more highly skilled construction work), earnings rates peak early and prior to the family's increased needs, such as when children are adolescents and parents require care (Oppenheimer, 1981). Lack of sufficient resources then affects the resources and types of assistance that family members can provide one another.

Social interaction in the working class is more local in orientation and more narrow in scope than in the middle class (Gardner, 1991). That is, middle class families place more emphasis on friendships and broader social networks, while working class families report higher rates of kin interaction, particularly for the wife's relatives, and interact with friends outside of the family less frequently (Allan, 1979, 1989; Gardner, 1991). This is due to the close proximity of kin, scarce financial resources, and an orientation that is more traditional and less open to new experience (Myers and Dickerson, 1990; Reiss, 1981). Other researchers have also noted higher rates of mutual helping activity among low-income family members, the result of economic scarcity (Brady and Noberini, 1987; Mutran, 1985; Myers and Dickerson, 1990).

In addition, working class women express a stronger family ideology vis-à-vis work roles than professional and middle class women. Although working class women still express relatively high levels of work enjoyment, their families are more important. In contrast, professional and middle class women emphasize work and its centrality to their lives. Working class women are more likely to have rigid work schedules that make it hard to integrate work and family (Burris, 1991).

In part to prepare their children for jobs in which they too will be in the lower rungs of a career chain, working class parents stress conformity, obedience, and authoritarianism in raising their children (Langman, 1987).

To differentiate themselves from the "lower classes," working class families stress respectability and traditional values. This is best exemplified by Rubin's (1976, 1994) findings that blue collar families were very strict with their children and allowed for little personal freedom. As such, young adult children were quick to leave home in order to gain the autonomy and privacy they lacked in their parents' home (whether through pregnancy, as was often found in Rubin's 1976 study, or more frequently in 1994 through beginning their own working class jobs). In addition, fathers stress a traditional masculine ideology in raising their sons, consistent with the overall gender division of labor and authority (Langman, 1987).

In Rubin's (1994) followup study, she found that the recent recession had only continued to exacerbate problems for working class families. Over one-third (35 percent) of the men had experienced episodic bouts of unemployment. Frustrated by low-paying jobs and mounting bills, over half (56 percent) of the families she originally surveyed had divorced. Still holding on to traditional values and a gender division of labor, husbands were embarrassed that their wives worked while the women themselves were haunted by the belief that they should be at home. Fragile family bonds were further threatened as families were pressed for time due to the multiple roles that wives assumed.

Middle Class Families

Based in part on higher levels of education, middle class families enjoy more stable incomes. Their positions range from lower echelon bureaucratic functionaries to small proprietors and midlevel managers. Consistent with the needs of their positions, their values emphasize personal autonomy, the ability to develop and carry out rational plans, and a high degree of individualism and independence. As such, parents are less likely to resort to physical punishments but instead use reasoning and a withdrawal of rewards to discipline children (Eshleman, 1994; Langman, 1987).

Middle class families also emphasize the ideal, at least, of an equality of status between men and women. As such, they are less likely to espouse a gender division of labor (Eshleman, 1994; Hochschild, 1989). Women are more likely to give work a high priority (versus family) due to structural advantages, such as job flexibility and available child care, which make work and family compatible. Middle class parents are more likely to stress autonomous achievement for both sons and daughters (Eshleman, 1994; Langman, 1987).

The middle class family is more child-oriented than the working class family. Relationships with children are egalitarian and reciprocal. Parental warmth facilitates attachment to the family network in comparison to the authoritarianism and hierarchy of parent-child relations in the working class (Langman, 1987).

Class Differences in Later Life

These class differences continue into later life families. In a classic study of twenty-seven working class and fifty-three middle class households in Cleveland in 1956, Sussman found that 100 percent of middle class and 93 percent of working class families had been involved in either the giving or receiving of interfamilial assistance in the last month. Nearly half of the adult children had helped their parents during an illness, accounting for 92 percent of the reported illnesses in the past twelve months (Sussman, 1988). However, middle class families provided one another with more financial aid (in terms of the amount exchanged), valuable gifts, care of children, and advice (both personal and business). Help during illness was provided equally, and for both groups the flow of financial aid was from parent to adult child (Sussman, 1988).

Other researchers have demonstrated higher levels of intergenerational contact in working class than in middle class families. Hill (1970) found that working class men engaged in more intergenerational contact than white collar men. Cantor (1975) also found that the lower the social class, the greater the extent of supportive relationships, as measured by both the frequency of interaction and the amount of help given and received.

Class differences also persist into caring for elderly parents. According to a review by Horowitz (1985a), lower class caregivers were more likely to live with the elder and to provide direct care. Similarly, Archbold (1983) found that women of higher economic status and in socially valued career positions were more likely to be career managers who identified resources and managed their parents' care versus care providers who provided direct care. Hoyert (1991) attributed this finding to the close proximity of working class families, while others (Abel, 1990; Glazer, 1993; Walker, 1983) attributed it to a lack of financial alternatives.

While higher socioeconomic status decreased the likelihood of one's self providing actual physical care (what we normally think of as caregiving), other researchers have found that having financial resources did increase the likelihood of providing financial gifts or procuring services. Less educated children endorsed weaker norms of obligation for parents than more highly educated children (Lawton, Silverstein, and Bengtson, 1994). This likely reflected the greater financial capability of more educated children to fulfill the responsibility of supporting older parents.

Such differences persist throughout the world. In a review of sixteen countries at different stages of development, Kosberg (1992) concluded that, although impoverished families had fewer resources to share with elderly relatives, they upheld more traditional values of family caregiving. More affluent families provided only a perfunctory role in family caregiving. Throughout the world, wealthier families were more likely to purchase alternative lodging and care for elderly family members.

Discussions of class differences in social support are not without debate. While many researchers, like those cited above, argue that social networks in the lower social classes are extensive (Sokolovsky and Cohen, 1981), others believe that lower class standing is associated with diminished social support (Krause, 1991; Krause and Borawski-Clark, 1995; Turner and Marino, 1994). They found, for example, that elders from the lower social classes had less contact with friends, were less satisfied with support, and provided support to others less frequently (Krause and Borawski-Clark, 1995). In addition, older adults in the lower classes were less likely to anticipate that others would help in the future, should the need arise (Murrell and Norris, 1991). These results pertain to relationships with others in general. It is argued here that when it comes to relationships between elderly parents and adult children, norms of family interdependence in the working class will result in greater support to parents. Much of the above research also includes the poorest families in which working class norms of assistance may not exist.

Whereas other studies of caregiving have focused on a cross section of the population (Abel, 1991; Kaye and Applegate, 1990), this study focuses on the experience of working class caregivers relative to that of middle class caregivers. The need to focus on the working class is due to the many differences in family behavior and values noted earlier. For example, we know that working class children have more contact with elderly parents and are more likely to provide direct assistance. But how do these norms continue to manifest differences in the caregiver role itself? Since this study focuses on those already providing care, it examines how class continues to affect dimensions of the role beyond selection of the caregiver. I ask, how do the lack of financial resources, expectation of providing care one's self, and family interdependence affect the caregiving role for the working class? Are working class caregivers more willing to volunteer for the role? How do they manage to accommodate caregiving with rigid work schedules? Are extended family more likely to provide assistance? These are among the many issues that are addressed.

As is clear from Rubin's (1976, 1994) studies, working class families are under extensive financial stress. As such, they have fewer options to purchase care as a substitute and are more likely to provide the care directly. This study examines whether this difference continues into the caregiving experience, so that middle class caregivers are also more likely to purchase *assistance* with their caregiving tasks. In addition, resources within the family are limited for buying necessary equipment or making structural accommodations to one's home for an elder to become co-resident. Accordingly, this study asks whether working class children are less likely to co-reside with the elder and investigates how they are able to pay for the expense of an additional person in the household when they do co-reside. Similarly, the stress within the family resulting from an unstable, and often insufficient, resource base is likely to cause strain on family relationships. Thus, is the impact of caregiving on the caregiver's own nuclear family more severe within the working class, and does the caregiver have a more difficult time finding other family members who will provide assistance?

In addition, working class families emphasize a strict gender division of labor, with a higher status given to male members of the family. How will this attitude then affect the participation of male members of the family? While Kaye and Applegate (1990) focused on men providing care (including two-thirds who were spouses), they did not consider how class affected the participation of men in general. This study addresses whether daughters have a more difficult time involving brothers, spouses, and other male members of the family in caregiving in working class families and the role of male members of the family in sibling networks.

Working class families also place a greater emphasis on family interdependence and authority to parents, while middle class families stress individual autonomy and independence. How will this difference then translate into their caregiving experiences? Despite the scarcity of resources, working class caregivers may not perceive of caregiving as a burden, particularly if they have fewer leisure and career mobility opportunities that conflict with family responsibilities (Eshleman, 1994). As such, working class caregivers may be more likely to volunteer for the role, whereas middle class caregivers will do so when no one else is available. Nuclear family members may also be less likely to object to the caregiver's involvement in the working class and may be better able to form sibling networks because of the emphasis on family versus individual achievement.

Finally, how will the flexibility, or lack of flexibility, of working class jobs affect caregiving? Low on the rung of a career hierarchy, working class caregivers are heavily dependent on the policies and attitudes of their employers. As such, this study investigates whether working class caregivers are more likely to quit their jobs to provide care, whereas middle class caregivers are more likely to accommodate their work and, if so, how? The accommodations that employers can make to ensure that work and caregiving are compatible are also considered.

Class differences in later-life families have received little attention. Thus, examining the above questions will make significant contributions to the study of social gerontology, for class status clearly has important implications for family life that extend into later life. It is also essential for those who determine social policy or who work with individual families to know what those class differences are to more effectively make changes.

ETHNICITY

Along with class, ethnic variations in family roles and responsibilities affect family caregiving. T. Johnson (1995) argued that while Anglo-Saxon families operated with a tradition of self-sufficiency and hyper-individualism, other ethnic groups were more likely to rely on one another in help-seeking. Among the various ethnic groups, Italian daughters and daughters-in-law, in particular, placed a strong emphasis on caring for elderly parents (C. Johnson, 1995). Intergenerational conflict may erupt, however, as children take on additional roles and responsibilities in the dominant culture (such as daughters having careers) which make it difficult to meet the cultural expectations of their parents for elder care.

Several of the families in this study were the first generations born in the United States, their parents having immigrated from Canada, Italy, France, or Ireland. In this work, ethnic variations in how family roles and responsibilities are defined and distributed, as well as cultural variation in help-seeking, are considered as they relate to the individual families. Also to be examined are the implications for children of trying to meet the expectations of their ethnic heritage when they conflict with the obligations of current American society.

THEORETICAL PERSPECTIVE

Studies of caregiving often focus on one particular point in the caregiver's life, the time in which they are providing care. Caring for an elderly parent affects and is affected by additional events in the life course, including prior caregiving or nurturing experiences. Caring for an elderly parent may be regarded as part of a series of nurturing activities across many women's lives. Additional roles that the caregivers may hold in their life courses, such as employment or parenting, also affect caregiving. Therefore, in order to fully understand the caregiving experience, one must take into account a life course perspective that promotes the examination of various transitions and interlocking trajectories such as work, health, and family that occur over the life span. In so doing, the life course perspective examines age-graded life patterns and how they are affected by the social institutions in which they are embedded and the historical changes that shape them (Elder, 1992; Hagestad and Neugarten, 1985; Winton, 1995).

A life course perspective emphasizes the importance of two main themes. First, social change is expected to produce change in individual life patterns. That is, caregiving (for example) is affected by the changes and events in the larger society (Elder, 1992; Hagestad and Neugarten, 1985). Thus, any examination of caregiving should take into account the impact of women's labor force participation (as more women work outside of the home) and changes in gender ideology of what is appropriate for men versus women with regard to family obligation.

The second theme emphasizes the cumulative patterns and role trajectories. Events in the life course are shaped by earlier experiences and in turn shape the life course. Thus, caring for an elderly parent is likely to be altered by earlier caring experiences and prior relationships with one's parents. The involvement of siblings and the caregiver's attempts to enlist their help will also be affected by prior family experiences and relationships (Elder, 1992; Hagestad and Neugarten, 1985).

In addition to being cumulative, a life course perspective emphasizes the interrelatedness of careers or role trajectories across the life span (Elder, 1992; Hagestad and Neugarten, 1985). One's work, family, and health careers are all interrelated. Changes in one produce changes in the entire trajectories of the others. Any examination of caregiving should therefore take into account how changes in the caregiving career affect work and other family roles and vice versa.

The life courses of family are also interrelated. Each generation is bound to the fateful decisions and events in the other's trajectory. As such, life transitions are contingent on those of other family members (Elder, 1992; Hagestad and Neugarten, 1985). The present research investigates how transitions in and out of the work role are dependent on the health career of an aging parent and how caregiving is dependent on the competing roles of other family members.

Other researchers have argued that to fully understand caregiving, it must be considered along three separate axes. These include a spatial axis that takes into account the key individuals and groups involved in caregiving, a temporal axis that includes the time frames relevant to caregiving, and a transactional axis that focuses on the processes involved (Kahana, Kahana, Johnson, Hammond, and Kercher, 1994). In examining the caregiving career, I discuss the changes within these three axes over time.

The timing of caregiving may also be in conflict with the historical context of other societal structures and institutions. As argued in this book, the difficulties and lack of resources for family caregiving are in large part a result of structural lag. That, is societal norms, institutions, and practices have not kept pace with the shifting realities of contemporary life (Riley, Kahn, and Foner, 1994), the aging of the population, and the increase in female labor force participation resulting in many caregivers working outside of the home. It is argued that we need a transformation of the workplace, offering greater flexibility in the time and timing of work to more easily integrate family needs (Moen, 1994). Greater resources and provision of social services are also necessary to meet the new circumstances of an aging population at a time when adult children have fewer available siblings to assist in caregiving as well as increasing obligations outside of the home.

PLAN OF THE BOOK

The purpose of this book then is to examine how "plain folk" manage caring for a frail, elderly parent while simultaneously working outside of the home. This analysis is done within the framework of a life course perspective that considers the context of other societal institutions and structures, such as health services resources for the elderly and gender role expectations within the family, the interrelatedness of role trajectories including work and caregiving careers, and the interdependence of the life courses of successive generations.

This research is based on fifty in-depth interviews with working and middle class caregivers. Additional family members were also interviewed when present in the home. Ten interviews were conducted with the care receivers, spouses of the caregivers, and their children. In addition, a subset of seventeen (out of twenty randomly selected) caregivers were reinterviewed eighteen to twenty-four months later to examine the caregiving career. See the Appendix for greater detail.

The outline for *Caring for Elderly Parents* is as follows: chapter 2 provides the reader with an understanding of what it means to be a caregiver. The activities of seven different caregivers who varied in the level and type of care that they provided are presented to show the range of caregiving circumstances and the high degree of involvement. Chapter 3 focuses on the different pathways by which children became caregivers and the salience of gender and the "in-law" relationship in determining which pathway a caregiver took.

Chapter 4 addresses the extent to which siblings formed caregiving networks and the conditions under which these networks existed. How caregivers attempted to involve their siblings and whether or not there was conflict are also considered. Gender and class differences are highlighted. Chapter 5 documents the effect of caregiving on employment. Special consideration is given to class differences in work and family accommodations and to the strategies that caregivers use to work during the day while simultaneously providing care.

Chapter 6 focuses on the stress of caregiving and the circumstances in which stress is greatest. Also considered are the implications of (and involvement in) caregiving for the caregiver's own nuclear family. Chapter 7 examines the effect of the in-law relationship on being a caregiver. In particular, the differences between daughters and daughters-in-law as caregivers are focused on in terms of the involvement of other family members, motivation for being a caregiver, impact on one's own nuclear family, and how the caregiving career might vary. A sufficient number of sons-in-law could not be located to compare with sons.

Chapter 8 focuses on the caregiving career and how the caregiver's role changed over time. Based on information from a subsample of the caregivers who were reinterviewed eighteen to twenty-four months after the initial study, the differences in tasks performed, assistance by other family members, and any changes in the use of formal services are examined. Chapter 9 summarizes the class, ethnicity, and gender differences, while chapter 10 focuses on the policy implications. Chapter 11 concludes the study with a discussion of implications for the state of the family.

CHAPTER 2

Illustrations of Caregiving

Earlier research on family caregiving provides descriptive statistics regarding the amount and type of care that caregivers provide. We know that nearly 80 percent of caregivers provide assistance seven days a week. While approximately half (47 percent) spend two or fewer hours per day on caregiving, one-quarter (25 percent) spend five or more hours per day, a significant amount of caregiving. Nearly half (44 percent) of caregivers have been caregiving for one to four years, while one-fifth had been caregiving for five years or more. Two-thirds of the caregivers (67 percent) assist with personal hygiene functions such as feeding, bathing, dressing, or toileting, while four out of five assist with household tasks (Stone, Cafferata, and Sangl, 1987). Thus, caregivers provide intensive forms of assistance for long periods of time.

Although these statistics provide an overall summary of caregiving in the aggregate, they do not offer detail on the daily lives of caregivers. The following illustrations are intended to describe what it means to be a caregiver. The examples are chosen to illustrate the variety of caregiving situations that family members may find themselves in. The caregivers who are detailed in this chapter are also referred to frequently throughout the text.

BRENDA: PROVISION OF PHYSICAL ASSISTANCE FOR MODERATE DISABILITY

Brenda and her husband, Tom, had four children between the ages of 8 years and 10 months. The children were very involved in sports and school activities. Brenda worked part-time in Customer Service for an insurance company. She was the primary caregiver for her mother-in-law, June, who could not walk on her own, dress, or bathe herself and who needed assistance around-the-clock. June, however, could feed herself and was continent. While Brenda provided care by herself during the day (except for when she worked), she and her husband shared care at night and on weekends. Brenda had been a caregiver for less than a year.

June had spent the previous winter in Florida when she had a stroke. She was living alone and had no relatives in the area. Tom and his siblings (two sisters and a brother, all of whom lived in the area) flew down to be with their mother during her initial medical treatment. Tom flew down a second time to make arrangements to have his mother sent back to their hometown. Once back home, June was in the hospital for several weeks and then in a rehabilitation center. Her physicians said that she would need 24-hour care and would probably never walk again. Tom did not want his mother to go into a nursing home. With his siblings unwilling to care for their mother in their homes, he volunteered his wife as caregiver during a family meeting.

Tom got June up in the morning and made her breakfast while Brenda readied their children for school. A visiting nurse came in the morning to dress and bathe June and then left her with Brenda for the day. June spent most of the day in a wheelchair, watching television and occasionally playing with the children. As part of her physical therapy, Brenda helped June walk back and forth to the bathroom rather than use the wheelchair. As often as every thirty minutes, Brenda walked her mother-in-law to the bathroom, helped to undress her, waited, dressed her, and then walked her back to her chair. This took anywhere between fifteen and twenty minutes and continued throughout the day. This was the primary source of ADL (i.e., activities of daily living, including eating, bathing, dressing, toileting, getting in and out of bed, and indoor mobility) assistance that Brenda provided.

At lunchtime, Brenda prepared her mother-in-law's meal but did not have to feed her. On the two days that Brenda worked, June attended an adult day health center. June paid for only part of this service, the remainder being subsidized by Elder Home Care. A van picked June up in the morning and dropped her off in the afternoon. Brenda also helped her mother-in-law to get in and out of the wheelchair in order to take a nap or to sit in another chair.

In the evening, a visiting nurse returned around 7:00 to get June ready for bed. Both of these visits by the nurse were covered by June's insurance. However, the nurses came at a time when Brenda was trying to get her own children fed and bathed in their small home.

> It gets crazy, especially on the days that I work. They are in the bathroom with June, so I can't give the kids a bath. I am trying to get them fed. It is hard having strangers in your house. Sometimes I get embarrassed.

Tom and Brenda divided their responsibilities so that Brenda got up with their children at night and Tom got up with his mother. In the beginning, Tom was waking up as often as seven times a night to take his mother into the bathroom. After only a few weeks of this, Tom installed a female urinal on his mother's bed so that he had to get up only two or three times. Brenda mentioned that days were most difficult for her when she had been up the night before with both her mother-in-law and her 10-month-old. At the end of the interview, Brenda confided, "I am not sure how much longer we will go on like this though. We have her on a waiting list at [a local nursing home]."

Although Tom had three siblings in the area, he and Brenda received very little assistance. After demanding several times from his sisters that they help more (to be discussed in chapter 4) one of his sisters sometimes took their mother for the weekend so that Tom and Brenda could spend time with their children. The other sister occasionally helped with the laundry but did not "offer" to do more. She was unwilling to have her mother stay with her overnight despite the fact that she lived in her mother's house. *Brenda's* sister actually came over to help care for the children so that Brenda could catch up on the housework.

Brenda felt that the main difficulty in being a caregiver at that point in her life course was that she also had four young children. "We just don't have enough time with the kids. We used to take them places on the weekend, now we can't. . . . They are just little once." She described caring for her children and her mother-in-law as both being very demanding. "It gets so crazy. . . . The other day I was taking her [mother-in-law] to the bathroom because she had diarrhea. My 10-month-old was chasing me. My 3-year-old was yelling that he was hungry. The older kids needed to be picked up."

In this example, Brenda provided a moderate level of assistance (primarily helping her mother-in-law in going back and forth to the bathroom and getting in and out of her wheelchair). June would have needed much more care from Brenda, however, if it were not for the extensive assistance that she received from visiting nurses and from her son, Brenda's husband. In the following two examples, elderly parents required greater physical care.

ABBY: PROVISION OF EXTENSIVE PHYSICAL CARE

Abby was a retired registered nurse with two grown children living on their own. Abby's husband was also retired. They had intended to travel together in their later years, but they had not been able to because of Abby's caregiving. Although Abby's husband had never voiced disapproval of her caregiving, he did not provide assistance beyond helping to lift his mother-in-law when she fell or otherwise needed to be carried.

Ten years ago Abby's mother, Grace, first became forgetful and could not be left alone. At that time, Abby's father was able to care for Grace. Several years later, Abby's father died in his sleep while her mother was having a bladder operation. Abby's oldest sister volunteered to take care of their mother during the week while Abby and her other two sisters alternated taking Grace for the weekend. At that time, Grace just needed assistance getting in and out of the bathtub and had to be watched so that she would not wander outdoors. This caregiving arrangement lasted until Abby's sister developed her own medical problems and could not do it alone. At the time, Abby had lost her job and was considering retiring early. Her other two sisters, who also provided weekend care, had retired as well. So she and her three sisters arranged to each care for their mother one week a month.

Abby's mother, Grace, required assistance with everything except eating. In the morning, she was usually thoroughly soaked because she was incontinent. So, the bedding had to be stripped and washed every day. This was relatively easy for Abby since her washer/dryer were on the same floor. For two of her sisters, who were in their early 70s, it was more difficult since their washer/dryer were on a lower floor and they were somewhat frail themselves. Grace also had to be cleaned every morning, but none of the sisters was able to get her into a bathtub anymore. So, Grace had a real bath only once a week at the adult day health center. Abby stated, "That is why we are trying to hold on so long to day care. Otherwise, we cannot wash her."

Because she was incontinent, Grace wore a diaper. Each of the sisters helped their mother into the bathroom, and occasionally she did relieve herself there. They did so because it was much easier and less offensive than changing her diaper. When Grace returned from day care, however, she was too tired to sit on the toilet so Abby and her husband carried her into bed, waited until she rested, and then carried her to the toilet. One of Abby's sisters did not have a bathroom on the first floor, so she kept a commode in her kitchen. According to Abby,

> I really feel sorry for her. Taking the dirty diaper off in the morning can be a wretched smell. To do it in the kitchen for so long, that is hard. My other sisters also have to keep her bed in their living rooms because they don't have a first floor bedroom. So my husband and I are lucky.

Grace required assistance in walking around the house. Abby held her mother's hands and walked backwards with her. Still, her mother fell quite often. Knowing that she would not be able to catch her, Grace tried to ease her mother's falls. Once she had fallen, however, Abby had to wait for her husband or call a neighbor to help lift her mother up.

Grace attended an adult day health center three days a week, and Abby felt that it was very taxing for her mother. Still, it was the only way that her mother could have a bath and she and her sisters could have a break. On the days that she was not at the center, Grace spent most of her time sleeping and recuperating.

Although Abby's mother spent a large part of the week at the day care center, being a caregiver was both physically and emotionally stressful for Abby. "By the end of the week, I am wiped out. When my mother is tired at the end of the day, we practically have to carry her in. With all the lifting and heavy work, I am exhausted."

For Abby, the most difficult part of caregiving was that she herself was easily taxed (being in her mid-60s), but her mother required extensive lifting and sometimes carrying. In addition, her mother often fell and had to be steadied as she walked. While Abby provided care only one week a month, it took her the other three weeks to recuperate. She was also concerned that she have adequate time when her grandchild was born to be able to care for him or her. Abby intimated that if she had to choose between caring for her mother or her grandchild, she would pick her grandchild since her mother had "lived her life already."

LIZA: PROVISION OF CARE FOR SEVERAL FAMILY MEMBERS

Like Abby, Liza provided extensive physical care with the coordinated assistance of her siblings and later, her daughter and nieces. Liza cared for her father for six years until he died and then her mother for two years. She and her older brother coordinated the care and told their siblings that they must help, with little or no resistance from them.

Liza's father first had a stroke in 1985. At that time, her mother "fell apart" and could not be relied on for either household maintenance or caregiving. Unable to care for himself, Liza and her five siblings moved their father back home (from the hospital) where he would be more comfortable. They divided the week into shifts for which each of them would be responsible. One of the brothers moved from another state to be closer to home. They fed their father, bathed him, changed his diaper, and kept him free of bed sores. At the time, he was unable to walk around even with assistance or to use a wheelchair. Liza stated, "If my father had been a son-of-a-bitch, we wouldn't have done it. But he was a good man. He always worked several jobs for us, to make ends meet. We wanted the best for him."

This went on for several years until Liza's father had a second operation, which left him dependent on a respirator. After a family meeting, Liza and her siblings decided that their father would not want to be on a respirator and gave his doctor a letter informing him of this. After several arguments with his physician, they took their father home, expecting him to live for only a few days.

Because of the medical equipment that their father was using, Liza and her brother hired several private nurses to care for him. They did not, however, cease to provide additional care and they continued to provide twenty-four hour coverage. After their father's savings began to dwindle, Liza's oldest brother suggested that they resume the care of their father alone. This included all that they had done before, as well as monitoring stomach tubes and other medical equipment. George had been watching what the nurses were doing, and believed that he and his siblings could provide the same skills. Only George, however, could handle the stomach tubes. At that time, they needed two family members for each shift. Liza spent all of her evenings, lunch breaks, and several nights a week at her parents' home while maintaining a full-time job as a nurse's aide. During this time, only three of her siblings were able to help, and her own husband was dying of cancer. This arrangement lasted six weeks until their father died.

While her father was sick, Liza's mother required some assistance with bathing and getting around indoors. At the time of the interview, she required help with dressing and using the toilet, although she could feed herself. Because they felt that their mother could not be left alone, Liza and her family continued to divide their mother's care over a twenty-four hour day. Two weeks after the interview, however, Liza's mother was placed in a nursing home due to progressive dementia. Liza said to her siblings, "On Thursday we are taking Ma to put her into a nursing home and we are all going to be there. We are all going to share the guilt of putting her there."

Liza has provided care for her children, both of her parents, her husband, and one of her sisters, who died of diabetes. When referring to the time that she cared for both of her parents and her husband simultaneously, she stated, "I was a bitch then. You ask anyone. . . . I had everyone praying for me." Her husband, who had a lung tumor, was able to manage on his own during the day and needed assistance only during the morning and evening. For Liza, being a family caregiver has been a lifetime activity.

These examples illustrate the kind of care that is required for elders suffering primarily from physical impairments. Dementia and cognitive deficits, however, result in different needs on the part of the elder. The following examples illustrate caregiving for a cognitively impaired parent.

CELIA: PROVIDING CARE FOR AN ALZHEIMER'S PATIENT

Celia's mother-in-law, Kay, was diagnosed with colon cancer two years prior to the interview. Unable to care for his wife alone and not comfortable with having paid help come into his home, Celia's father-in-law accepted Celia and Patrick's offer that the elderly couple move in with them. Later diagnosed with Alzheimer's disease, Kay required constant supervision.

During the day, Celia's father-in-law was primarily responsible for his wife while Celia and Patrick, the son, worked. However, Celia did take Kay to day care twice a week as well as to most of her doctors' appointments during the day. This was because Celia was better able to "handle" Kay when she refused to do what the doctor asked or made a scene in the hospital, and her father-in-law did not like driving in the city.

Kay was physically able to do most things for herself. Because of her Alzheimer's, however, she was not able to remember *when* or *how* to provide her own care. For example, unless someone monitored Kay's dressing, she would put on two tops and no pants. Or she might put her underwear on one leg and put her shirt on backwards. During a previous blizzard, the family was "at their wit's end" because they were afraid that she would burn the house down with candles. Celia said, "I practically kept her chained to me." For example, not knowing what to do when she could not flush the toilet, Kay covered her feces with a poinsettia. Thus, out of fear that she would hurt herself or others, someone from Kay's family stayed with her at all times.

Kay talked nonstop and repeatedly asked the same questions, but she could not complete sentences. As a result, talking with her was very frustrating. She wandered at night, but Celia and her family felt that it would be cruel and unsafe to lock her into her bedroom. So, they listened at night in fear. During the day, Kay went from room to room, getting into drawers and moving items to other rooms. "Nothing is ever where you left it. You never know where your things are. She rearranges every room." Kay also asked constantly to "go home" and who each of the family members was.

Celia felt sorry for Kay. She spoke of her mother-in-law as someone whom she loved and hated at the same time. Celia added,

> At night she will get this far-off look and she starts scanning the room. She doesn't know who we are or where she is. She tells us that she has to go home to her family. We tell her that we are her family, but you can tell that she doesn't believe us.

Celia's primary responsibility for Kay was in the evening when she got home from work and on the weekends. On the weekends, she shared that responsibility with her husband. Celia said that she must keep her mother-in-law within eyesight at all times. However, the only physical care that she provided was to help Kay to bathe and to be with her while she used the toilet. This was so that Kay did not "take care of things herself" (i.e., insert her finger into her anus). Celia also helped her mother-in-law to dress and undress. The most frustrating part for her was repeatedly answering the same questions and always having to be with her mother-in-law. For example, Kay would often ask where her husband was and how she could get to him. Celia would then have to take her by the arm and guide her through the house.

Celia resented the fact that her home could not be a happy place for her three adult children to visit. They also could not have many friends over because of Kay's appearance and incessant swearing. Although Patrick had three siblings (two of whom lived nearby), they did not help because of their mother's history of alcoholism [to be discussed in chapter 4].

Thus, although cognitive impairment did not require extensive physical assistance, it was still extremely stressful and as time-consuming as many instances of physical assistance. Parents' behavior was unpredictable, and assistance was often thwarted and unappreciated. Although adult children knew that their parents were not responsible for their behavior, they often could not recognize their parents as the people they had known all of their lives.

SUSAN: PROVIDING CARE FOR HER PHYSICALLY AND COGNITIVELY IMPAIRED MOTHER

Susan, the manager of a university bookstore, was divorced with an adult daughter still living at home. She had been providing care for her mother and father for a year and a half. Susan's mother, Elizabeth, was first diagnosed with Alzheimer's two and a half years ago. Her father, Howard, provided most of Elizabeth's care until he had a stroke a year and a half ago. From then on, Susan provided care for both.

Howard was fairly self-sufficient. Although he had some difficulty speaking (e.g., he could not remember some words), he was able to get around their apartment and to take care of his own physical needs. Elizabeth, however, required assistance with all six of the activities of daily living (eating, dressing, bathing, toileting, getting in and out of bed, and indoor mobility). Although she was capable of raising a fork or spoon to her mouth, she would try to eat too much and choke herself. So, usually Susan or Howard fed her. She could walk to the toilet with assistance, but was unable to control her urine and bowel movements and therefore had to wear a diaper. Like Abby's mother, both Elizabeth and her bedding had to be cleaned and changed every morning.

What Susan found most exasperating about her mother were not her physical impairments but her cognitive disabilities. Elizabeth repeatedly asked the same questions of both Susan and Howard. In addition, she was unable to remember things that she was told or asked to do. For example, Elizabeth repeatedly took things (such as canned items from cabinets) and moved them someplace else. When Susan or Howard looked for them, she could not remember where she had put them. Elizabeth also wandered at night. Her family was afraid that she would go downstairs into the street or set the house on fire by turning on the stove. To discourage the wandering at night, Susan and her father tried very hard to prevent Elizabeth from napping during the day. This ensured her sleep at night.

Although Susan did not live with her parents, she went to their house every morning before work to clean, bathe, and dress her mother. Irate at the extent to which her mother had soiled herself and her room, Susan often blew up at her mother in the morning. "The bed will be soaked, and she will be soaked. There will be shit everywhere. . . . I scream, 'Look what you have done. . . . ' Then I feel guilty." Before going to work, she would prepare her parents' breakfast and lunch and wash a load of clothes.

In the evenings, Susan would leave work early to make her parents' dinner and to finish their laundry. She also did their shopping and prepared her father's medications. On Saturday, she cleaned their home and took them for a drive. The only time that Susan had to herself was Sunday afternoon when her brother would care for her parents.

In Susan's case, caregiving was more exasperating because she was managing two homes. She commented, however, that her privacy and ability to have her own home were invaluable. Although some additional time was involved in caring for her father as well as her mother, Susan realized that she would not be able to care for her mother at home if her father were not there during the day.

Susan was the most frazzled of all the caregivers. Strained by the lifting and cleaning necessary from her mother's physical impairments as well as the emotional stress from her mother's cognitive impairments, Susan bore the demands of all aspects of caregiving. In addition, Susan managed two households while other caregivers reduced their overall work by having their parents move in with them. With no help from a spouse and limited assistance from her brother, Susan faced these challenges alone.

KATHY: PROVIDING MODEST CARE FOR A COGNITIVELY IMPAIRED PARENT

Kathy, the manager of a local store, usually worked sixty hours a week. She and her husband had no children. Kathy first asked her mother to move in with her a year prior when her conversations became confused and she would forget things, such as having turned on the stove. At that time, Kathy's father had recently died. Kathy's mother needed assistance mainly with dressing and bathing. In addition, her mother could not be left alone because she wandered outside and got lost.

Kathy's mother, Ann, was healthy enough to go to an adult day care center five days a week. At night, Kathy put out her mother's clothing for the next day and reminded her of what everything was. Then she helped her to undress and got her ready for bed. In the morning, Kathy woke her mother, helped her to bathe, and then helped her to dress. Although Ann needed someone to be with her at home, she did not need to be constantly "watched" like Celia's mother-in-law. Ann also asked many questions. Kathy believed, however, that her mother remembered when she told her the answer. Kathy stated, "Sometimes my mother gets confused and says, 'Where did Kathy go?' I say, 'I'm right here, Ma.' Then she says, 'Oh, that's right,' and she remembers."

The hardest part of caregiving for Kathy was coordinating fragmented care from her in-laws and paid help to cover the three hours each day when she was at work but her mother was not in day care. In addition, Kathy's expectations of her siblings' assistance were drastically undermined, and there had been extensive conflict in the family. These issues are addressed in chapters 4 and 5.

DOMINIC: A SON PROVIDING CARE

Dominic, a retired machine engineer, first cared for his father and then for his mother. When his father was ill, he needed to be bathed and changed as often as every ten minutes. According to Dominic, "My father demanded to be changed. No man wants to live like that. " Dominic continued this care for approximately a year until he could do it no longer, at which time he sent his father to a nursing home. Dominic believed that his father preferred to be in the nursing home because he knew that there were doctors and nurses there to help him. Dominic and his wife brought his father home for special occasions.

The main care that Dominic provided was to his mother who lived with him and his wife. Freeda required someone to be at home with her at all times. This was because she sometimes wandered off or forgot that she had turned the stove on. Dominic also helped his mother to dress and assisted her somewhat with indoor mobility. His wife did most of the cooking and cleaning but did not assist with caregiving tasks.

Dominic's main difficulty with caregiving, however, was that he had no time to spend with his wife or by himself. According to Dominic, they had to "beg, steal, and borrow" to get away. With his mother constantly around, Dominic said that they could not even hold hands together. In addition, his wife and his mother argued over how the house should be decorated. While Dominic and his wife had bought the house previously owned by his parents, his mother felt that it was still her home. Dominic said that his wife worked full-time because of the tension with his mother. He worried that she would divorce him because of his decision to care for his mother.

Dominic did not seem at all embarrassed by the fact that he assisted his mother with personal care. However, he did state that he would cease providing care when his mother became incontinent and that he considered it inappropriate for his wife to change his father because he was a man. Dominic also believed that he was not adequate company for his mother but instead that she needed other women to talk to. Dominic stated that he "had no life" himself due to his mother's dependency. Nevertheless, Dominic had retired early in part to fix up his parents' home and to care for them.

The above illustrations are intended to give the reader an idea of the vast array of caregiving situations and all that caregiving entails. Some of the caregivers lived with their parents (foregoing privacy), while others ran back and forth between their homes. While most of the children cared for only one parent, others actually provided care for two. Parents varied substantially in the type and amount of care that they required. Children seemed better able to cope with physical impairments. While this work was physically taxing, it was less frustrating for the caregiver. Caregivers for parents with Alzheimer's and other dementias reported extreme agitation. Although these caregivers often did not have to contend with incontinence and lifting the parent, they usually were with the parent constantly and responded to irregular behavior. With these backgrounds in mind, the following chapters examine the effect of caregiving on a number of aspects of the caregiver's lives.

CHAPTER 3

Becoming the Caregiver for a Frail Parent: Processes and Pathways

Despite the term *family caregiving,* not all members of the family actually become caregivers (Pratt, Schmall, and Wright, 1987; Snyder and Keefe, 1985; Spitze and Logan, 1990). In fact, certain characteristics increase the likelihood that one member of the family will become the more involved caregiver. "Primary" caregivers (usually defined as the person who has the main responsibility for the elder) are more likely to be female members of the family versus male members (e.g., daughters versus sons), geographically proximate children, and only children (Brody, 1990; Stern, 1996). Caregiving responsibilities usually fall to the child with the fewest competing responsibilities, including obligations to one's own spouse or children, work outside of the home, or being a caregiver for another family member (Brody, 1990). Stern (1996), however, argued that work responsibilities had no effect on a family's decision as to who would be caregiver. Instead, a family decides how to provide care based on the location of each family member, again pointing to the importance of proximity. Finally, favored children are often caregivers, while the child who feels rejected may attempt to *gain favor* by taking on the caregiver role (Brody, 1990).

Thus, while we know that certain demographic and social factors increase the likelihood of becoming the caregiver, we know less about the *process* by which children become caregivers. To date, Albert, Moss, and Lawton (1993) have investigated the role of the elders' impairment in the process of becoming a caregiver. They found that severe impairment in the elder preceded the start of caregiving. This would suggest that caregiving began definitively either after the onset of sudden chronic illness or after the accumulated buildup of several conditions that resulted in extensive impairments. In contrast, other researchers found that a period of sporadic assistance preceded entry into the self-defined career of caregiving (Dwyer, Henretta, Coward, and Barton, 1992). That is, they suggested that caregiving occurs more in spurts rather than at a definite starting point, as was implied by Albert, Moss, and Lawton (1993). Consistently, Walker and Pratt (1991) have argued that caregiving is an intensification of a preexisting pattern of aid-giving.

Robison, Moen, and Dempster-McClain (1995) also attempted to examine what they referred to as the different "pathways" that women born in different historical time periods followed in becoming a caregiver. In actuality what they examined were the different characteristics that increased the likelihood of becoming a caregiver rather than the process of becoming a caregiver. They found that in more recent cohorts, the size of the women's own families and whether or not they had sisters did not determine the likelihood of caregiving due to the increasing prevalence of caregiving. That is, even women with sisters cannot avoid becoming caregivers owing to the growing need for elder care. In more recent cohorts, even women with continuous employment histories must assume caregiving roles.

Whether caregiving begins sporadically or with a more definitive starting point, we must still address the separate question of how the process of selecting the caregiver occurs within the family. For example, do children step forth (i.e., volunteer) to become caregivers, or do other family members elect them? It is important to understand the pathways to becoming a caregiver, for they are likely to influence the remainder of the caregiving career and the experience of being a caregiver. For example, children who volunteer to be caregivers may be less likely to institutionalize a parent later in the caregiving career if they are taking on the role willingly. As such, the onset of the caregiving career is an important predictor of later life course events for both the caregiver and elder.

Also considered in this chapter is whether or not becoming a caregiver is a conscious decision. That is, is a decision made at a particular point in time, or does a person gradually become a caregiver without ever actually deciding to do so? Dwyer, Henretta, Coward, and Barton (1992) found that caregiving began sporadically. For those caregivers who gradually assume the role then, caregiving may not be a conscious decision but may instead occur without deliberation. In contrast, Albert, Moss, and Lawton (1993) found that caregiving began at the onset of severe impairment. For those family members who become caregivers as the result of a sudden need on the part of the parent, they may be making a conscious decision to be caregivers when that need arises.

Finally, this chapter addresses whether the process differs for daughters, sons, daughters-in-law, and sons-in-law. Given the literature on the gender differences in the amount and type of care that sons versus daughters provide, they will quite likely also differ in the process by which they become caregivers. Based on their involvement after they assume the role, daughters may be more likely to volunteer for the role, while sons may become caregivers by a process of elimination. That is, sons may become caregivers when no other available family members are available to be caregiver. As such, they are the "de facto" caregivers.

Studies in the life course describe the pathways in life (including work and family trajectories) along an age-differentiated, socially constructed sequence of transitions (Hagestad and Neugarten, 1985; Riley, Kahn, and Foner, 1994). Caregiving itself can actually be thought of as a career that may span the entire life course but is more often a shorter trajectory intersecting with other life course events. Caring for an elderly parent most often occurs in midlife but may well extend into late life. In addition, the pathway or transition to caregiving is a socially constructed family role. That is, the decision of who should be the caregiver and the process by which a family member is chosen to be caregiver differ according to family expectations, defined in part by class. As such, the pathway to caregiving should also vary by class. This chapter adds to our knowledge of the caregiving career by examining its initiation, the particular pathway one takes in becoming a caregiver. (The overall caregiving career is considered in chapter 8.)

PATHWAYS TO BECOMING A CAREGIVER

This section examines the various pathways by which adult children become family caregivers. The factors considered include who (if anyone) selected or volunteered the caregiver, particular circumstances in which the decision was made, and how the decision was arrived at when no one came forth (to volunteer or nominate another family member).

De Facto Selection

One of the most common pathways to becoming a caregiver was to be selected "de facto." Nearly one-third of the caregivers were selected this way (fifteen out of fifty). In this pathway, adult children assumed the role of caregiver because no one else was available or willing to assume the responsibility and the child saw no other alternative as feasible (such as nursing home placement). Thus, they were *left* assuming the responsibility. The decision was made, however, without the deliberations of a family meeting. This included three groups of children: (1) only children who believed that they had no other choice but to become a caregiver (16 percent; eight out of fifty); (2) those whose siblings were either not available or not adequate caregivers and who believed that they had no other choice (8 percent; four out of fifty); and (3) those who saw it as their sole responsibility to provide care despite other options (6 percent; three out of fifty).

Eight of the caregivers were only children who did not see nursing home placement as an option at the time. They therefore believed that they had no alternative in becoming caregivers. This included two out of the eight sons. For them and their wives, putting their mothers into a nursing home was not a "choice," at least at the time. Similarly, for only daughters, nursing home placement seemed like an offense to their parents. In addition, other family members (such as more distant kin) were considered to be less appropriate caregivers. To ask a more distant family member to provide care would be an admission of abandonment by the daughter (or son).

Four of the caregivers had siblings who were either not available or (in their opinion) not adequate caregivers. For example, two of the sons had siblings who lived on the west coast. Another caregiver believed that her siblings were unfit to care for their mother. She stated,

> Once when my mother's ankles were swollen and she couldn't walk, I called my brother over and asked him what he thought we should do. He said, "Leave her with me for the night, and I will take care of her with a pillow." I thought, "Great, why am I asking him for help?" . . . I called my sister when my mother turned 75 and asked her if she was ever going to call my mother. She said, "Why should I when she has you?" . . . They're not human enough to take care of my mother. So I figure I am in this by myself.

Susan, who seemed the most desperate and frazzled of all the caregivers, believed that her brother, who lived forty minutes away, was "out of the picture" in terms of being available because of his responsibilities to his own children. She stated, "My sister-in-law commutes two hours every day, so my brother picks up the slack with his kids. He helps them with their homework and things . . . so he can't help me." As a result of seeing her brother as unavailable to help and believing that a nursing home was not acceptable, Susan became a caregiver vis-à-vis the de facto pathway.

Finally, three of the daughters believed that they should be caregivers because they were the women of the family and, accordingly, it was their responsibility to provide care. According to Jody, "Well, I am the caregiver because I am the only girl. I know that sounds chauvinistic, but my brothers are uncomfortable. They don't know how. . . . They wouldn't even know how to take off her bra!"

Marie felt that caring for her mother was her responsibility because she was the oldest daughter. She said,

I am from a big Italian family—the oldest girl of nine. It is expected that the oldest son and daughter will take care of the parents. . . . Now I do most of what gets done or make arrangements. . . . This is how I was trained.

Daughters who were de facto caregivers because they felt that it was their duty as "girls" were more likely to come from working class backgrounds. All three daughters in this category were working class. One of the women was from a large Italian family; her parents were first generation. A second woman was also from a traditional family that adhered to a very strict gender division of labor. This emphasis on the separate responsibilities of male versus female members of the family is more common in working class families (Langman, 1987; Rubin, 1976, 1994). As such, working class women were more likely to "own" or feel solely responsible for the duties incorporated in their roles as daughters, including providing care for elderly parents.

A high proportion of the sons were de facto caregivers. Over half (five out of eight) of the sons were de facto caregivers compared to 24 percent (ten out of forty-two) of daughters and daughters-in-law (chi-square (1) = 7.0, $p < .01$). That is, sons became caregivers by a process of elimination rather than by being elected by another family member or volunteering. This is consistent with our cultural belief that kinkeeping, in general, is a woman's role. Thus, men became caregivers primarily when others were not available.

In general, children who became caregivers by a process of elimination (i.e., the de facto caregivers) did tend to be more "available" than their siblings. Their own children were grown, and their jobs were flexible so that they could either reduce their hours, work part-time, or even quit their jobs if they were near retirement. This is not to say, however, that such choices were made without sacrifices. In addition, these children were more likely to live close by.

Selection During a Family Meeting

Approximately 20 percent of the caregivers (ten out of fifty) were selected during a family meeting. While many of these meetings were set up (usually by the person who became the caregiver) at the onset of a medical crisis, others were called when there was a less pressing need for a change in care (such as when a child noticed a parent becoming forgetful). For these meetings to occur, at least one sibling had to be geographically proximate or willing to travel. Of the caregivers with siblings, all except two had at least one sibling within an hour's drive.

Family meetings were often called after an accident (such as a fall) or a sudden change in the parent's health status (such as a stroke or heart attack). Brenda's mother-in-law, June, was spending the winter in Florida when she had a stroke. Tom realized that his mother would not be able to live alone and that he and his siblings would have to make arrangements for some form of alternative care. Tom believed that it should be a joint decision with all his siblings, since it could theoretically affect them all. According to Brenda,

> My husband took the initiative to arrange a family meeting. His brother wasn't really involved enough to know what was going on with his mother. Tom's two sisters would just start crying every time you mentioned the stroke. So Tom made arrangements for everyone to get together. He told them [that] they *had* to come.

Family meetings were often called by the child who eventually assumed caregiving responsibilities. Whether because they were the oldest child or the child most willing to care for their parent, one child would take control of the situation in arranging a meeting (or several meetings). In situations in which siblings were sharing care, it was the child with the more commanding personality who would call family meetings.

Usually in these meetings, only one of the children was willing to care for his or her parent. That is, when the question of who would become caregiver was raised, other family members claimed that they were "unable." Consider Brenda's example:

> [During the family meeting], the other kids wanted to put her [June] in a nursing home. Tom's oldest sister said that she couldn't take her because she works. But her kids are grown and ours are still little. The other sister lives in her *mother's* house, rent-free. She isn't married; you would think that she would do it. But she says she can't because she works. Tom's brother told June that she could stay with him except that he lives alone

out in the country. Tom didn't want his mother to go into a nursing home, so he told his sisters and brother that his mother would come here. What could I say?

Other caregivers told similar stories of family meetings where siblings were unwilling to share the care because of their work. They often suggested institutionalizing the parent. In all cases, the child who was unwilling to have the parent go to a nursing home (although he or she also worked) would offer to become caregiver.

Family meetings, and the resulting conflict, often went on for several sessions before a decision was made. Sally called a family meeting with her three siblings when her mother wandered into a neighbor's yard at 2:00 A.M. She and her siblings met four times before it became clear that they could not agree on a care arrangement for their mother. Her siblings suggested a full-time nurse for their mother, locking her into her apartment, and nursing home placement, none of which was satisfactory to Sally. After their fourth meeting, Sally decided to take her mother into her home against her siblings' wishes.

In other families, care was divided equally during a family meeting. Liza's father first had a stroke in 1983. Although her mother was still alive, Liza did not believe that she would be able to care for her father. So Liza called a family meeting and told her siblings that their father needed constant care and that they were all going to have to help out. At that meeting, she and her siblings divided up care equally so that their father had twenty-four hour coverage. Since then, Liza had called other family meetings when there was a change in her father's health status. Perhaps because of their commanding personalities, it was usually she or her brother who took the initiative to arrange the meetings and coordinate the caregiving schedule. (This arrangement is discussed more fully in chapter 4.)

Three of the daughters-in-law (30 percent) spoke of their husbands' nominating them as caregivers during family meetings without their prior consent. Both Brenda's and Billie's husbands made the decision to care for their mothers in their homes (with the bulk of care being provided by their wives) during a family meeting. At these meetings, other siblings "made excuses" for why they couldn't do it, so both sons suggested their wives as caregivers. However, they believed that their sisters should have offered. Although neither wife objected, they had not been consulted beforehand. As Brenda intimated, "What could I say?" In contrast, the other sisters-in-law made the decision to be caregivers themselves.

Parent's Choice

One-fifth of the caregivers were actually selected by their parents (ten out of fifty). In these situations, the parent decided that they would prefer to be taken care of by one child rather than another or to living alone. In doing so, parents assumed that the chosen child would be willing and able to be a caregiver. In instances in which they were choosing among children, they perceived that several children were willing and available caregivers. This, however, was not always the case, as was explained by Deborah:

> Last Christmas he [my father] fell down the stairs and split his head open. His doctors told him that he couldn't live alone. He said that he would move in with his daughter without even asking me!! I was living in this one-bed-room apartment with my son, so I found this place and my father moved in. I thought that I was going to be able to go about my own business. Then about five days before I was going to move in, his doctor said, "You know that you will never be able to leave him alone?" Why didn't they tell me that before?! By then I had given up my apartment, and I couldn't pay for this alone. Besides, my father had spent $650 to move here. So, I was stuck.

In this situation, Deborah became the caregiver by (1) being chosen by her father and (2) being financially unable to reverse the process when she realized all that caregiving would entail. It is quite likely that Deborah would have relinquished her role as caregiver if she could have afforded to pay for her apartment on her own. By the followup interview, Deborah could not be located, although her father was still in an adult day health center.

Gladys's father also chose her to be the caregiver. In actuality, however, he was choosing to live in his own home. Since Gladys had always lived with her parents, she cared for her father as well. (Her mother was now deceased.) While her brother and sister were willing to have their father live at their house, Hank did not want to be a "burden" on his children. Hank, however, did not believe that he was a burden on his daughter.

Celia and her husband opened their home to Celia's in-laws at her father-in-law's request. He asked to live with them so that they would help to provide care for Kay, her mother-in-law, who had Alzheimer's.

> Two years ago, Kay was diagnosed with colon cancer and given only four to six months to live. My father-in-law was at his wits' end trying to take care of her. Our daughter was getting married, so we told them to stay after the wedding, for the summer. After they were here, my father-in-law realized that he would never be able to take her back. We do it to help out Dad. . . . As long as he wants to stay here, we will help out.

In other cases, the parents initially had some choice of where they wanted to live. For example, Billie's mother-in-law chose to stay with Billie (and Billie's husband) rather than her other son because her other son's house was both dirty and chaotic. Similarly, Mary's mother did not want to go to her son's home (but instead to Mary's home) because her son lived in a different neighborhood while Mary and her mother had lived for many years in the same neighborhood. In addition, Mary's brother had young children who bothered her mother. Neither of the two caregivers thought these alternative arrangements would have lasted very long if they had been tried.

Each of the five pathways to becoming a caregiver was followed by adult children from both middle and working class backgrounds. However, nearly all (80 percent, or four out of five) adult children who became caregivers as a result of their parent's choice were from the working class (chi-square (1) = 4.14, $p < .05$). Elderly parents in the working class may have felt that they had more of a choice in selecting a caregiver either because they had more children in the near vicinity or because there was an expectation of parental care. This latter interpretation is reinforced by the finding that siblings were more willing to assist the primary caregiver in the working class (see chapter 4.) It is also consistent with Archbold's (1983) findings that caregivers from lower socioeconomic backgrounds were more likely to provide care directly, while those from higher socioeconomic backgrounds were more likely to coordinate care but not to actually serve as a caregiver. Working class elders and adult children expected, and acted upon the expectation, that children would care for their parents.

"It Just Happened"

It was also quite common for the process of becoming a caregiver simply to evolve, whether due to co-residence or other circumstances. This occurred in eight out of the fifty cases (16 percent). In Frank's case, he had been a case manager for the state for many years when his mother first became ill. Because of his knowledge of the system, he had done a lot of "troubleshooting" for his mother. This included locating a wheelchair that would hold her, finding a visiting nurse who would tolerate his mother's "feisty" disposition, and helping his mother to secure an apartment in a building for seniors. Frank stated, "Then it just seemed like I was doing more and more, and she was asking for more and more. I had gotten so used to saying that I would take care of it, that I didn't know how to say no."

Thus, Frank's case was consistent with Walker and Pratt's (1991) findings that caregiving was an intensification of a preexisting pattern of aid-giving.

Children who co-resided with their parents also found that their role evolved into that of caregiver or that the process "just happened." As far as their siblings were concerned, co-residence incorporated caregiving responsibilities. As such, siblings were unlikely to offer any extensive assistance, and the child who lived with the parent reluctantly accepted the role of caregiver. Said one of the daughters:

> I am the caregiver because I was the one who was always around. My sister and I both work, but I have always lived with my parents. I used to live in their house, then I had some money to invest so I bought a house. . . . But I am the one that they always asked to do things, so when more needed to be done everyone thought that I should do it.

Many children made the decision to co-reside with parents before their parents required extensive care. Dominic and his wife bought his parents' home when his father could no longer manage the repairs. Shortly thereafter, his father got sick, and then his mother could not be left alone. As a result of their need for care and believing that he was the appropriate caregiver due to his co-residence, Dominic retired early to care for his parents.

Joyce's father moved in with her when he was fairly healthy. For awhile, he was even helping *her* out. "My father would pick up my kids after school or meet me when I had to take my car in." But Joyce's father has lived with her for twelve years now and has gradually become more dependent. While no conscious decision was ever made to be a caregiver, she became one over the years.

Although the relationship is not statistically significant, sons were more likely to become caregivers vis-à-vis this route than daughters. Two out of eight sons (25 percent) "just happened" to become caregivers compared to six out of forty-two daughters and daughters-in-law (14 percent) (chi-square $(1) = 1.31$). In contrast, sons were less likely to volunteer or to be elected by default because family caregiving is not a traditionally male family role. In particular, providing nurturance and physical care to one's mother is inconsistent with a male gender ideology, what men (and others) believe is appropriate for their role. Thus, to become a caregiver it had to "just happen" as an extension of co-residence (in the case of Dominic) or as an extension of prior family responsibilities that are more consistent with a male ideology (in the case of Frank). While this does not change the tasks that men perform, it legitimates the pathway that they take to caregiving.

Volunteering

The least common pathway to becoming a caregiver was for children to volunteer to care for their parents, without the deliberation or consultation of a family meeting (14 percent; seven out of fifty). These children believed that they actually had a choice whether or not to become caregivers. Usually, the acceptable alternative for them was nursing home placement or care by another family member.

Joan volunteered to take care of her parents at a point when her father had recently undergone open heart surgery and her mother was diagnosed with cancer.

> Neither of my parents was doing very well. They lived about ten minutes away. I used to get a lot of phone calls. I was always running around so I decided to have them move in. I never asked my brother or sister. They never showed any interest anyway, but my aunt would have taken care of them if I asked.

Melissa also volunteered to take care of her father when her stepmother had him placed in a nursing home. She explained, "I knew that my sister would agree with me [to take my father out of the nursing home]; I just didn't ask. I was so furious with my stepmother, I didn't care what *she* thought."

Other caregivers also volunteered even though they had alternative choices. Connie did not have siblings to meet with or from whom her mother might choose. Yet, she appeared to "volunteer" in a way that other only children, who felt that they had no alternative, did not. She stated,

> I had a choice to make. My mother could have gone into a nursing home; she was far enough along. Or she could come home and live with me. I talked to my husband and then my kids before I decided. It was going to affect everyone, and I needed their help if this was going to work.

Mark was the only son who volunteered to become a caregiver. However, upon closer examination, Mark volunteered to have his mother live in his home, which was once the family home. Mark provided some care in the evening, but the bulk of care was provided during the day by his sister-in-law in her home. He stated,

> I asked my mother if she wanted to come and live with me after my father died. Even then she needed someone to be with her. I'm here all alone anyway.

At first I could leave her alone. Now I take her over to my brother's during
the day, but she knows this house better.

It was quite likely that Mark would not continue to care for his mother at
home when she became less self-sufficient and needed more personal care.

Among those who volunteered to be caregivers (including those who
volunteered during a family meeting), the vast majority (thirteen out of
seventeen; 76 percent) were nurses or members of the medical profession.
For these women, medical knowledge may have increased their confidence
(and the confidence of other family members) that they could care for their
parents. It may have also provided them with a more realistic picture of
alternatives such as nursing homes and thus increased their willingness to
care for their parents themselves. As one of the registered nurses commented, "I know what nursing homes are like. They are institutions. You get
in line for everything. You have no choice. I would like to keep my mother
out of them for as long as I can." The same registered nurse as above added,
"Sometimes I wish that I didn't know what I do. Ignorance can be bliss."
Still, the nursing home was an option, and her willingness to provide care
was voluntary.

A FAMILY LIFE COURSE PERSPECTIVE

Within the life course trajectory, the process of assuming the caregiver
role was affected not only by the timing of events in one's own life, such as
being the parent of a young child or being preretirement, but by the timing
of events in one's siblings' lives and for sons, their wives' lives. Thus, the
pathway to caregiving was subsumed under a family life course that was
distinct but encompassing of all the individual life courses of its members.
This is consistent with Rossi and Rossi's (1990) findings of the interlocking
nature of the life course within family systems.

Broader social change produces change in individual life patterns (Elder,
1992). In this example, the availability of what were seen as acceptable
alternatives to home care within the formal health care system influenced
one's decision to become a caregiver and the particular pathway one took
in becoming a caregiver. Adult children who saw the formal care system as
an unacceptable source of care for their parents believed that they had no
other choice but to become caregivers and thus became de facto caregivers.
If nursing home placement becomes a more normative alternative (due to
the aging of the population), those remaining family members who do
become caregivers may be more likely to assume the role out of choice.

Increases in women's labor force participation, an important social change, likely decreased the proportion of daughters who volunteered for the role, while the gender role revolution increased the likelihood of sons volunteering for the role.

OTHER DETERMINING FACTORS

Previous research has found several factors to be significant determinants of who in the family becomes the caregiver. These factors include gender, geographical proximity, being an only child, being a favored or rejected child, having fewer competing responsibilities, and being particularly nurturant (Brody, 1990). However, this research indicates that additional factors increased the likelihood of being a caregiver. At least one of the caregivers felt that he was the only one in his family who could effectively manage his mother. Although he was not a favored child, he was the only one who could "stand up to" his mother. Thus, having a special rapport with his parent increased the likelihood of being the caregiver. He added,

> I am the caregiver because I am the one that she listens to. I cut off all of her arguments as to why she can't do something. I will only put up with so much from her. She abuses other people and they get fed up.

In addition, a significant proportion of the caregivers, nearly one-third, were nurses or other medical helpers (such as home health aides). This is consistent with previous findings that caregivers tend to be particularly nurturant (Brody, 1990). However, it has not been noted in previous studies.

THE IMPORTANCE OF GENDER IDEOLOGY

Gender role ideology played an important role in the pathway taken to becoming a caregiver. Perception of what was appropriate for one's gender greatly influenced willingness to assume caregiving roles and thus the process or pathway by which a child became a caregiver. For example, sons were less likely to volunteer for the role of caregiver. Out of the seven caregivers who volunteered, only one was a son (14 percent). Unlike women, this may have been partly due to the conflict between their gender ideology of what it was to be a man versus a caregiver. However, several sons who felt they had no choice did take on the role, although they delegated much of the responsibility to other female family members.

Mothers were also less likely to choose their sons as caregivers. Only one mother chose to live with her son, although her daughter-in-law was actually her caregiver. Again, this was partly due to gender ideology and one's belief of what was appropriate for a son versus a daughter. It may be that mothers, in particular, were uncomfortable having their sons assume their bodily care. They may have questioned whether a son can truly provide adequate care given traditional assumptions that this is a female role. Lastly, mothers may have been more reluctant to interfere with a son's career versus a daughter's due to the higher importance placed on a man's career in this generation of men and women.

Fathers also chose daughters over sons to provide care. Of those fathers who had both a son and a daughter living in the area, all except for one chose their daughters over their sons to provide care. This is inconsistent with previous findings that caregivers tend to be the same gender as care receivers (Lee, Dwyer, and Coward, 1993). What it tells us is that fathers would *prefer* their daughters as caregivers, but that when sons do provide care, they are more likely to provide it to a same-sex parent. In addition, what is more important than having a same-sex caregiver are our cultural notions of the appropriateness of women as family caregivers. Whether because we believe that women are naturally more nurturant or that men's work should not be compromised, mothers *and* fathers looked to daughters rather than sons for care. Only one father chose living with a son (and daughter-in-law) over a daughter. However, it was Patrick's *mother* who received his and his wife's care. According to the daughter-in-law, Patrick and his father had always been very close since the mother became an alcoholic.

Men and women were more likely to take different pathways to caregiving in working class families owing to the greater emphasis on sex role segregation. According to Langman (1987) and substantiated by the findings of Rubin (1976, 1994), working class families emphasize traditional sex role patterns for husbands versus wives and acknowledge the husband as patriarchal authority in the home. These sex role patterns also determined the pathway to caregiving. For example, daughters who saw it as their duty as women to be caregivers, and thus followed the de facto pathway to caregiving, were more likely to be from the working class.

LACK OF VOLUNTARISM AND ITS IMPLICATIONS

While many of the caregivers cited either filial obligation or parental love as the motivating factor for being a caregiver, a little more than one-third (seventeen out of fifty) of the caregivers volunteered for the position. This included family members who agreed to be caregivers during a family meeting (sometimes only because they did not want the parent to go to a nursing home) and those who volunteered but without the deliberations of a family meeting. For the remaining caregivers, the decision was made by additional family members (without their consent), in a process of elimination or as a result of prior commitments. For these caregivers, just how willingly did they take on the role?

While all of the caregivers were making heroic efforts to combine caregiving, employment outside of the home, and responsibilities for their own families, the ways in which caregivers were selected suggests that most were not willing recruits to the role. Although they did it when faced with (what they saw as) no alternative, only a minority eagerly sought the role. This was certainly not an unexpected finding given the difficulties and stresses of providing care during this period of the life course when the adult child has many additional responsibilities. It is in sharp contrast to the romantic picture of family caregiving, which is sometimes assumed when noting the high numbers of family caregivers. An example is Brody's (1995) reminder that families provide between 80 and 90 percent of the personal and instrumental help to older people. Such statistics inaccurately portray large numbers of men and women eagerly volunteering to significantly alter their lives to come to the aid of their aging parents. The results of this study suggest that the process was less of offering and more of seeing no alternative.

That caregivers were not volunteering in large numbers was perhaps due to their inadequate training or resources to care for an aging parent. Time, one of the most necessary resources, was most difficult to manage for those who were simultaneously working. In a sample of nonworking caregivers, rates of voluntarism might be much higher. Extra money to make the necessary alterations to one's home were less available in working class families, and lack of medical training may have prevented family members of severely impaired elders from offering assistance.

Children also may have been less likely to volunteer because of the lack of assistance in caregiving. If siblings and other family members could be counted on to share caregiving or if respite and other home care services were more common, rates of voluntarism might have been higher. Similarly, if the workplace offered greater flexibility (making caregiving more compatible with work), children might have been more likely to volunteer for the role. These issues are discussed in greater detail in chapter 10.

If adult children are providing care while not being fully trained in such tasks as managing dementia, accessing community assistance, or providing low-skilled nursing care, they may find the experience a more arduous one than is necessary. The stress and strain on the caregiver and on his or her family may be elevated. The elderly persons themselves may receive poorer care or inadequate treatment. In addition, nursing home placement may occur sooner when the pathway to caregiving is not a voluntary one. Those who are not trained to be caregivers may find the responsibilities over-whelming and unmanageable. These questions, emanating from the results, remain to be tested but certainly warrant further investigation.

CONSCIOUS DECISION OR NOT?

For most of the caregivers in this study, the decision to become a caregiver was a conscious one. This did not mean that all of the caregivers "wanted" to fulfill these tasks. However, they consciously accepted the role. In fewer than one quarter of the cases did the adult child believe that becoming a caregiver had occurred without deliberately making the decision to take on the caregiver role.

Although adult children consciously accepted the role of caregiver, what was not evident was if, in doing so, they realized all that caregiving entailed. Clearly, those in the medical profession had prior knowledge of their parents' likely needs. Although this study did not include those who had quit being a caregiver, there was at least one woman who admitted that she would like to quit caregiving, but she was financially dependent on her father's pension. Many others commented that caregiving was more than they bargained for, but that they were not ready to give up yet. Many of the caregivers sustained high levels of stress throughout the caregiving career and institutionalized parents only when medically necessary. The issues of stress and the remainder of the caregiving career are discussed in chapters 6 and 8.

CHAPTER 4

Siblings and the Division of Labor: Conflict and Cooperation

Research on filial care has often focused on one adult child as the sole provider of care, neglecting consideration of the family as a caregiving system. In response, recent studies have demonstrated the importance of exploring ways in which children other than the primary caregiver may or may not participate in systems of parent care (Matthews and Rosner, 1988; Stoller, Forster, and Duniho, 1992; Tennstedt, McKinlay, and Sullivan, 1989). Families, and adult children in particular, provide care to elders in a variety of ways. Some families do this via a "network" where more than one sibling takes primary responsibility for care. A network does not imply, however, that everyone shares equally in the task of caring for a parent; instead there can be variations among siblings in their participation in the caregiving process. For example, according to Cicirelli (1992), siblings coordinated their efforts in half of the families, provided partial coordination in one-quarter of the families, and each sibling helped with care as he or she wished in the remaining one-quarter of the families. In yet other families, siblings provide no help.

Matthews and Rosner (1988) identified the conditions under which these varying styles of participation occurred. They found that the participation style of each member of the network depended on family structure (size and gender composition) and the extrafamilial ties of the children. In smaller families, there were only two styles of participation; children provided routine care or backup for routine care. Routine care—regular assistance to the elderly parent that was incorporated into the child's ongoing schedule—included activities such as household chores, running errands, and visiting. Caregivers who provided backup care were not regularly involved in providing services, but could be counted on when they were asked to help out.

In larger families, however, additional styles of participation were found. These included circumscribed care that was highly predictable but carefully bounded, such as taking a parent for a drive every Sunday afternoon. The styles of participation also included sporadic care, or occasionally calling one's parents, as well as near total dissociation from caregiving. Daughters were more likely to use the routine and backup styles, while sons were more likely to follow the circumscribed, sporadic, and dissociated styles. Stoller, Forster, and Duniho (1992) found that geographic proximity was also central in explaining whether adult children participated in these networks.

Secondary caregivers, including siblings, provide a wide range (and thus degree) of assistance (Penrod, Kane, Kane, and Finch, 1995; Tennstedt, McKinlay, and Sullivan, 1989). Included in this are families where one adult child tends to take primary responsibility, while siblings provide only minor or insignificant assistance or remove themselves from caregiving (Cantor, 1979; Johnson, 1983; Pratt, Schmall, and Wright, 1987; Snyder and Keefe, 1985). According to one study, only 43 percent of caregivers received any help with caregiving from family members and only 28 percent said that family assistance was consistent and regular (Snyder and Keefe, 1985). Consequently, assistance from helpers has no effect on either the hours or type of care that the primary caregiver provides. That is, assistance from helpers does not serve as a substitute for what the primary caregiver provides, possibly because it is so inconsistent.

Whether adult children form networks or one sibling provides the bulk of care, conflict with siblings is a likely result of filial care. Strawbridge and Wallhagen (1991) found that nearly 40 percent of adult children providing care experienced serious conflict with a sibling, usually due to lack of sufficient help. How caregivers attempt to involve their siblings and further consideration of the conflict are matters that have not been explored.

Family dynamics, including sibling conflict and cooperation, are best understood by using a life course perspective that highlights the interdependence among the lives of family members and examines how the life course is embedded in joint "family time" as well as in historical time (Hagestad and Neugarten, 1985; Kahana et al., 1994). For example, in applying a life course perspective, one takes into account how the timing of events in one's siblings' lives also affects one's caregiving career. A life course perspective also recognizes that for some siblings, perhaps much older and much younger children, the role of caregiver for an elderly parent may be inconsistent with their stage in the life course. Such children may already be caring for an elderly spouse (in the case of an older sibling) or may be forming their own families or still in school (in the case of a younger sibling). Consistent with this approach is the recognition that caregiving patterns (or lack thereof) are also a reflection of family history which affects the ability and willingness of siblings to work together and to help a parent. For example, adult children who are bitter that their parents have always favored another child may believe that it is the other sibling's responsibility to care for the parent. Similarly, families that have never worked together as a team may be unable to form networks as adults.

The life course perspective also considers how age-related transitions are socially constructed. Normatively based turning points in the life course, such as when and if one becomes a caregiver, provide road maps for human lives and outline life paths. The occurrence, and perhaps timing, of these turning points are likely to differ by class. For example, an emphasis on family interdependence and the need for help created by financial conditions in the working class (Myers and Dickerson, 1990) may increase the likelihood that working class siblings expect to become caregivers as part of their life course. In contrast, in middle class families, at least some siblings may not expect caregiving to be a part of their life course at all due to the lack of emphasis on family interdependence and assistance. As a result, networks may be less likely to form.

It is important for researchers to investigate the issue of sibling assistance since adult children perceive their effectiveness as caregivers to increase when other family members assist and cooperate with them (Townsend and Noelker, 1987). Conflict with siblings in middle age may also have important implications for sibling relationships which are central in later life (Bedford and Gold, 1989; Cantor and Little, 1985; Cicirelli, 1985; Goetting, 1986; Gold, 1989a, 1989b). This chapter furthers the study of later life families, families whose children are grown and living on their own, by addressing new questions regarding adult sibling relationships with respect to caregiving. Many researchers have already noted the lack of assistance from siblings. Some adults are even unwilling to allow their siblings to help, despite their complaints of lack of assistance (Altschuler, Jacobs, and Shiode, 1985). Researchers have not considered, however, whether and how caregivers attempt to involve their siblings and have not examined the conflict that arises when siblings do not help. In this chapter, I ask, What was the caregiver's reaction to the lack of assistance? Why did they perceive that siblings did not help? According to the caregiver, how will this arrangement affect future relationships with siblings? Also examined is whether and how the caregiving arrangement was a reflection of other family patterns. That is, how did the history of the family affect sibling participation? The chapter begins by examining the extent to which siblings formed a caregiving network.

LIMITATIONS

Several limitations of this study may have impacted the results. Caregivers who attended support groups or who sent their parents to adult day health centers may have been less likely to receive assistance from their siblings. This selection bias would have overestimated the number of caregivers who received little or no help from their siblings. In addition, the caregivers' interpretation of how much assistance their siblings provided may be different from what was actually provided. Lerner et al. (1991) found in their study of sibling pairs that adult children did perceive their siblings as contributing less than themselves. As such, it is emphasized that this study focused on the caregivers' perceptions.

THE EXTENT OF SHARING WITH SIBLINGS

The following findings are based on those caregivers who had one or more living sibling(s) (forty out of fifty caregivers). (In the case of daughters-in-law, their husbands had to have one or more living sibling.) Among the forty caregivers, all except for one son had a second sibling within a thirty-mile radius. This is consistent with Lin and Rogerson's (1995) findings that for families with two or more adult children, the closest two children lived within thirty miles.

Assistance to siblings was not common. The vast majority of caregivers received little or no help from their siblings (twenty-seven out of forty or 68 percent). Consistently, only a small number of caregivers said that they were part of a network of siblings who shared in caregiving tasks (five out of forty, or 12 percent). The remainder of the caregivers received some help from siblings, although it was limited (eight out of forty, or 20 percent).

Sibling Networks

Liza and her five siblings shared equally in the care of their father until he died and are currently doing the same for their mother. Liza described their network as follows:

> We worked hand-in-hand. We all had one shift at night from 6:00 P.M. until 8:00 A.M., and we took turns on the weekends. My niece was there then from 8:00 A.M. until 1:00. Then my sister Mary did it from 1:00 until 6:00. She also got them dinner. Then the other five of us did the evenings. Later, when we took my father off the respirator, there had to be two of us [per shift]. By then, Ellie [another sister] had died and Mary couldn't handle it anymore and Alice was too sick. So there was my two brothers and me and two of my nieces and my daughter. We had my father in the dining room and my mother in her room, and we slept in chairs.

Since all except for one of Liza's siblings also worked outside of the home, their ability to synchronize care to provide twenty-four hour coverage is remarkable. Liza and her siblings have experienced little conflict in negotiating this arrangement.

> Nobody has to be made guilty to do it. . . . We usually all agree on something before we do it, like taking my father off the respirator. Either my oldest brother or I will call the family meetings. . . . We all knew that everyone would have to help. It had to be a family thing.

Previous research has suggested that daughters overwhelmingly provide assistance with personal care (Dwyer and Coward, 1991; Horowitz, 1985b; Matthews and Rosner, 1988; Montgomery and Kamo, 1989; Stoller, 1990). Yet, Liza's brothers helped as much, if not more, than her sisters, even though one had to move to the area and commuted an hour to work to care for his parents. This sharing was likely the result of the history of a close-knit French-Canadian family. Indeed, the children have cared not only for their parents as one unit, but for one another as well. For example, when Alice was dying of diabetes-related complications, her siblings, not her children, fulfilled her wish to be cared for and to die at home.

Abby also rotated the care of her mother with her four sisters. In the beginning, Abby's oldest sister provided care during the week, leaving her remaining sisters to alternate caregiving on the weekends. However, her oldest sister's health worsened, and her younger sisters retired. As a result, each sister began providing care for one week at a time. According to Abby, "If I didn't have so many sisters, I wouldn't be able to do this. My turn rolls around fast enough as it is. At the end of the week, I am so happy. I yell, 'Yeah, it is May's turn!' ' "

Adult children who received help from siblings were more likely to be working class, consistent with Archbold's (1983) findings that care providers (versus managers) were more likely to come from lower socioeconomic backgrounds. Whereas 48 percent of working class caregivers were either part of a sibling network or at least received "some" help from siblings, only 12 percent of the middle class caregivers received comparable assistance (chi-square (1) = 5.81, $p < .025$). This result was also consistent with additional findings from this study that parents of working class children felt that they had several children from whom they could choose a caregiver, perhaps because more children were willing to provide assistance in working class families.

The association with class was not due to a larger family size in the working class. In fact, 22 percent of the working class caregivers (five out of twenty-three) but 24 percent of the middle class caregivers (four out of seventeen) had five or more siblings. Furthermore, 39 percent of the working class (nine out of twenty-three) and 53 percent of the middle class (nine out of seventeen) had three to four siblings (chi-square (2) = 1.02, not significant).

Receiving at least some help from siblings was more common in the working class also because of cultural prescriptions for family interdependence and the need for help created by financial conditions. (These concepts were teased apart in the work by Myers and Dickerson [1990]). That is, there may have been a greater understanding in the working class versus the middle class that siblings, even as adults, share in contributing to the good of the family rather than pursuing individual goals and that children should provide care to aging parents. This was consistent with Langman's (1987) findings that extended family ties were central to the lives of working class families and that they maintained these ties even as adults. Working class siblings may have also provided care because they could not obtain other sources of assistance, such as financial help or the ability to manage care.

Several of the adult children who formed caregiving networks were also the first generation born in the United States from European Catholic groups. According to C. Johnson (1995), these ethnic groups are noted for their intimacy and interdependence. Italian Americans, for example, place a strong emphasis on filial responsibility and caring for one's parents (Squier and Quadagno, 1988). The family would be dishonored if the parent were placed in a nursing home. Norms of filial responsibility are particularly strong among those embedded in Italian neighborhoods, which was the case for Marie and Dominic. Although Dominic's siblings did not provide assistance, it does explain why Dominic was so appalled by their lack of involvement.

Receipt of Some Sibling Assistance

Family size did affect whether or not caregivers received only some assistance. Approximately one-fifth of the caregivers received some help from siblings, although it was limited. Three-quarters of those who received only some help had only one brother or sister. If that sibling was unavailable or could provide only minimal assistance, the caregiver had no one else to turn to. These caregivers had fewer sources of assistance, and the sources were not generous with their help. Consider the example of Susan, who had one brother living forty minutes away:

> My brother comes on Friday night to cook their dinner and then again on Sunday to spend the day. But he says that he can't do more to help me. . . . I have no one else to help.

Lack of assistance from siblings in smaller families may have important implications. Uhlenberg and Cooney (1990) found that in smaller families, there were fewer high-quality relationships and more poor-to-average quality relationships between mothers and adult children. This was the result of the fact that relationships were less harmonious when children did not share the responsibility of aging parents. Thus, in smaller families, siblings may be less likely to provide help because of a smaller pool of available assistants and subsequently because of the lower quality relationships with their mothers.

Brothers were more likely to receive some assistance from their siblings than sisters and sisters-in-law (chi-square = 7.53, $p < .01$). The reason may be that sons were more likely to demand help from their siblings (discussed below). Our cultural beliefs that men are not good caregivers and that it is not an appropriate part of their life course may also account for the results.

Receipt of Little or No Assistance

Even though all but one-quarter of the caregivers had at least one sibling within a one-hour drive, the vast majority (68 percent) received minimal or no help from their brothers and sisters. There was some evidence that the sex composition of siblings, particularly having only brothers, increased the likelihood of being in this category. Among the six caregivers who had only male siblings, all received little or no help from siblings (chi-square $(1) = 3.53, p < .01$).

Do Siblings Form a Caregiving Network?

While there appeared to be some sharing of caregiving tasks among siblings, it was certainly not common. Instead, it was more typical for one child to provide the bulk of care. This was not necessarily in contrast to the findings of Matthews and Rosner (1988). They, too, found a variety of participation styles. Moreover, much of what Matthews and Rosner called a filial network was one or two sisters providing the bulk of care with minimal and inconsistent help from siblings, similar to the results of this study.

ATTEMPTING TO INVOLVE SIBLINGS IN CAREGIVING

Among the caregivers who received little or no help in caregiving, three-quarters (twenty out of twenty-seven) tried to involve their siblings. Their requests ranged from hinting that they could use more help to demanding that their siblings help more. Nearly half tried for a prolonged period of time (many still trying), while more than a quarter argued and cajoled with siblings for awhile and then gave up.

Of those who had not attempted to involve siblings, at least two of the daughters believed that their siblings were "unfit" to take care of their parents. According to Deborah, "I wouldn't leave my worst enemy with my brother. He is more than irresponsible. It doesn't even begin to describe it." Jody also did not ask her two younger brothers to help because they were men. According to her, they would not know how to help.

> My youngest brother, Joe, has lived here [at the mother's house] with his son since he got a divorce. . . . We pay my niece to come over and get dinner. Joe is home, but he can't be bothered to cook. He would rather do things with his son, and my mother can't be eating junk food all the time. He doesn't stick around to take care of my mother, so I come over on weekends too. He is 40, but he acts like 14 when it comes to undoing a bra or any of her personal hygiene.

Requesting Help

Caregivers commonly requested that brothers and sisters provide occasional respite or substitute care. Only one out of twenty-three daughters (4 percent) consistently demanded this help from her siblings; the others "asked" for help. In comparison, six out of seven of the sons with available siblings (86 percent) demanded help. Rose had taken a leave of absence from work to move home and provide care for her mother who was bedridden and who kept her awake all night screaming. She was typical of how sisters requested help:

> My brother and sister say that they feel sorry for me and what can they do. So I tell them that it would help if they would come over and spend the night sometime so that I could sleep, or the evening so that I could go out. But they aren't willing to do it. . . . It doesn't help if I say anything. I shouldn't have to ask; they should just pitch in.

Sons commanded assistance (and often received it) whether they themselves or their wives were the caregivers. According to Brenda, one of the daughters-in-law:

> We had a meeting with the family. My husband put his foot down. He said, "Look, you have to help out. We need a break. You come once a week and you just sit here and visit. You don't help out. We are with her twenty-four hours a day, not just a couple of hours a week." This happened a couple of times. Now one of the sisters takes her weekends. Another sister comes over and does the laundry. It helps.

Frank, too, demanded that his brothers and sisters help out when he found himself being overwhelmed. Frank said, "Family is family, but I won't let it take over my life. I make sure the others help, and they listen. I just tell them, 'This is the way it has to be.' "

In comparison to adult children who wanted siblings to provide assistance on a regular basis, other caregivers asked their siblings to come and take their parents occasionally so that they could spend some time with their own families. According to Dominic,

> My brothers and sister are not available, if you know what I mean. They are too busy, but they are not too busy to go fishing and camping. . . . The thing we miss most is time together. Time to hold hands. We have to beg, steal, or borrow to get away together. My brothers will never do it [provide help occasionally].

One of the caregivers, Sally, was able to get her sister to come over and stay with her mother one weekend so that Sally could go away with her husband. Sally's sister, however, charged her $100 a day. Sally said that since then, her sister has been unwilling to help further. Caregivers also requested that their siblings just visit more, particularly on holidays, for the benefit of the parent. According to Joan, "I know that they aren't going to help out, but I get angry when Father's Day and his birthday comes and he doesn't even get a card."

Perceptions of Why Siblings Did Not Help

When asked why they believed that their siblings did not help with caregiving, many of the caregivers echoed reasons similar to why they were chosen as caregivers in the first place. That is, siblings were not available because they had small children, work, or activities that they could not (or were not willing to) relinquish. However, asking a sibling to help occasionally is quite different from asking him or her to be the primary caregiver. The daughters-in-law, in particular, were amazed that their husbands' families did not help more, as is suggested in the following:

> I thought we would get more help from Tom's family. My family helps more than theirs. My sister comes over and does the laundry and takes care of the kids to help me out because I can't do it all. . . . I asked Tom's sister, the one who isn't married and lives in her mother's house, "How can you not help to take care of your mother? She is your mother. I would do anything to help my mother, to keep her out of a nursing home." She says she can't do it because she works, but I tell her that there are visiting nurses. . . . Hey, you make do. You have to.

Several caregivers said that their siblings had very "flimsy" excuses for not helping. Rose's sister said that she could not help because she slept late, while Sally's sister could not help because she went to Cape Cod so often. Dominic believed that his brothers should help, but he did not believe that they would. He kept saying over and over again, "That is the way it is. What can you do?"

Dominic also suggested that his siblings' lack of assistance was an extension of prior family patterns or was embedded within the family life course. He stated,

> My sister lived here for sixteen years after she got a divorce without doing a lick of work or paying the rent. She never made her own bed or dried a dish or did her own laundry. My mother spoiled her. . . . My mother and her daughter never got along. Now she comes occasionally, but she never calls.

Celia, too, felt that her in-laws' history with their mother prevented them from helping with caregiving. She added,

> I think that what is at the root of all of this is that their mother is an alcoholic. They still resent her alcoholism and are not as committed to helping out. It reminds them of what she was like when she was dependent before and needed to be taken care of. I tell them, "Yes, but it is hard for Dad too. He needs your help."

Billie's husband, Steve, was willing to be interviewed separately. Steve believed that his brothers did not help his wife because that was "woman's work."

> My brothers don't help because there is not much that they can do. My mother needs to be bathed and washed and things like that. But they know that they are lucky that Billie will do it. . . . My sisters-in-law don't help; well, one is too flaky. The other takes care of her own mother and has six kids. My sister takes care of her mother-in-law. What can you do when it is your husband who asks you? You can't say no. [Billie said separately, "He makes excuses for his sister. I wouldn't let any sister-in-law take care of my mother!"].

Finally, Sally felt that her siblings did not help her because she took her mother in against their wishes. Other caregivers voiced similar sentiments. "They are afraid that I am going to get all of the inheritance. It still comes up, so they stay away."

CONFLICT

Powerful feelings were unleashed by many caregivers as they discussed the difficulties of battling with their siblings. Over half of the caregivers (twenty-four out of forty or 60 percent) who tried to get their siblings to help experienced a high degree of conflict. Most often this took the form of continuously arguing with their siblings that they should help more. The potential for conflict appeared to be most acute when the parent lived with the caregiver, making visits from siblings captive situations for bickering.

Kathy tried for over a year to get her brother and sister, both of whom lived nearby, to occasionally take their mother or to stay with her at Kathy's home.

> I really thought that my brother and sister would do their part, no questions. My brother and I used to do things together; now we are farther apart than

ever. Whenever I call, we end up in a big fight. My sister-in-law usually answers. I say, "Doesn't your husband know how to dial?" . . . My brother and sister say, "Well, you chose to do this." And I tell them, "And you chose not to. How can you live with yourself?"

Marie was from a first-generation, close-knit Italian family. One of nine children, all of whom lived in close proximity, she argued with her siblings over who was going to do what for their mother. Marie contended that her siblings would fight for the *right* and *privilege* to provide certain tasks for their mother but did not carry them out. When Marie pointed out to them that they needed to help more, they were offended. However, if she arranged for someone else to provide that task, they were also offended.

I wanted the [adult day health center] to give my mother a bath. My sister said, "Why should we pay them to give our mother a bath when she has three daughters? *We* should do for our mother." I said, "Well, you don't do anything. I want to hear what it is that you are going to contribute. I give my mother a bath once a week. What will you do? . . . " She said to my oldest brother, "Why is she making all the decisions? She is pulling rank. *I* want to take my mother to the doctor." This battle went on for two nights with all nine of us. I kept saying to myself, "What has happened to this nice family? We are at each other's throats!"

Sometimes parents became involved in the conflict. When Rose argued over the phone with her sister for not helping, her mother asked for the receiver and also screamed at her daughter. While Rose's mother liked to invite the other siblings to stay for dinner when they visited, Rose refused to cook for them because they did not provide help. As such, Rose's mother had less opportunity to spend time with her children. Parents' knowledge of the conflict between siblings also heightened their own sense of being a burden on their children.

Working class caregivers were more likely to acknowledge conflict with siblings (78 percent versus 35 percent, or eighteen out of twenty-three versus six out of seventeen; chi-square $(1) = 5.73, p < .025$). While working class caregivers may have felt more comfortable admitting that such conflict existed, cultural prescriptions in working class families that children should care for parents and should assist their siblings may also account for this result. Consequently, when siblings did not provide assistance, the caregiver felt that they were not living up to their responsibilities. In contrast, caregivers from the middle class believed that they had taken on the responsibilities themselves and that other family members were not obligated to help them.

Conflict in the family was also related to the way in which adult children became caregivers. Among those children who "just happened" to become caregivers, three-quarters (nine out of twelve) had not experienced conflict with their siblings. Caregiving was an extension of prior roles. It is quite likely that any conflict with siblings was resolved earlier on when the caregiver undertook the role or that the caregiver had become resigned to the lack of assistance. In contrast, among those who volunteered for the role, another three-quarters (71 percent or six out of nine) had experienced conflict with siblings. Although they were volunteering, they still had expectations of assistance from others. In fact, volunteers may have been more willing to accept responsibility because they assumed that their siblings would help. Conflict erupted when siblings "let them down," as many caregivers phrased it. Children who volunteered may also have felt more obligation to kin and expected greater obligation from their siblings as well.

Consistent with the expectations of Walker (1996), conflict also arose when family members, who did not see themselves as the appropriate caregivers, became resentful of those who "should" have been caregivers. For example, daughters-in-law were often resentful that their husbands' sisters did not assume the caregiver role. This suggests the existence of a pecking order based on cultural assumptions of who is most and least appropriate as caregivers. According to the results of this study, daughters were seen as most appropriate followed by either sons or daughters-in-law, dependent on gender role expectations in the family. Conflict then arose when that pecking order was not followed.

While researchers had previously focused on sibling networks of caregivers as either being present or absent, they did not emphasize the conflict surrounding these networks. Nor did they document the anger and frustration that resulted when siblings did not mobilize to assist the child providing the bulk of care. Thus, this newer image is one of fragmented families, with elderly parents sometimes caught in the middle.

REFLECTION OF FAMILY HISTORY

Several caregivers portrayed the lack of assistance from their siblings as a result of their family's history. Dominic, for example, believed that his sister did not help out because she had always been spoiled and was never expected to make a contribution to the family, even when she lived at home as an adult. He also believed that his sister did not help because she and his mother never got along. In addition, Dominic also pointed to the prior relationship between his parents as a cause of his siblings' lack of assistance. He suggested that his sister and brothers might help out more if his *mother* were not as "spoiled," the result of more than fifty years of his father "doting" on his mother. "My father has left us with, well, a monster to take care of. All those years, he made the coffee, he did the dishes, he did all for her. Now she expects us to do it all."

Celia believed that her brothers-in-law and sister-in-law did not help more because of her mother-in-law's history of alcoholism. She argued that her husband, in contrast, was willing to help in caregiving because he alone had cared for his alcoholic mother when he was a child. As such, caregiving was an extension of prior family patterns.

Judy's example, however, was probably the most vivid illustration of the effect of family history on the willingness of siblings to participate. Judy had ten siblings, four of whom lived in the same town. When asked early on in the interview why she believed that her siblings did not help her to care for their mother, she commented, "My brothers and sisters do not have the same love for my mother as I do. I am the only one who lived with her my whole life." Judy confided that her mother had abandoned her other ten children when Judy was an infant, the youngest of the children. Taking only Judy with her, the other children lived with their abusive father and step-mother. "I guess my brothers and sisters are still bitter that I got the better of the two deals. They don't include me in family get-togethers, so why would they help me in taking care of my mother?"

These results were consistent with earlier findings that family history plays an important role in the configuration of family caregiving. According to Bedford (1992), adult offspring who were more unfavored in childhood felt less affection in their relationships with parents in later life. Growing up in a divorced single-parent family was also associated with reduced solidarity between parents and children. Adult children of divorce perceived relationships with both mothers and fathers to be of lower quality, although the effect was generally two to three times greater for fathers (Webster and Herzog, 1995). Such effects may reduce the likelihood of children providing care later in life, as well as siblings forming a network, particularly for elderly fathers. Similarly, parental divorce may have less of an impact for older children in the family if their childhoods were not affected like those of younger siblings, thus decreasing the likelihood of younger children helping older children in the family.

THE EFFECT OF CONFLICT ON FUTURE RELATIONS

Several of the caregivers believed that the conflict with siblings would not be shortlived. Celia, one of the daughters-in-law, believed that the tension between her husband and his siblings would continue beyond the death of their parents. Kathy believed that things would never be the same with her siblings. "We were all very close. Now we just barely talk. I know that it is the result of all of this."

For Judy, whose mother abandoned her other ten children, there was always some distance between herself and her siblings. Judy believed that things were worse, however, since her mother's recent death. She stated, "My mother left me all of her money since I took care of her and they didn't help. Now they won't even speak to me. My sister hired a lawyer. She is going to try to get some of the money."

CAREGIVING NETWORKS AND THE LIFE COURSE

Family members appeared to take different pathways through the life course. To begin with, not all children recognized this transition, the caregiver role itself, as a normal part of their life course. Cultural values, particularly for the middle class, of individual independence and autonomy led people to overlook the obvious fact that aging parents needed direct assistance from them. Furthermore, they may have recognized the role of caregiver as part of their siblings' life course, but not as a part of their own due to differences in availability, their own belief that their siblings were better caregivers (as a result of gender or personality), or family history. As a result, they did not recognize that their siblings needed help in providing care. Family members may place caregiving within a context of family roles, to be performed by those whose additional family roles are most compatible or consistent.

The caregiving career, as part of the overall life course, continued to be affected by siblings and the choices they made. Caregiving careers varied in terms of whether and how much assistance the caregiver received from siblings and how much conflict resulted. Middle class caregivers, as well as daughters, were less likely to receive substantial assistance from siblings, but they were also less likely to acknowledge conflict with siblings.

This interdependence of the life courses of family members must be underscored. Siblings' williness to provide assistance was greatly decreased if they were unavailable due to work or family commitments. Thus, the caregiving career was highly embedded in the timing of events in one another's lives. For those adult children who chose not to ask for any help from siblings or who gave up asking for help, siblings' choices and actions had little effect on their caregiving role. In these instances, caregivers were independent of siblings and their life courses. Such independence could be short lived if siblings moved from a dissociated role to a more active role in caregiving, even if it was to provide only sporadic or circumscribed assistance. In addition, the initial decision to provide care alone was affected by siblings and their life choices.

This study found both class and ethnic differences in whether siblings provided help. Other differences, such as racial variations, are also likely. In fact, the continued application of the life course perspective to later life sibling interactions and the transitions in their relationships is likely to yield important findings. As such, further theoretical development in this area is warranted.

LATER LIFE FAMILIES AND FAMILY HISTORY

The caregiving network was anchored by family history. History affected who was selected and how they were selected, the division of labor between siblings, and the ensuing conflict. Earlier family patterns and events, such as divorce and subsequent custody issues, influenced children's willingness to care for a noncustodial parent, particularly if they felt abandoned by that parent. In one family in which there had been an adoption, the natural child argued to her adopted sister, "Why should I help? She [her mother] has you!" Children who were not taught to contribute early on in the family were also less likely to assist in later life, according to their siblings. In addition, children who were favored earlier were more likely to be selected by the parent as a caregiver.

The effect of family history may continue across the life course. If so, there will be important implications for later life social support. Several researchers (Bedford and Gold, 1989; Cantor and Little, 1985; Cicirelli, 1985; Goetting, 1986; Gold, 1989a, 1989b) have described the importance of siblings in later life as a source of social contact and a meaningful relationship, particularly when one's spouse is deceased. While a minority of seniors have actually received social support from siblings, a majority believe that siblings would be available in a crisis (Connidis, 1994). Thus, conflict with siblings in midlife over caring for an elderly parent may mean the loss of an important source of support, or it may require the substitution of a long-term friend or neighbor for a displaced sibling. It is also possible that, although the family "is never the same again," new understandings and a respect for one another's place in the family can result despite sibling conflict. Earlier research found that levels of sibling conflict and affiliation were independent (Bedford, 1989). It is important for gerontologists and those who work with later life families, however, to recognize the potential impact of sibling conflict on later life social support.

Future research should also consider the importance of inheritance in the provision of care to elderly parents. Such studies would examine both the existence of an inheritance and whether children need or desire it enough that it becomes an incentive in parent care, factors that may be related to class. While several of the caregivers in this study mentioned inheritance as a source of conflict with siblings, none cited it as a motivating factor in the provision of care. This is an extremely sensitive issue and would require closer examination.

THE FUTURE OF THE FAMILY

Caregivers were asked what they thought would make caregiving easier in the future. Of those who tried to get their siblings to help more, nearly all said that assistance from siblings, occasional relief and respite, would make it much easier. According to one,

> What would be ideal would be if my sister would take my mother for the whole afternoon so that I could go shopping or whatever. The most that she ever does is take my mother for an ice cream. That just is not enough time.

What we did not know, however, was the siblings' interpretations of the caregivers' requests. While the caregivers said that all they wanted was occasional relief, siblings may have believed otherwise. They may have been afraid that if they helped at all, more would be expected in the future and that they would have to make the same sacrifices and accommodations that the caregiver made.

The caregiving experience is not expected to remain stable. In the future, new generations of caregivers may be less likely to experience conflict with siblings, for the decrease in fertility will lower the number of siblings one has (Maugans, 1994). Each successive generation of women since 1900 gave birth to fewer children until the mid-1970s, when the fertility rate leveled off (Maugans, 1994). Thus, elderly women will continue to have fewer adult children to turn to up into the second decade of the twenty-first century.

Adult children in the future may still be as frustrated and depressed that they are taking on the tremendous task of caring for their parents alone. Yet, they may not have the anger and disappointment of unsuccessfully trying to share tasks with siblings. Those who would otherwise share care with their siblings will be left on their own as increasing numbers of only children reach middle and later ages. Such changes will underscore the need for a renewed contract with the formal care system to meet the needs of the growing population of elderly.

CHAPTER 5

The Race from Home to the Office:
Managing Work and Caregiving

While research on working mothers with child care responsibilities has overwhelmed the literature on work and family for several decades, only more recently have we begun to pay attention to the prevalence of employees who care for older adults. Estimates regarding the proportion of employees who provide care to an elderly person range from 23 percent to 32 percent (Scharlach and Boyd, 1989; Travelers Companies, 1985; Wagner, Creedon, Sasala, and Neal, 1989). That is, at least one-quarter of all U.S. employees care for an aging parent outside of their work hours.

An alternative way of gauging the extent of the overlap across roles is to ask how many caregivers of the elderly are also employed outside of the home. According to Abel's (1991) study of adult daughters who provide care in the Los Angeles area, nearly 42 percent were employed full-time while another 12 percent were employed part-time. Results from a national survey suggested that nearly 31 percent of all caregivers were working, while 44 percent of daughters and 55 percent of sons worked full-time (Stone, Cafferata, and Sangl, 1987).

Given the inherent difficulties of juggling both of these roles, researchers have examined the impact of work on caregiving and the reciprocal effect, the impact of caregiving on work. Results are mixed. With regard to the effect of work on caregiving, most studies suggest that employed caregivers provide as many hours of care as nonemployed caregivers, simply timing tasks so that they can be done on the weekend or in the evening (Brody and

Schoonover, 1986; Matthews, Werkner, and Delaney, 1989; Scharlach and Boyd, 1989). Other researchers, however, have found that the extent of employment does affect the amount and type of care that caregivers provide, with the major distinction being between full-time and part-time work rather than employment versus nonemployment (Lang and Brody, 1983; Olson, 1989; Stueve and O'Donnell, 1989). While daughters working full-time interact less with parents and are less available to provide instrumental support, daughters working part-time provide similar levels and types of care as nonemployed daughters (Stueve and O'Donnell, 1989). These studies, however, did not take into account the effect of accommodations made by employers (which will be discussed in this study). No research has been done on the effect of employment on the amount of care provided by sons.

Alternatively, how does caregiving affect employment for those who pursue both roles? Most studies suggest that caregiving causes people to quit their jobs, accommodate their work (i.e., take an unpaid leave, reduce work hours, or rearrange work schedules), or at least consider one of these options (Brody, 1985; Brody, Kleban, Johnsen, Hoffman, and Schoonover, 1987; Franklin, Ames, and King, 1994; Neal, Chapman, Ingersoll-Dayton, and Emlen, 1993; Olson, 1989; Scharlach and Boyd, 1989; Soldo and Myllyluoma, 1983; Stone and Short, 1990). Perhaps the greatest effect is to quit one's job. Between 12 and 28 percent of caregiving daughters leave the workforce to provide care. They lose salary and benefits, retirement pensions, social networks, and work satisfaction (Boyd and Treas, 1996). Employed caregivers also pass up opportunities for advancement, change jobs to be more available, and often feel tired on the job (Abel, 1991).

When caregivers accommodate their work, they do so at the point of becoming a caregiver rather than later in the caregiving career. There is an immediate impact of acquiring the elder care role on employment adaptation (Franklin, Ames, and King, 1994). Although caregivers are not chosen based on who does or does not work, primary caregivers must decide whether or not to reduce their work hours once they have been selected (Stern, 1996).

Certain factors increase the likelihood of experiencing conflict between work and family. According to Gottlieb, Kelloway, and Fraboni (1994), providing assistance with activities of daily living or elder care management activities and the number of elder care crises to which the employee responded each placed the respondent at greater risk of family and job costs. Crises often demanded immediate attention, and since elder care management could only be done during the day, conflict with work resulted. Others have found that providing more hours of care and caring for an elder with special care needs increased rates of absenteeism, while resources such as having a partner and finding outside care decreased rates of absenteeism (Neal, Chapman, Ingersoll-Dayton, and Emlen, 1993). In addition, having flexible job responsibilities lowered levels of work interference (Scharlach, Sobel, and Roberts, 1991).

Not all workers have the option of cutting back their hours or rearranging their work schedules. While the above studies included caregivers from a wide array of income and occupational levels, the present study focuses exclusively on (and compares) working and middle class children, omitting the poor, upper middle class, and upper class caregivers. I ask how, among "ordinary folk," caregiving impacts their paid employment. Do working and middle class caregivers have the option of cutting back on their hours or rearranging their work schedules, or do they differ in their ability to accommodate their work? Mutschler (1994), for example, found that workers in different occupations had different opportunities available to them for adjusting their work and care demands. For example, production workers did not have the option to rearrange work schedules or reduce hours but instead took unpaid days off. Executives and professionals had greater flexibility in scheduling their work activities but also had fewer opportunities to switch to another job. Given these differences, this study focuses on how working and middle class employees, who hold occupations as service workers and factory operatives to small proprietors and midlevel managers, are able to accommodate their work to meet the demands of caregiving. It is expected that consistent with prior research, women in higher status positions will be better able to accommodate caregiving to work because they have more flexible work schedules (Archbold, 1983), but they will feel more conflicted and report more work interruptions and missed job opportunities (Brody et al., 1987).

In addition, this study asks whether there are more subtle effects on employment which have not been captured in previous research. While caregivers may not necessarily have to quit their jobs in order to be caregivers, they may be less able to concentrate at work or less inclined to take on additional projects or work hours. This would likely affect their productivity and career mobility, which are often already limited for working class employees.

Based on the role accumulation perspective that stresses the increased benefit of multiple roles, this study also investigates whether working outside of the home can actually ease the strain of caregiving. Although additional roles do contribute to the overall burden of being a caregiver, they are also associated with improved well-being (Stoller and Pugliesi, 1989). Scharlach (1994) found that the negative aspects of combining work and caregiving roles were outweighed by the positive aspects, such as a sense of accomplishment, enhanced interpersonal relationships, and opportunities to compensate for limitations in each of the separate roles. This study asks whether such positive benefits of combining work and caregiving are also found in working class careers where workers may not have a sense of accomplishment and other opportunities to outweigh the negative aspects of juggling both roles.

While other researchers have investigated how caregiving affects employment among the general population, to date no one has investigated the strategies that caregivers use to fulfill both roles. If adult children are working all day long, how do they care for frail parents as well? In this chapter, I examine just how caregivers manage to fulfill (what appear to be) conflicting roles.

Class differences in the strategies utilized to combine work and caregiving are anticipated. It is expected that working class caregivers will rely more on family support, while middle class caregivers will seek formal care, whether subsidized or purchased, as a strategy to combine work and caregiving. This is assumed given Archbold's (1983) findings that care managers, who coordinated care for a parent, were more likely to come from higher socioeconomic backgrounds whereas care providers, who directly administered care, came from lower socioeconomic backgrounds. It is expected that in seeking assistance to combine work and caregiving, caregivers will seek similar types of help.

The work and family linkage is also affected by macrolevel issues, particularly national family leave policy and employer-based policies. We therefore examine how, according to the caregivers, individual employer policies (whether formal or informal) affected their ability to combine work and caregiving. Implications of the Family and Medical Leave Act of 1993 are also discussed.

Any discussion of work and caregiving careers should be considered within a life course perspective. This framework emphasizes the timing of events such as work and family responsibilities across the life cycle, with a recognition that such events may occur simultaneously, referred to as interlocking trajectories. To date, however, there has been little discussion of what happens when some events or roles (such as work and caregiving) clash or cannot interlock. This conflict is likely to be responsible for the lack of overlap in the timing of work, education, and leisure which Riley and Riley discuss (1993a). In order to understand the timing of events (such as when one works), we must also understand what other events (such as family roles) might preclude that event and the strategies that are utilized by those who manage both roles.

The life course perspective also emphasizes how our life patterns are embedded in the context of the larger society. As such, events in the life course are subject to class and gender role expectations and to the changing nature of women's labor force participation. According to this theoretical framework, any effort to make sense of individual behavior should be informed by the societal context in which it takes place. As such, the impact that changes in women's work and gender role expectations have had on individual life courses is discussed where applicable.

THE EFFECT ON WORK

On the surface, it appeared that few of the caregivers made drastic changes in their employment due to caregiving. Only two (4 percent) of the caregivers stated that they quit their jobs to provide care. On closer examination, however, a much larger percentage of caregivers (50 percent) made significant changes that were at least spurred on by caregiving demands, if not totally attributable to caregiving.

Only two of the caregivers clearly stated that they quit their jobs because of caregiving. Before leaving work to take care of her parent, Sally had just gone back to teaching after taking time off to care for her daughter until she started kindergarten. Because of this circumstance, she and her husband were financially accustomed to living on one salary. As a result, Sally was probably more willing than others to quit her job in order to care for her mother. Nine years later, Sally still had not gone back to teaching.

A second daughter was working for a temp agency before she quit work to care for her mother. She stated, "I was sick and tired of doing things at night. It would not be fair to rearrange my schedule at work. I would have gotten fired anyway, so I quit first."

Other caregivers had also terminated their employment (while caring for their parents), although they did not say that it was totally due to caregiving. Three of the caregivers (6 percent) retired early, at least partially because of caregiving demands. That is, they moved up the timing of one event (scheduled usually for "old age") as a result of the family demands of later middle age. For example, around the time that Abby's niece requested that Abby and her other sisters more fully help to care for their mother, Abby had just been given a pink slip from the teaching hospital she had worked in all of her life. Abby had to decide whether to retire early and care for her mother or to look for another job in nursing in her early 60s. Abby commented, "It means that I have less money to live on than I planned, but I can get by."

Ten other caregivers (20 percent) were not working either because they were on Disability Leave or because they were in between jobs. In all cases, however, being a caregiver was involved in their decision to not work. Judy, typical of the others, said that she quit her job because it was stressful. She later added that racing back and forth to her mother's home during the work day and receiving phone calls from her mother at work added to the stress of her job.

Caregivers from the working class were more likely to not work than middle class caregivers. Among those caregivers currently on Disability Leave or looking for a job, all ten (20 percent) were working class. However, all had been employed at some point while caregiving. It may have been harder for these caregivers to find a job since they had fewer job skills or more limited resources. Yet, an additional explanation is that they may be more likely to not work in order to stay home with their parent rather than sending him or her to day care or to a nursing home out of a desire to be the direct providers of care. The one caregiver on Disability Leave stated that even if she physically could go back to work, she would not do so because her mother could not afford to hire someone to care for her and she wanted to care for her mother herself.

Caregivers also cut back their workloads. Four caregivers (8 percent) reduced their work from full-time to part-time, while another switched to a less demanding (although still full-time) job. These caregivers thus managed the conflict that is often inherent in this stage of the life course by reducing the obligations of one role. Beth was working as a full-time dental assistant when her mother was diagnosed with pancreatic cancer. With her mother being given only six more months to live (approximately four years ago), Beth waited for a position to open up as a part-time receptionist. Although her mother had improved tremendously and was no longer living with Beth, she vowed that she would not go back to full-time work. "I am afraid to go back into that situation again. I have no idea when Meme will need me again. This way, I will be able to manage." At the time that she changed her job, Beth was remarrying, making it more feasible to take a cut in pay. Six other caregivers (12 percent) already worked part-time when they started caregiving.

Deborah, a single mother, also reduced her workload from a full-time to a part-time hair stylist when her father moved in with her and her son. She stated,

When I was working before, my father paid someone $140 a week to stay with him. So, I said, "Look, I only bring home $70 and you are paying out $140. That makes no sense." So, I quit. Now I only work on Saturdays.

When I probed Deborah as to why she did not work on the days that her father went to day care but instead worked on the day that he could not attend, she commented that she had started to school her son at home. "I work on Saturdays because that is when [her son] goes with his father." It became clearer that caring for her father made it financially feasible for Deborah to quit her job in order to stay home with her son. Similar situations in which family members became caregivers for personal gain were rare.

Few caregivers took leaves of absence. In most situations, caregivers did not believe they could leave work for longer than personal and vacation days. At the time of the interview, Rose had managed to provide care for her mother for the last two years by taking extended leaves of absence (usually for two weeks) as needed. Because of her accumulated sick days and vacation days as well as her seniority in the company, Rose managed to do this without losing her job. Rose realized that this could not go on indefinitely, although she did not know what she would do in the future.

Other caregivers accommodated their work in a less drastic manner. Four of the caregivers (8 percent) reduced their hours, but not to part-time work. Connie, who was the director of nursing in a local nursing home, reduced her work by approximately fifteen hours a week. She commented,

> It is the kind of job that I can leave early if I need to. That makes all of the difference. My boss said, "You know what needs to be done. I don't care what hours you do it in." I used to be to work at 7:30; now I don't get there until 9:00 to make sure my mother gets on the van. But I can bring my work home with me at night and do it. If it weren't for the flexibility of my job, I would not be able to do this.

Other caregivers found that they could not reduce their hours because of the demands of their work. Susan tried to reduce the number of hours that she worked, but she said she could not get her work done when she did so. Rearranging her schedule and working at home did not help since she was too tired to work by the end of the day.

Caregivers in this sample were as likely to cut back on their hours as in other samples. In this sample, 16 percent reduced their hours (including to part-time work) in comparison to 20 percent of employed caregivers nationwide (Stone, Cafferata, and Sangl, 1987). Caregivers in this sample were much less likely to take time off without pay (4 percent versus 25 percent of daughters and 14 percent of sons nationwide). This suggests the increased difficulty of taking time off without pay when one focuses on the working class. Although caregivers may be able to reduce their hours, they cannot get by financially without pay. These findings may also suggest the scarcity of working class positions that offered leave without pay before the Family and Medical Leave Act of 1993 went into effect.

More often, caregivers rearranged their schedules to coincide with caregiving needs. Marie was able to rearrange her schedule because she was self-employed. However, the increase in responsibilities required working very long days. Marie spent all day Sunday and Monday with her mother. On Tuesdays she did all of her mother's shopping and laundry (as well as her own) and prepared both of their meals ahead for the week. "It means though that from Wednesday to Saturday, I work from 7:00 in the morning until 8:00 at night."

There were gender differences in who accommodated their work and who did not. Among the eight men who were designated as caregivers, only one (13 percent) retired early to stay home with his mother. As for the others, only two occasionally missed work in order to take their mothers to doctors' appointments but did not accommodate their work further (chi-square (1) $= 5.36, p < .025$). Sons did not reduce their work hours, rearrange their work schedules, or accommodate their work in any other way. Nor did any of the daughters-in-law report their husbands' work as being affected, and no daughters reported their brothers' work as being affected. In contrast to women, men provided care in addition to their work role only up to the point of conflict, suggesting the greater importance placed on the work role for male versus female caregivers. Based on our societal assumptions that family care is the wife's/daughter's responsibility, women provided care even when it conflicted with other life course events.

Although all of the adult children in this study worked outside of the home at some point during their caregiving experience, only 4 percent said that they quit their jobs because of caregiving. This was in sharp contrast to estimates given in other studies. According to Abel's (1991) study of caregiving daughters and data from the National Long Term Care Survey (Stone, Cafferata, and Sangl, 1987), 16 and 12 percent of caregiving daughters, respectively, quit their jobs to provide care. Upon closer examination, however, fully 30 percent were not working, whether because they retired early, were on Disability Leave, or in between jobs, despite the fact that they had been working earlier in the caregiving career. Although none other than the 4 percent said that their decision was due totally to caregiving, they did state that their decisions were at least partially prompted by caregiving demands. Another 8 percent cut their work back to part-time and 12 percent reduced their hours, substantially rearranged their schedules, or took leaves of absence.

Why was there a difference in results? The higher estimates (30 percent in this study versus 16 percent and 12 percent in Abel's study and the National Long Term Care Survey) of caregivers not employed due to caregiving may be the result of the more liberal coding used in this study to include those who have quit work even if not fully due to caregiving. The estimates may also be higher due to the focus on the working class. In fact, thirteen out of the fifteen (87 percent) caregivers who were not employed were working class (chi-square $(1) = 13.8$, $p < .001$). They may have been more likely to leave a job because combining work with caregiving was more difficult (e.g., they could not take work home) and thus stressful. In addition, working class positions may have offered fewer intrinsic rewards or incentives to remain employed. There was also some evidence that working class children were more inclined to not work so that they could provide care for their parents directly.

ADDITIONAL SUBTLE EFFECTS ON WORK

Although not discussed in prior research, caregivers also noted more subtle effects on their work. Judy, a tax auditor for an insurance company, used to get a dozen or more calls from her mother during the day. Judy explained that her boss complained about the frequency of calls, increasing the level of stress that she felt at work. Although a subtle effect at first, this stress later caused Judy to quit her job.

Several of the caregivers commented that their ability to concentrate at work was affected. Susan noted,

> Caregiving hasn't hurt my work, but I am thinking about them [her two parents] all day. I cannot remember things instantaneously like I used to. Other people don't know it, but I have to stop and think first. I know it though. My focus isn't the way it should be, and I am tired a lot.

Barbara ran her own business making silk decorations at home. She said that she constantly had to put her work down (thus interrupting her concentration) to run down to the basement to care for her mother-in-law who shared their home. Barbara said, "It is okay most of the time, but she doesn't care if I have a customer or not when she yells. That makes it hard to be professional."

Finally, Beth sometimes brought her mother to work with her. Before she was able to switch from a full-time dental assistant to a part-time receptionist, Beth would sometimes take her mother to work with her after day care and have her wait in the waiting room. Although Beth's employer agreed to this situation, having her mother in the waiting room distracted from Beth's ability to work. Beth used this arrangement for only a short period until she switched to part-time work.

Although these effects were subtle, the impact on the caregiver's longer range career may be more substantial. For example, not being able to concentrate at work can have long-lasting implications for one's career mobility if productivity is diminished or if the caregiver makes more mistakes. In general, to the extent that family interferes with work, caregivers may be seen as less effective employees.

MANAGING WORK AND CAREGIVING

Caregivers who continued to work despite providing care for a disabled parent somehow managed to fulfill both roles. The following section lists some of their strategies and the circumstances that allowed them to manage both roles. For those who eventually terminated their employment, the strategies they used while still working are discussed.

Co-Residence

For many of the caregivers, having their parent move in with them made caregiving a much more manageable set of tasks. In all, 60 percent of the caregivers co-resided with their parents. Although we often think of co-residence as being for the sake of the elder, it can also be for the sake of the caregiver as well. One-half of the caregivers who co-resided with their parent (sixteen out of thirty or 53 percent) mentioned that they were always running over to their parent's house before they asked their mother or father to move in. Co-resident caregivers also had only one house to clean and one set of meals to prepare once their parents moved in with them. According to Connie,

> That was the worst time. I didn't have the money to pay someone to stay with my mother. She lives 20 minutes away from work and I am 20 minutes away from work, so it wasn't easy. And it wasn't just the time. I always felt guilty because she wanted me to stay longer and I couldn't. It was sad seeing her so lonely.

Among those who did not co-reside, 70 percent (fourteen out of twenty) reported "racing back and forth." Judy exemplified the increased difficulty of caregiving when the parent was in a separate residence.

> In the morning, I go over and strip the bed and clean her because she is incontinent. I have to be to work at 7:00, so I get to her house at 6:00. . . . On the days she doesn't go to day care, I go to her house during my lunch hour to get her lunch and feed her. . . . Then I go back at night after work to get her ready for bed as much as I can. I stay an hour or so. Then I go home to fix dinner for my own family and clean my own house.

Having a parent co-reside did not in itself make it possible to work while being a caregiver; it just eased some of the burden. Instead, it was necessary to have someone care for the parent during the day while the caregiver worked. Caregivers employed the following stagies to care for parents while they worked: using adult day care, having the other parent at home, sharing care with siblings, sharing care with wives and other female kin, hiring help, and caring for parents with minimal needs.

Adult Day Care

Using adult day care provided many caregivers with the opportunity to work during the day. Although one-third of the sample of caregivers were recruited from adult day care centers (thus biasing the sample in the direction of those who used them), nearly two-thirds of the caregivers (thirty-two out of fifty) had their parents in day care one or more days a week. Twenty-two (44 percent) of the caregivers depended on day care as the source to care for their parents while they worked.

On average, most elders attended the program three days a week. For those caregivers who worked full-time and had no one else to help with caregiving, elders were more likely to attend five days a week. Approximately 65 percent of the elders received financial assistance with the cost of the program, either through Medicaid or Elder Home Care which reimbursed on a sliding scale. In all cases, the parents themselves paid for the additional cost of the program with either social security/pension funds or with savings.

Six of the caregivers (12 percent) managed to work and provide care through a combination of adult day care and sharing care with their own nuclear families. In one case, the daughter's in-laws also helped to take care of her mother. Kathy's example is typical of the varied substitutes that caregivers needed:

> On Tuesdays and Thursdays my in-laws pick her up [at day care] at 3:00. She stays with them until my husband can pick her up at 6:00. Then he stays with her until I can get home, another two or three hours. On the other days, we pay a woman to stay with her until my husband gets home. [The money came from her mother's social security.] My husband or my in-laws stay with her every Saturday, and my sister-in-law stays every fourth Sunday when I work.

Kathy's rotating schedule made it difficult to find a steady source of care for her mother. In addition, she often had to work with very little notice, requiring her to then find someone to care for her mother. Thus, her in-laws' willingness to provide care occasionally and at the spur-of-the-moment were a "godsend."

Connie had a similar arrangement. Her mother went to day care four days a week. Since her husband worked nights, he took care of his mother-in-law during the day if she needed to stay home because of an illness and on the fifth day when she did not go to day care. In the afternoon, Connie's three teenage daughters stayed with their grandmother and cooked dinner before their mother got home at 6:30.

> The whole family pitches in to take care of my mother. That was settled before we asked her to move in because one person cannot do it alone. My mother doesn't like my husband to be involved though, particularly with the colostomy bag . . . but I need everyone to fill in after [day care].

Adult day care was a particularly effective strategy for caregivers who worked part-time. By arranging day care on the days that they worked, adult children working part-time were able to find full care for their parents through this one source. When Beth worked full-time, she sometimes had to take her mother to work with her after day care. By switching to part-time work, Beth was able to fully cover her time away with adult day care. Of course, not everyone could afford to work part-time, nor did all occupations offer such a luxury.

At least some of the caregivers originally used adult day care to permit their parents to have social contact with others their own age. Later, however, it became impossible to leave the parent alone. At that point, caregivers used day care as a solution to the work–caregiving conflict, often signing their parents up for additional days of care.

Working class caregivers were substantially less likely to depend on adult day care than middle class caregivers. Of the eighteen caregivers who did not use adult day care, 100 percent were working class. Although middle class caregivers did use formal services more frequently (primarily adult day care and occasionally visiting nurses), they were still paid for primarily by Medicaid or Elder Home Care, with the remainder of the bill being covered by the parent with social security or pension funds.

Having the Other Parent at Home

Four of the caregivers (8 percent) who worked full-time were able to combine work and caregiving because the other parent (in-law) was also at home during the day to provide coverage. In all four cases, the fathers provided needed supervision during the day, but the bulk of the caregiving tasks fell to the children (in-law). It is just that their "shift" began after a full work day.

Celia cared for her mother-in-law who had Alzheimer's. Celia's husband got his mother dressed and fed in the morning before he went to work, while her father-in-law cared for her during the day. After a full day of working, Celia then cared for her at night. This included bathing and feeding Kay and constantly monitoring and soothing her. Celia believed that if her father-in-law were unable to care for Kay during the day, they would not be able to keep her at home.

Sharing Care with Siblings

Other caregivers (ten out of fifty or 20 percent) were able to work full-time because they shared caregiving with their siblings. Six of the caregivers relied exclusively on siblings to provide care while they worked (sometimes substituted by other family members), whereas four of the caregivers relied on a combination of siblings and adult day care. Liza and her siblings were able to divide care for their father (and now for their mother) for nearly eight years before their father died. Each of the siblings had a shift one night a week, and they took turns on the weekends. (For more detail, see chapter 4 on siblings and the division of labor.)

To maintain the caregiving network, new caregivers must be added as others drop out of the network. One or more relatives is also needed to provide care during the day while the others are working, or they must have complementary work schedules. In addition, when siblings divide up care in shifts, as Liza and her family did, all of the caregivers, including the brothers, must provide personal care rather than simply assisting the caregiver.

All except for one of the caregivers who shared care with siblings was working class. The one caregiver who was not working class was the first generation from her family born in the United States. The greater willingness of siblings to share care in the working class suggests a higher level of family interdependence. Indeed, working class caregivers were more likely to emphasize the importance of family as the major source of care for the elderly as compared to middle class caregivers. Although it is quite likely that their parents could have afforded formal care given state subsidization, they preferred to rely on family assistance.

Sharing Care with Wives and Other Female Kin

While daughters were more likely to share care with siblings, sons were more likely to share care with their wives or other female kin while they worked. This is consistent with previous findings by Horowitz (1985b). Use of the term *sharing* may be misleading, however, since much of the care was "shifted" to female kin. Five out of the eight sons (63 percent) had others who provided care for their mothers at least part of the time while they worked. Two of the men relied on their wives who did not work, while the other three relied on a sister, sister-in-law, or, in the last case, two aunts. It is not clear whether they would have become caregivers if these female kin were not available and if caregiving interfered with their employment. All of the men, however, did provide regular assistance and were named by others as the caregiver. In situations in which sons did not provide regular assistance, it was their female kin who were interviewed.

The following are three examples of sons receiving assistance from female kin. In George's case, his mother required minimal supervision during the day which his wife provided. At night, either George or his wife helped their mother (in-law) to take a bath. Mark's sister-in-law cared for his mother during the day at her home (and often late into the evening and on weekends), while Mark helped his mother to dress and gave her her evening medication at the home that they shared. Doug's sister came to his home in the morning and late at night to get his mother bathed and dressed, and she stayed with her after day care until his wife came home from work. Doug did get up with his mother at night, however, to take her to the bathroom and to give her her medications. He and his wife took his mother to church and to doctors' appointments. In contrast, none of the daughters received as much assistance from their husbands.

Hired Help

Two of the caregivers (4 percent) hired someone to provide care for their parents while they worked. In one instance, a daughter hired someone to clean the house while she worked. This also fulfilled the need for someone to watch over her father while she worked, although he did not agree that he needed a caregiver. In the second situation, the mother hired someone to help her get ready for day care in the morning because her daughter had to be at work early. Her daughter then cared for her in the evening. In both situations, the daughters eventually quit their jobs, one on Disability Leave and the other in between jobs, at least partially due to their parents' needs.

Parent's Needs Are "Minimal"

Other caregivers were able to work because their parents' needs were relatively minimal. Four elderly parents required help only with bathing or dressing. Two others needed assistance with getting in and out of bed as well (12 percent total). As a result, their children were able to work during the day and provide assistance in the morning and evening.

For caregivers who did not live with their parents, this required a great deal of running back and forth. But at this point in their parents' health trajectory, they were able to do both. New strategies may be needed, however, when (and if) their parents' health worsens so that they require assistance throughout the day.

While this sample may be biased in that caregivers were more likely to have a second parent living at home or other relatives who could care for their parent at least part of the day, the consistency of these findings suggests that these are the resources that are necessary to combine work and caregiving. A separate study might address whether working children without such resources are more likely to institutionalize their disabled parents.

STRATEGIES MAY NOT BE FOOLPROOF

These "strategies" were not foolproof. Many of the caregivers said that they did not know what they would do if their parent had an emergency or, for those who could be left alone for awhile, required more care. Using extra vacation days for doctors' appointments, at least some of the caregivers even questioned what they would do if their parents required a modest change in care. That is, there was little leeway in their schedules for any increase in care. Kathy noted,

> So far, luckily, my mother hasn't gotten sick. I am not sure what I will do if she does. I am a manager, so it isn't easy to take time off. I guess I would

have to find someone to stay with her all day and that gets pretty expensive. Right now, her money is going out fast.

Although use of adult day care was a common solution to the work–family conflict, many of the caregivers pointed out that going to the center could be very tiring for their parents. In particular, elders needed time in between visits to rest and recuperate. Therefore, full-time day care may not be in the best interest of the elder in the long run, although it certainly made it more feasible to work full-time.

WORK AS A GODSEND

Although we often think of work (outside of the home) and caregiving as being conflicting obligations, one-quarter of the caregivers volunteered (without prompting) that their work was a "godsend" that made caregiving a little easier. According to Liza, "I need my job to get my mind off them [her parents]. It is my sanity." Similarly, Brenda commented, "Work is a break. I can finally use my brain. I am so busy, it takes my mind off everything here [at home]. I wouldn't want to give it up."

All of the caregivers who found their work to be helpful in alleviating the stress of caregiving also enjoyed their jobs very much. While some enjoyed the satisfaction of knowing they had done a job well, others enjoyed the people they worked with or the particular tasks they performed. This was true for working class caregivers as well, suggesting that working class jobs also offer intrinsic rewards that balance the difficulties of caregiving. For all, it was the one area of their lives where their contributions were recognized. Susan commented, "My work is very important to me; I love it. I do a very good job, and I know it. If I lost that, it would be the hardest thing for me."

The fact that working outside of the home made caregiving a little easier is consistent with previous findings and with the role accumulation theory (Moen, Robison, and Dempster-McClain, 1995; Scharlach, 1994; Stoller and Pugliesi, 1989). According to this theory, as people gain roles, they accumulate satisfaction and achievement. Workers, including those in the working class, gain psychologically from their role in the form of status, social relationships, and self-esteem (Moen, 1992; Verbrugge, 1982). Multiple roles also allow one to compensate for limitations in each of the separate roles (Scharlach, 1994). In this study, it was the workers who enjoyed their work the most and who derived the most satisfaction from it who suggested that work was a "godsend." As such, work may compensate for the difficulties of caregiving.

LIFE COURSE STRUGGLE

Caring for an elderly parent is usually confined to that period of the life cycle, middle age, when sons and daughters have yet to retire. The trajectories for the careers of work and elder care therefore interlock, each being affected by the timing of events in the other. However, they more than interlock; they actually clash due both to the amount of time it takes to be a caregiver and to the constancy required in providing assistance. Being a caregiver does not necessarily cause one to quit one's job. Instead, caregivers find strategies to combine these opposing trajectories and are sometimes fortunate to have employers who offer flexible work hours.

Further along in the life course, when caregivers no longer participate in work outside of the home, additional roles may be substituted that will also conflict with parent care. These may include the onset of caring for one's own spouse or (less frequently) grandchildren. How these same caregivers would reconcile conflict within the same career trajectory, family care, would be an interesting followup study.

EMPLOYERS' ACCOMMODATIONS

Nearly all of the caregivers stated that the flexibility offered by their employers made it possible to combine work and caregiving. This included being able to work part-time, determine one's own schedule, and work at home. By far, the most common concession made by employers was to allow their employees to arrange their own schedules, within certain limits. Edith, typical of the others, started work fifteen minutes late because she had to wait for the van from day care to pick up her mother-in-law. Her supervisor agreed that this was no problem as long as Edith worked her full eight hours. Although Mutschler (1994) found that some working class positions did not allow for rearranging work schedules, results of this study suggested that both working class and middle class caregivers had this option. It should be noted, however, that there was sometimes less latitude for working class positions.

Other caregivers observed that it was helpful to take work home with them. Connie and Susan, both middle class, could take at least part of their work home with them. Connie's boss said that he did not care where she did her work as long as it got done. Susan added that sometimes at the end of the day she was so tired she could not possibly work at home. Although the option was available, it did not make work and caregiving more compatible. Several caregivers also worked in their own homes, including Billie who was a foster parent and Barbara who made silk decorations. At times, however it was very difficult for Barbara to get her work done owing to her mother-in-law's needs. Other working class caregivers did not have the option of working at home.

Several caregivers also noted how important it was to be able to leave work and come back. This allowed them to take their parents for doctors' appointments and other errands or to run to their parents' homes in the case of an emergency. While some of the caregivers made this time up by working late, others credited time away from work toward their "personal days." The nurses (except for the home health aides), managers, and the owner of a small beauty shop argued that they could not take time off in the middle of a shift. Clerical staff, however, whether working or middle class, were most likely to say that they took time off during the day.

Several caregivers also mentioned the importance of being able to make and receive calls during the day. Whether to check on their parents or to arrange appointments, phone calls allowed them to be "caregivers-in-absentia." Only in one case did a supervisor intervene when Judy was receiving a dozen or more messages from her mother during the course of a day.

Less frequently did caregivers have the option of working part-time in the same job. While Deborah was able to switch to part-time work as a beautician, Beth had to change jobs (from being a receptionist to a dental hygienist) when she wanted to work part-time. In Beth's situation, this involved a cut in pay (both the hourly wage and overall compensation for the number of hours worked), benefits, and prestige. Similarly, consistent with Mutschler's (1994) findings that professionals had fewer options to change jobs, part-time work may be less of an option for middle class occupations.

IMPLICATIONS

Despite the prevalence of adult children who provide care to elderly parents, society offers little assistance to the family. Instead, social policy reinforces the ideology of familism, that the family is the appropriate provider of care and does not need support (Walker, 1996). Results of this study suggest that although family members do wish to provide care themselves, they are also crying out for assistance from other family members, employers, and the government. The following is a discussion of the policy implications with regard to work.

Adult Day Health Centers

In terms of the linkage with work, caregivers in this sample pointed to the need to improve adult day health centers. In particular, caregivers who used adult day health as the source of care for their parents while they were at work stated that they needed day care to extend throughout the afternoon. Elders returned home as early as 2:30 in the afternoon, long before their adult children were home from work.

Adult day health care is limited in other ways as well. For example, caregivers needed temporary care for their parents while they were sick (since they could not go to the adult day health center) or when the adult day health center was closed due to snow. Four of the caregivers (8 percent) had other family members who were available to provide care during such occasions, while the others said that they had to take the day off from work. Finally, caregivers pointed to the need for greater subsidization of day care since they found it to be very expensive. Eight of the caregivers (16 percent) wanted to send their parents to day care more often but could not afford to do so. The source of funding for increased subsidization of day care would likely come from a progressive tax.

The Family and Medical Leave Act

Only two months shy of being fully introduced at the time of this study, the Family and Medical Leave Act (FMLA), which went into effect August 5, 1993, provides up to twelve weeks of unpaid leave to workers at companies with fifty or more employees for the birth of a child or the care of a seriously ill relative, such as a parent. It is unlikely that this piece of legislation will help working and middle class caregivers who cannot afford twelve weeks without pay. Said one caregiver of an earlier time when her mother was left totally in her care while her sister, the primary caregiver, traveled: "I could no more afford to take those three weeks off as I could to quit permanently and take care of my mother." In addition, the vast majority of caregivers were not even aware that this option existed. Interviews were conducted in June and July of 1993 when the FMLA was receiving much attention. Only three of the caregivers (6 percent) knew of the Act and the possible implications for themselves. In addition, half of the caregivers currently employed worked for small companies with fewer than fifty employees and, therefore, would not benefit from the legislation.

The FMLA may have been a welcome relief for those caregivers who occasionally needed to take a day off (for emergencies, for example) but who had already used all of their sick or vacation days. Under these circumstances—the option of losing a day's pay or leaving an ill parent at home—most of the caregivers probably would have forfeited the money. Prior to the FMLA, they risked losing their jobs.

A higher commitment to a guaranteed leave with pay for large and small companies is needed. The financing of such a program would clearly be a hardship for any company. However, the cost could be more effectively shared by state and federal governments if paid leave reduced rates of institutionalization and the spending down of savings which then resulted in the need for nursing home reimbursement. Such benefits could also be phased in to minimize economic disruptions (Ferber and O'Farrell, 1991) and could be offered as one of several benefits to choose from (Wagner, 1991). That is, funds would be available in a dependent care account to be used as necessary by employees. Remington, for example, established a spending account to reimburse employees for the cost of needed services. The company set up a system for processing claims and helping employees to gain access to in-home respite services (Wagner, 1991). In addition, companies might find that extended leaves of absence are no more costly than high rates of absenteeism and low worker productivity or retraining employees (Ferber and O'Farrell, 1991; Scharlach and Boyd, 1989).

Additional Workplace Initiatives

At the outset, employers need to be more responsive to the caregiving needs of adult children. While employers are aware that elder care is an issue for their employees, less than 10 percent have studied the problem and even fewer have developed policies (Seccombe, 1992). Those programs that do exist are informal or are confined to larger companies such as Travelers Insurance (Wagner, 1991). Although 2,500 of the nation's 44,000 largest employers offer child care services to their employees, elder care policies in the workplace are so new and innovative that one author referred to them as "still at the threshold" (Magnus, 1988).

Policy analysts suggest that the workplace should offer additional programs to accommodate the family needs of their employees. They argue that employers and unions should support the development of resource and referral programs to provide employees with information on available services, employee assistance programs to provide counseling and education, and direct and indirect assistance for the care of dependent family members. This would include direct on-site day care and respite as well as indirect reimbursement (whether partial or full) for care during the work day (Ferber and O'Farrell, 1991; Wagner, 1991). These services would be considered part of an overall benefits package.

Employer-based initiatives have been found to be successful. In one study of employed caregivers in Portland, Oregon, researchers found that respondents who worked for companies with more family-friendly policies provided fewer hours of help and less health care, social support, and home maintenance (Starrels, Ingersoll-Dayton, Neal, and Yamada, 1995). Employers with more flexible personnel policies may have also offered more information on alternative sources of care, thus reducing their employees' need to provide extensive care. The caregivers in this study also agreed that the referral programs would have been helpful at the very beginning of caregiving and that it might have been easier if the adult day care were at their work site, but that they would not jeopardize relocating their parents at this point.

It has also been suggested that employers offer flexible benefits packages that allow employees to choose among options that are more fitting to their life cycle needs (Ferber and O'Farrell, 1991; Voydanoff, 1987; Wagner, 1991). Thus, while parents of young children might choose child care subsidies, adult children of older parents would have access to long-term care insurance or subsidies for formal health care services. In their early and middle years, employees would pay into a dependent care account, to be used if necessary for the care of young children or elderly parents or to be returned upon retirement if not fully used.

Businesses and supervisors who currently offer little or no flexibility to their employees need to consider innovative ways to restructure the workplace to allow such needed flexibility. Although employees in working class positions did have some flexibility in rearranging their work schedules, options were limited for taking work home or leaving for a short period in the middle of the day. Similarly, employees in middle class positions often could not work part-time, and they, too, were sometimes limited in leaving work during the middle of the day. Given the importance of such flexibility to the caregivers in this study, employers may find worker productivity and morale enhanced by offering flexible hours to caregivers. Such a question is certainly worthy of further investigation.

The high number of women working for small businesses also suggests the need to expand benefits coverage beyond large companies. It may be more difficult for small businesses to provide such benefits. However, the fact that the majority of caregivers were concentrated in this area suggests that it in fact be the target of change.

The results of this study cry out for the need to support adult children caring for elderly parents. The initiatives discussed here will be costly to taxpayers and employers. Yet the current lack of policy is also costly to families and indirectly to employers and taxpayers by accelerating institutionalization and employee absenteeism. By supporting family policy, we will promote intergenerational linkages that will be beneficial to us all, whether now or in the future.

CHAPTER 6

Stress and Implications for Family Life

Researchers have noted that emotional stress and strain are by far the most pervasive and severe effects of caregiving (Brody, 1990; Kaye and Applegate, 1990; Montgomery, 1992). For both sons and daughters, interference between caregiving and one's personal or social life is a central source of strain. For daughters, the strain is caused specifically by a poor relationship with their parents and interference with work, while for sons, the causes are behavioral problems on the part of the parents and having few informal helpers (Mui, 1995). The effects do not stop here. The strain in turn leads to increased levels of depression, exhaustion, eating problems, and other psychiatric and health-related problems for caregivers (Abel, 1991; Braithwaite, 1996; Brody, 1990).

Not everyone is at similar risk of stress. In fact, some caregivers do not experience any stress, at least not at high levels. Caregivers who are most affected include women, older caregivers because they are in poorer health, and those who co-reside with the elder (Brody, 1990; Cantor, 1983; Moen, Robison, and Dempster-McClain, 1995). Family members who care for elders with more disabilities or with degenerative conditions also have higher rates of emotional stress, as do those who provide hands-on personal care or who care for elders with disruptive behaviors (Braithwaite, 1996; Brody, 1990; Kaye and Applegate, 1990; Levesque, Cossette, and Laurin, 1995; Noelker and Townsend, 1987; Pruchno and Resch, 1989; Stoller and Pugliesi, 1989).

The stress effects of caregiving are moderated by other contexts as well. Factors associated with lower amounts of burden or stress include higher levels of affection for the care receiver and assistance or support from others (Clipp and George, 1990; George and Gwyther, 1986; Thompson, Futterman, Gallagher-Thompson, Rose, and Lovett, 1993; Townsend and Noelker, 1987). Among daughters providing care, being married significantly decreases the strain from caregiving and lowers depression, suggesting support from husbands (Brody, Litvin, Hoffman, and Kleban, 1992). Daughters with better relationships with the mothers they care for are also less likely to experience frustration, anxiety, and a feeling of insufficient time (Walker, Martin, and Jones, 1992). Caregivers with prior high emotional well-being report high well-being as caregivers (Moen, Robison, and Dempster-McClain, 1995). This suggests a cumulativeness of advantage, those with superior emotional health being better equipped to take on caregiving responsibilities. Those with a higher level of caregiver mastery also report reduced role strain, suggesting the importance of the caregiver's "sense of control" (Miller, Campbell, Farran, Kaufman, and Davis, 1995). Nonfamily roles are also other important buffers. Women who are currently working and have been caregivers report being better off in terms of self-esteem and life satisfaction than nonemployed women (Moen, Robison, and Dempster-McClain, 1995).

Results are mixed regarding gender differences in perceived levels of stress. According to one group of researchers, daughters reported higher levels of burden or stress than did sons (Kramer and Kipnis, 1995; Montgomery, 1992 for overview; Mui, 1995). This difference may have been due to the greater investment of time, physical energy, and emotion that characterized caregiving by daughters. Indeed, Kramer and Kipnis (1995) found that the gender difference in caregiver burden decreased once they controlled for care provision tasks, work role strains, and resources. Similarly, Stoller and Pugliesi (1989) found no gender differences in levels of stress for sons and daughters caring for parents living in the community as the daughters (as well as sons) in their sample did not provide hands-on personal care. Montgomery and Kamo (1989) also reported no differences between sons and daughters in levels of objective and subjective burden. They attributed this lack of difference to the high level of care provided by sons (as well as daughters) for this substantially impaired population. Thus, levels of burden reported are more comparable when sons and daughters provide similar types and amounts of care.

Although most studies of caregiving focus on the implications for the caregiver, they omit consideration of the caregiver's family (Abel, 1991;

Kahana, Biegel, and Wykle, 1994; Kane and Penrod, 1995; Kaye and Applegate, 1990). However, particularly for adult children in the earlier stages of the family life cycle, their own nuclear families are likely to be severely impacted by caregiving. Those few studies that do exist suggest that caregivers have less time with family members (Brody, 1985), which is likely to be particularly troublesome for mothers with young children. But what about the impact on older children as well? Are their lives affected by their parents' caregiving in ways that we have not considered in focusing on younger children? In addition, we know that caregiving affects marital satisfaction over the short run (Suitor and Pillemer, 1994). In fact, 66 percent of husbands report strain from their wives' caregiving (Kleban, Brody, Schoonover, and Hoffman, 1989). But what about the impact over the long run? In addition, how does caregiving affect the day-to-day interaction with spouses? Finally, it is expected that family members will have less privacy, particularly if the older person is co-resident, and may even resent the caregiver's involvement. These issues and others are examined in this chapter.

This chapter then examines the stress from caregiving and the implications for the caregiver's nuclear family. The chapter begins by considering the context in which stressful caregiving takes place. Also in this chapter, the implications of stress for family life and relationships with spouse and children are considered, including family members' attitudes toward the caregivers' involvement in caregiving and whether or not there is assistance from nuclear family members. How stress affects the caregivers' health and leisure time are also considered. In particular, there will likely be class differences in expectations of both health and leisure, which will differentially impact working class caregivers' perceptions of whether or not caregiving has a negative effect.

CAREGIVING AND STRESS

All of the caregivers agreed that caregiving was very stressful. However, the strain in their voices and the pain with which some of the caregivers talked of forgone leisure and time with family as well as sleep deprivation indicated that caregiving was more stressful for some caregivers than for others. Consider the following accounts:

> Sometimes I am really dragging. . . . It is worse when my kids are sick and on the days that I work. . . . I'm up until 11:00 or 12:00 [at night] doing housework and then I get up at 6:00 [in the morning]. I told my own mother

that I wished I didn't live here anymore. . . . It is just too much, you know? You don't have a life anymore, you know?

It is like living three lives. I can't take my mother-in-law anywhere. But we don't have anyone in because my father-in-law is embarrassed. . . . It is like being the mother of young kids again. You are never relieved. We are always worried that she will wander into the woods or water. Sometimes we sneak out and go places. My husband says we should give his dad a break, but I say, "NO, we need to see our son too!" Then I worry about them all of the time because they don't know how to get in touch with us.

At times, the stress reached dangerous levels. According to one caregiver,

Sometimes I just feel like I am going to blow up. I am working so hard here [at work], at home, at my mother's. Then I see that she messed herself again, and I scream at her. I just want to shake her, but what good would that do?

Only a minority of caregivers (four out of fifty or 8 percent) volunteered that they had been abusive to their parent, although a much higher percentage admitted being near abuse. Caregivers who were abusive had handled their parent roughly, shaken or pushed their parent, or withheld food or changing. Another daughter admitted to locking her father in the basement and pinning him to the floor when he was disruptive, although she did not regard this as abusive.

Certain caregivers were at greater risk of stress than others. Anxiety levels were quite high for those children who felt that caregiving was their responsibility but who had no one with whom they could share that responsibility. Often in these situations, children could not consider institutionalization as an alternative. As a result, they felt a heightened sense of inescapable burden. Susan, the most frazzled of all the caregivers, believed that she had to provide care for her mother for as long as was "humanly" possible. Divorced and with only some assistance from her brother, Susan felt total responsibility for her parents. She stated,

I don't go anywhere without leaving my parents a number. Then I worry all night. I call before I go, and I call when I get back. . . . The only time when I am not with my parents is Sunday afternoon when my brother comes. But then I have to catch up on everything at my house and so I will have clean clothes for work. I just iron the parts people see. I don't see my own daughter or have flowers in my yard. . . . What can I do though [crying]?

In contrast to those who felt they had no alternative, at least two of the daughters-in-law suggested that caregiving was an option they could relinquish if it became too much for either them or their families. As such, they did not report as high a level of anxiety from caregiving. According to Brenda, "I told my husband that we would try it. But I don't know. We have our names in [at the nursing home] just in case it doesn't work out." In addition, caregivers who shared the tasks more equally with their siblings reported more flexibility in spending time with friends and seemed to feel less strain from caregiving.

Consistent with findings from the literature (Brody, 1990; Pruchno and Resch, 1989), caregiving was also more stressful when the parent wandered or repeatedly asked the same questions or was "unmanageable" in other ways. In contrast to prior research, the extent of hands-on personal care needed did not increase strain as much. According to Susan, whose mother had Alzheimer's and whose father had some physical disabilities, "I am more patient with my father, but my mother is extremely frustrating. I have to tell her the same things over and over again. It never clicks." For Rose, it was her mother's constant screaming which was most stressful. She stated,

> I don't mind the cleaning and feeding. But the grief and aggravation my mother puts me through. She is never happy; it is never enough. She screams all the time and I just can't stop it. I can't stop it [crying].

Celia had to watch her mother-in-law, Kay, continuously because she wandered. As a result, her time at home was strained by needing to monitor Kay while simultaneously accomplishing tasks around the house. In addition, her mother-in-law repeatedly asked where her husband was and how to get to him, although he was just in the next room. Not remembering her way around the house, Celia had to guide Kay to her husband. At night, Kay begged to go "home," even though she had lived with Celia for several years. Sometimes driving her mother-in-law around the block in a car was enough to convince her that she was home. Also adding to the strain was Kay's inability to remember either Celia or her husband. She believed that they were nice people whom she was visiting.

In the process of becoming caregivers, adult children and their own nuclear families endured many adjustments. However, there was one adjustment that often goes unnoticed by researchers. Of the children who had their parents move in with them (60 percent), half made some physical alterations to their homes in order to accommodate their parent. Both working class and middle class families sometimes finished off a part of the basement that the parent could live in. Only one middle class family was able to add on another room to the house, although many families mentioned that they would like to do so if they had more money. Another caregiver from the middle class installed special equipment, a walk-in shower, for her mother. Two families from the working class needed similar showers (or sunken tubs) but could not afford them. Deborah also found a larger apartment to share with her father, although it was her father who paid the rent. Others managed to get by with what they already had in their homes.

Caregiving stress did appear to be related to gender but only indirectly. Daughters were more likely to report high levels of stress from caregiving and to describe caregiving in very stressful terms. That is, twenty-eight out of thirty-two (or 88 percent) of daughters versus four out of eight (or 50 percent) of sons reported high levels of stress (chi-square $(1) = 3.49; p < .10$). This may have been due to several factors. Brothers were more likely than sisters to receive assistance from siblings (see chapter 4). Consistent with previous findings (Clipp and George, 1990; George and Gwyther, 1986; Townsend and Noelker, 1987), receipt of assistance (especially from a relative with a similar level of responsibility) reduces the amount of stress that the caregiver experiences. In addition, daughters appeared to care for elders with both greater physical needs and more extensive dementia. Of the most severely impaired elders (whether cognitively or physically), all were cared for by daughters (and daughters-in-law). These results are consistent with the findings of Stoller and Pugliesi (1989) that gender differences in levels of stress were due to the greater personal care provided by daughters. Findings from this study suggest that cognitive impairment and disruptive behavior were the most anxiety-provoking for caregivers. Finally, prior research suggests that for daughters, but not sons, interference with work causes strain (Mui, 1995). This research shows that sons were less likely to experience work disruption. Thus, daughters were more likely to experience strain.

A useful comparison of sons and daughters is to consider the examples of Frank and Susan. Frank insisted that his relatives help with caregiving and believed that a nursing home was a viable option should he no longer be able to provide care. Although his mother was constrained to a wheel-chair and was cantankerous, she did not require extensive assistance and did not suffer from dementia. As a result Frank did not experience a high level of stress. He stated,

> I have my priorities straight. . . . I have limits of what I am willing to do and I just tell her when I can't do something. . . . I think family is obligated, but I won't let it take over my life.

In comparison, Susan's mother suffered from Alzheimer's disease and had extensive incontinence. Susan's only "free time" was Sunday afternoons and occasionally Friday evenings when her brother cared for her parents. Compounding the stress was Susan's belief that she was obligated to provide care for as long as she could. Susan seemed the most frazzled of all the caregivers. She stated,

> My mother always said every day of her life, "I hope that God takes me . . . before I have to go into a nursing home." I have that implanted on my mind. . . . I have to give her that wish.

Daughters were more likely to voice similar feelings of limited alternatives, while sons were more likely to receive assistance and to believe there were alternatives to caregiving.

Stress, however, was not related to the length of time caregiving. Nor was there a curvilinear relationship with both groups, those who had just begun caregiving and those with many years of caregiving being highest in terms of caregiving stress. Such a relationship would have suggested that stress decreases as caregivers adjust to their role and gain self-confidence in caregiving and then increases again over time. Regarless of how long someone had been caregiving, stress was instead related to the caregiver's perceptions of having total responsibility for the parent as well as caring for "unmanageable" parents.

IMPLICATIONS FOR RELATIONSHIP WITH SPOUSE

One of the most frequent comments from adult children was that caregiving impeded on their time with their own families, both spouses and children. While nearly one-quarter of the caregivers had minor children in the home, slightly more than half were married. In terms of spending time with their spouses, nearly all of the middle class caregivers commented that they no longer had the opportunity to go out to dinner. Working class caregivers were less likely to mention going out to dinner but did say that they could not do things with their friends for the evening such as visiting at one another's homes. Families with small children found that "regular babysitters" were not appropriate for disabled parents, so there was no convenient overlap allowing them to go out. Nor did they feel that they could spend money for nursing care beyond what was required to cover their work hours or very special occasions. Several families with older children said that they were able to go out at night if they planned events after the parent had gone to bed and if one of their children would stay home. Still, it was not the carefree life that they had known earlier. Both working and middle class caregivers reported activities with their spouses being curtailed by caregiving, although the activities themselves varied.

Although none of the caregivers had divorced during their caregiving careers, nearly all stated that caregiving was hard on their spouses, often causing strain in the marriage. For example, one of the daughters volunteered the following,

> The thing that caregiving has affected the most is my marriage. My mother is needy. She always wants to be with me. But sometimes she can be intrusive. My husband works nights, so we don't have much time together. When we need some quiet time to talk things over, it may be hard to get. We can be in our bedroom, and she will knock on the door until someone answers it. So if we need to have a private conversation, we have to go *out*! It is also hard to fight. . . . She thinks we are fighting about her.

Susan, who was divorced, mentioned that caregiving made it difficult for her to date. At the time of the interview, she had been seeing someone steadily. However, she was concerned that her constant fatigue and inability to get away more than one night a week would drive her boyfriend off. She sighed, "I finally meet a nice guy and I can't stay awake through dinner. But how can I pick a boyfriend over my parents?"

Although the caregivers believed that their spouses were frustrated by not being able to spend time together, only one of the caregivers implied that his spouse was opposed to the caregiving arrangement. Dominic bought his parents' house many years ago, in part to make necessary improvements to the family home that he and his father built but also to be available to care for his parents. He did this against his wife's wishes. Dominic stated,

> [Referring to buying the house . . .] My wife never forgave me. That is why she works. Two women in one house. . . . It never works. This is my wife's house, but my mother thinks of it as hers. My wife can't decorate like she wants. She has to work around my mother. There have been problems. . . . I have been in the middle.

It may be that Dominic's wife was more opposed to living in her mother-in-law's home than she was to Dominic providing care. Still, caregiving was difficult because it impeded on their time together.

It is harder for my wife than it is for me. She is ten years younger than me, so she should be enjoying herself. She has raised her kids. We are never alone to hold hands, not even for ten minutes. We can't go out to dinner without hurrying or go away by ourselves. This is no life for her. It isn't her mother. I am afraid that if something doesn't give, I may be divorced.

Several other caregivers mentioned that they did not invite their parents to live with them because it would "destroy [their] marriages." Donna, for example, was in the process of finding a nursing home for her mother in order to protect her marriage from the next step in caregiving, having her mother move in with her.

The fact that Dominic was concerned that his wife would consider divorce is consistent with previous findings that marital satisfaction decreased due to caregiving when the caregiver's spouse did not provide emotional (Franks and Stephens, 1996; Suitor and Pillemer, 1994) or instrumental support (Franks and Stephens, 1996). It was not clear whether Dominic himself was dissatisfied with their marriage. He did, however, seem to be highly distressed by the tension between his wife and mother. Earlier findings suggest that emotional support from *husbands* mitigates the strain of caregiving for daughters (Kleban, Brody, Schoonover, and Hoffman, 1989). Results of this study suggest that the situation extends to sons and their wives as well.

The other spouses, however, did not resent the caregiver's decision to provide care, including both sons-in-law and daughters-in-law. Many of the married caregivers (fourteen out of twenty-nine or 48 percent) referred to the positive relationships between their spouses and parents, pointing out that the spouses were willing to make these sacrifices because they, too, loved their parents-in-law. This suggests that perhaps spouses recognize caregiving as part of their partner's life cycle or their own family life cycle. While it is not surprising that sons-in-law would recognize this, it is worth noting that daughters-in-law also perceived of caregiving as part of their husbands' role as sons. It may be that Dominic's wife was resentful, however, because she did not recognize caregiving as part of her husband's life cycle and, according to Dominic, saw it as more appropriate for Dominic's sister. In addition, it may be that in situations where the children-in-law do not have a good relationship with their parents-in-law, adult children do not become caregivers.

Other caregivers also mentioned that they no longer had the opportunity for a family vacation. This problem was more common for middle class caregivers than for working class caregivers (sixteen out of twenty-six versus eight out of twenty-four families) (chi-square $(1) = 5.14$; $p < .025$). Two of the middle class daughters remedied this problem by taking their parent with them on vacation. For example, Jen took her father to visit her daughter during a family vacation. She stated, "We had a fairly decent time with him there. My daughter is good with him. But it wasn't really a vacation. I mean, it wasn't restful." In addition, taking a parent on vacation was possible only for healthier elders.

Other caregivers tried to piece together a series of substitutes to cover them during rare vacations. Susan managed to get away once by asking distant relations and friends to each make her parents' dinner once a week and by paying an aunt to clean her mother in the morning. "It is a lot of work to put it all together, however. And I have to have backups for people who forget. It will be harder now that my uncle is sick. He can't make dinner." Susan also paid her aunt back beyond financial compensation by listening to her aunt boast of all that she had done for her, which Susan found to be very difficult.

The effect of caregiving on one's obligations to a spouse was greatest during times of crisis. Four of the daughters were caring for elderly parents while their husbands were also dying. Only one of the women temporarily put her mother in a nursing home so that she could devote more time to caring for her husband. Another woman's husband died within months of being diagnosed, so the period of conflicting obligations was relatively short. For the remaining two women, several years were spent simultaneously caring for their husbands and their mothers. One of the women said that she managed by bringing her mother over to her house so that she could be with both of them at the same time. "They would both be on one couch in the living room, and they would keep each other company. Then I could do things around the house." The fourth woman spent most of her time with her husband who required a great deal of care, but she still managed to bathe, shop, and cook for her mother. All of the women did agree, however, that caring for their mothers took time away from their husbands when they were needed the most.

THE EFFECT ON CHILDREN

Time with children was also adversely affected by caregiving. While we often think only of minor children as being affected, caregivers with grown children lamented not having time for them and their families. Celia, one of the daughters-in-law, was disappointed that she and her husband could not be available to support their adult children, particularly their youngest son who had recently married. She added,

> It is hard for the kids to come over. It just is not a happy house anymore. My older daughter-in-law lets what my mother-in-law says roll off her back. But it is hard on my younger daughter-in-law. So I don't get to see my kids as much.

Other caregivers mentioned wanting to help their daughters with new babies but not being able to because of the time that it took to be a caregiver. Susan said that she would like to do something as simple as take her daughter out to lunch now and then, but she just never had the time.

Lack of time with younger children was also a pressing issue. Brenda had four children between the ages of 8 years and 10 months. She said that she and her husband would have to consider a nursing home for his mother because they simply did not have enough time for their children. Her husband Tom was most angry at his siblings' lack of assistance because it deprived him of time for his kids. Susan stated, "We used to spend all weekend taking our kids to soccer practice and doing fun things with them. We still do a little of it, but not nearly as much."

Caregiving was hard on children in other ways that we often do not consider. Children who lived with their grandparent (including all eleven cases of minor children in the home) had to adjust to the physical and cognitive impairments of the elder such as grandparents no longer remembering them. One of the granddaughters came home from school to find that her grandfather had "attacked" her mother and pinned her to the floor. Their parents' involvement in caregiving deprived them of other advantages that they were used to as well. For example, Deborah related the following:

> Scott understands that we have to take care of his grandfather because he is old and he needs us. He understands respect, but sometimes he asks why he has to live here. My father won't let him play or watch TV if he is noisy. Scott can't understand my father, so he just ignores him. He wants to go to a mother-son sleepover with Boy Scouts, but I can't leave my father alone that long, so he is disappointed.

Children experienced difficulty when their grandparents did not live with them as well. In several situations, children resented their parents being called from the home so often. Eddie's children were angry that their grandparents might call "at the drop of the hat," causing the family to have to change their plans. Although their grandparents' needs were minimal, their parents' caregiving was still a disruption in the children's lives.

For Connie's three daughters, who ranged from 14 to 19 years of age, living with their grandmother was particularly difficult because of their own extensive involvement in caregiving. Each day, the two youngest children came home from school to care for their grandmother and later to cook dinner until their mother arrived home at 6:30. Caring for their grandmother included monitoring and changing her colostomy bag, seeing that she did not wander, administering medications, and generally keeping their grandmother occupied. According to Connie,

> [Changing] the colostomy [bag] is very hard on the kids. . . . There is a fine line between what is appropriate for them and what will rob them [of their childhood]. They need to learn these things and know what the real world is like, but there is a point. So I monitor it.

Connie's oldest daughter felt that caregiving was too much for her sisters. Connie explained,

> We just recently had a family powwow because my oldest daughter is upset. She came home from college and thought that my mother required too much care now . . . that it was unfair to her sisters. I told her that we would have to put Grandma into a nursing home at some point, but I did not think that it was time yet. I couldn't give her a date like she wanted, but I told her that the time would come. But for now, we will just have to work it out. They know that I have veto power. . . . I am sure that we will have more meetings before this is over.

The presence of Connie's mother also disrupted family norms. Connie's daughters found it difficult that their grandmother did not like them to argue with or to challenge their parents, a family style that Connie and her husband had encouraged. "My mother thinks my kids are being disrespectful, so she gets after them. It frustrates them to no end." Thus, the impact on children went beyond just a decrease in time available from parents and affected older children in the home and their lives as well.

Boyd and Treas (1996) argued that while there currently was not a significant number of women with both minor children and elderly parents, demographic trends would result in more "women in the middle" in the future. By the time that today's elderly parents require assistance (after age 75), only a tiny fraction of women still have children at home. However, as women postpone childbearing, adult children return home in greater numbers, and the young-old experience higher levels of chronic disease, there will be more women in the future caring for children and frail parents simultaneously, thus posing greater challenges to later life families.

PATTERNS OF SPOUSAL AND FILIAL ASSISTANCE

Although the majority of the spouses and children were supportive of the caregiver's involvement with their parent (in-law), the emotional support did not necessarily translate into instrumental support. Twenty of the caregivers (40 percent) had either grown children living in the area or teenagers living at home. Of these, only eight caregivers (40 percent) received assistance from their children, half from the working class and half from the middle class. In some cases, children were part of the caregiving network, such as Liza's and Connie's children, and provided fifteen or more hours of care per week. More often, however, children helped out when they were around, such as Billie and Celia's children. In these situations, children would watch their grandparent to give the caregiver a break, help indirectly by cooking meals, or less frequently, stay with their grandparent while their parent went out.

Caregivers were only slightly more likely to receive help from spouses than grown children. Of the twenty-nine caregivers (58 percent) who were married, fourteen (48 percent) received at least some assistance from their spouses. These statistics are consistent with Penrod et al.'s (1995) findings that half of primary caregivers in general received help from their spouses. Similarly, Brody et al. (1992) found that married daughters received more socio-emotional and *instrumental* support overall in comparison to nonmarried daughters. But assistance and support from a spouse more than just decrease the overall amount of care that must be provided. Other researchers have found that they are important in buffering the negative effect of high levels of stress on the caregiver's physical health (Franks and Stephens, 1996; Uchino, Kiecolt-Glaser, and Cacioppo, 1992).

Based on previous findings, daughters-in-law who were providing care were expected to receive less assistance from their respective spouses than sons who were providing care (Walker, 1996). In this study, however, it was the daughters-in-law who received the most assistance. This may have been because daughters-in-law who were caregivers in this study were also working, thus needing their husbands' help. In addition, our cultural assumptions regarding the appropriateness of daughters-in-law over sons as caregivers may be changing due to less rigid gender roles and, again, an increase in daughters-in-law working. As such, the greater assistance given to those whom we consider less appropriate (according to cultural assumptions) for the caregiving role is going to daughters-in-law relative to sons. It is not clear, however, whether this would extend to the general population or only to the working and lower classes.

It was the daughters who received the least assistance from their spouses, perhaps because of the peripheral role of sons-in-law in the family (Rossi and Rossi, 1990). In only one instance did a son-in-law provide enough support to be considered part of the caregiving network. Kathy's husband cared for his mother-in-law several nights a week until Kathy got home from work. He watched her so that she did not wander off and occasionally fixed her meals. He did not help with bathing or dressing his mother-in-law, however. Although sons helped their mothers with personal care tasks and daughters helped their fathers similarly, children-in-law did not provide personal assistance to a parent-in-law of the opposite gender due to barriers of intimacy in in-law relationships. All of the daughters-in-law were caring for mothers-in-law.

While sons were more likely to receive assistance from *siblings* than daughters, unexpectedly, sons were only slightly more likely to receive assistance from their *spouses* than daughters. Half of the married sons (three out of six) received help from their wives. This is in sharp contrast to expectations based on the role of sons in caregiving that sons would receive a great deal of help from their wives due to the gendered nature of caregiving tasks (Coward and Dwyer, 1990; Dwyer and Coward, 1991; Montgomery, 1992; Spitze and Logan, 1990; Stoller, 1990). All of the sons still provided assistance with at least one activity of daily living, despite their wives' assistance. Of the three wives who provided help, one wife cared for her mother-in-law during the day while her husband worked. The other two wives helped their husbands with personal care tasks, but it was their husbands who provided the bulk of care. Of the three married sons who did not receive assistance from their wives, one son received substantial help from his sister. Dominic and Frank, though both married, cared for their mothers alone. Of the four wives who worked outside of the home, only one provided assistance.

IMPLICATIONS FOR RELATIONSHIP WITH PARENT

Unexpectedly, the stress and sense of isolation from caregiving affected relationships with parents in only a few cases. In two of these situations, caregivers described relationships with their fathers prior to caregiving in negative terms as well. In these cases, being "tied down" by their parent increased the caregiver's resentment. At the time of the followup interview, one of these caregivers had ceased providing care and could not be located.

In a third case, Dominic was very open in pointing out to his mother how much he resented caring for her. About midway through the interview, Dominic's mother, Freeda, joined the interview against the interviewer's objections. Following Dominic's lead, the interviewer allowed Freeda to remain for a few minutes and then later reasked the questions of Dominic, probing for additional information that he might have left out during his mother's presence. The following exchange suggests the strain in his relationship with his mother:

> *Dominic*: I keep telling my mother that things cannot always be like this. When am I going to have a chance to live? I have no life. I can't go anywhere for more than an hour. But she doesn't understand. She doesn't know how I am suffering.
>
> *Freeda*: But you will be going away next month for a few days. [Looking quite sad] I wish that I could go too.
>
> *Dominic*: But Ma, that is 4 days out of 365. I need to live a little. [Turning to the interviewer] Some day I will become just so bitter, and then I will have to find some place for her. It will happen very suddenly.
>
> *Freeda did not like this at all and snapped*: This is the way that it *has* to be. This is the way that it has to be. You will have to find someone to take care of me. This isn't so bad. It is our life.
>
> *Dominic*: Some life!
>
> *Freeda*: I cannot stay here alone.

Seemingly at ease, Dominic also added in front of his mother that he would never expect his children to care for him given how much they would "lose" in doing so. It seemed throughout the interview that Dominic's resentment toward his mother stemmed primarily from the constraints of caregiving rather than from prior problems in their relationship. By the time of the second interview, Dominic's mother had died, and he spoke of his period of caregiving as being much less burdensome. Adult children may therefore modify their views of their relationships with parents following their death or the termination of caregiving.

LEISURE

Nearly all of the caregivers reported having no time for leisure. Those who were able to continue activities had interests that could be combined with caregiving. For example, Rose loved to garden. She explained that although her garden [at her mother's house where she lived] was not as large as it usually was, she was able to maintain it because it could be done in conjunction with caregiving activities. For example, she said, "I can be out here [in the yard] and still hear my mother when she wakes up."

A few caregivers also mentioned that they had reserved time for exercising. Beth felt that she needed time to work out "to keep her sanity" but had no one to care for her mother while she did so. Seeing no alternative, Beth took her mother with her to the gym. She would bring her mother a donut to eat while she rode the exercycle. This situation could not be maintained during times when her mother was severely ill.

Caregivers who had backup care were also able to reserve a night or two for themselves. They tended to use the backup care sparingly and to treasure the time for themselves. Celia stated,

> Thank goodness my husband belongs to the Knights of Columbus. We know that we can get out once a week. We used to pick people up on the way. Now we don't so we can have a little time alone. My father-in-law stays with her that night.

While nearly all of the caregivers reported having no time for leisure, working class caregivers tended to pursue leisure time activities that could be combined with caregiving. As such, it was easier for them to maintain some involvement. The example of Rose and her garden, above, illustrates this. Working class caregivers also saw the sacrifices that they made as less of a hardship than middle class caregivers. This may have been because they did not have high expectations of leisure prior to caregiving. With little extra money and a lifestyle centered around family, they had limited expectations of recreational pursuits outside of the home (Rubin, 1976, 1994). In contrast, middle class caregivers, who were more likely to seek activities beyond home and family, such as belonging to clubs and organizations (Langman, 1987) as well as eating out and attending plays, movies, and the like, had a more difficult time combining leisure and caregiving. Also, with higher expectations prior to caregiving, they cited more restrictions on caregiving than working class caregivers. According to one of the middle class caregivers,

> Our kids were grown . . . so we took advantage of it. . . . We were really active. . . . I was involved in the Shriner's Women's organizations. . . . It is parade season now, but we can't go because of my mother. My husband goes alone sometimes.

Co-resident caregivers noted a loss of privacy in their lives. Celia and her husband lived in a large house, but she felt that she was living in one big room with her mother-in-law. Her mother-in-law would enter all of the rooms in the house, moving belongings from their proper place and placing them somewhere else. At one point Celia was so frustrated that she demanded that her husband put a lock on their bedroom door so that they could have one room to themselves. "I told him, 'If there isn't a lock on that door by Sunday, I am walking.' I was so upset; then I calmed down. The next day I heard him drilling the hole."

When Kathy's mother moved in with her and her husband, they also lost a precious chunk of their privacy. Needing some space between herself and her mother, Kathy and her husband made their basement into a family room.

> So when my mother goes to bed on the second floor, we can go into the basement and have a whole floor between us. That's how we get privacy. Plus on Sunday mornings, which is our only day off together, I tell my mother not to get up and I will get her up. Then we have a little more time together too.

Given the frequency with which caregivers sought to create privacy for themselves, results suggest that maintaining some degree of privacy is central for ongoing caregiving. Those who work with the families of the elderly may wish to focus on ways to help adult children maintain privacy when parents become co-resident.

THE EFFECT OF CAREGIVING ON HEALTH

Unexpectedly, few of the caregivers believed that caregiving had negatively impacted their health. Two of the caregivers had back problems that they related to all of the lifting they did while providing care. Beth, who was quite petite, had been both lifting her mother and helping her up and down stairs for over four years. Beth assisted her mother into the bathtub at least once a week, tried to grab her when she fell, and helped her to keep her balance when she walked. This was not easy given that Beth's mother was quite large, weighing approximately 170 to 180 pounds. Still, Beth was adamant that her own health was a price worth paying for her mother. She stated, "The stress did affect my health. I have health problems of my own now. But it wouldn't have stopped me from doing it."

These results are consistent with Lieberman and Fisher's (1995) findings that it was the severity of the elder's illness, not the amount of caregiving, that affected the health of the caregiver. Regardless of how often Beth provided other forms of assistance, the fact that she had to lift her mother due to the extent of her mother's dependence was the cause of her own health problems. The fact that Beth had been doing this lifting for over four years likely exacerbated her back problems.

Rose, too, believed that caregiving had negatively impacted her health. According to her, the source of the problem was not lifting but the stress and "running around" that caregiving entailed.

> I have inside shingles from all of this. My doctor says that it is because of all that I do for others, that I am always giving instead of doing for myself. My oldest brother also has shingles from this. He says it is from all of the fighting and bickering. One of my sisters isn't good either.

One final caregiver also believed that providing care had hurt her health, but only indirectly.

> I have weight problems and high blood pressure that my doctor says I need to do something about. But when I am running from work to my mother's at lunch, I don't have time to eat right. . . . I grab a burger. Then at night when I come home after cooking her dinner. . . . I eat a big meal because I am so hungry. I am always on the go. How can I worry about what I eat?

None of the male caregivers reported health problems from caregiving. Instead, they were more likely to say that they would give up caregiving if it became too much for them. In addition, they were more likely to share caregiving with siblings which lessened any "running around" that needed to be done, and they were less likely to be physically taxed from lifting elderly parents. Caregivers who did have health problems, both working and middle class, accepted poor health as a necessary part of caregiving or of meeting family obligations in general.

Although the length of time caregiving was not related to stress, it did have a cumulative effect on the caregiver's health status. Beth pointed out that although her back problems started after about six months of caregiving, the pain became chronic after years of lifting. For Rose, it took several years of stressful caregiving before any health problems appeared. It was not the number of hours spent caregiving at one point in time that mattered but instead the years of caregiving which had a cumulative effect.

MOTIVATIONS TO CARE

Given the stress and negative effects on leisure time, health, and relationships with one's own family, the logical question to ask is, Why do adult children provide care? Are there any positive aspects of providing care for the caregiver? No matter how difficult it was, only one of the caregivers expressed regret at providing care. Deborah intimated that she would not have provided care if she had known how much was involved. The other forty-nine caregivers had no regrets because they were pleased that they had fulfilled their obligations or had done what was best for their parents.

While caregivers may have been motivated to provide care by several factors, the first answer that they gave was considered to be their primary answer. Only a minority of the caregivers, eight (16 percent), expressed receiving something positive back from caregiving when asked what motivated them to be caregivers. Beth, for example, said, "She [my mother] is really a joy. . . . I get a lot from her too. . . . I don't feel like I owe her, I like to do it." Marie echoed, "You get everything back when you are a caregiver. I feel like I am the lucky one."

While other caregivers did not say that they received something back from caregiving, they did express additional beneficial reasons for providing care. Eight caregivers (16 percent) said that they provided care out of love for the parent, "pure and simple." Billie, one of the daughters-in-law, said, "You just have to love her. She is this little tiny French woman who tells you just what she thinks." When providing care out of love, adult children did not always treat parents equally. Donna, for example, was willing to care for her father in her home but not her mother. "With my Dad, I can feel his approval. We love each other, but I didn't always like her [my mother]."

The most common motivating factor for providing care, however, was a sense of obligation or reciprocity. Nearly one-third of the caregivers (sixteen adult children) cited either of these two factors when asked what motivated them to be a caregiver. While it was sometimes clear that one of the two was more salient, in other instances the two factors were intertwined. Among the adult children who provided care out of a sense of obligation, Kathy said that children should provide care and that she would not be able to live with herself otherwise. Another caregiver felt that it was morally and religiously appropriate. According to Deborah, "I think that it is biblical that we should take care of our parents. They took care of you, didn't they? A family shouldn't have trouble taking care of an elderly person as long as they can walk." Sally felt that, in general, family members have a duty to care for one another and that the difficulty of that care should not matter. She stated, "I don't believe in putting people away just because they are inconvenient. I don't see *people* as inconvenient. . . . I am from a long line of farmers. . . . I believe in taking care of your own." These children were more likely to see caregiving not as a choice but as a duty that they could not avoid.

Other adult children provided care to pay back parents who had worked hard all of their lives. Sylvia related, "My mother was always good to me. . . . It was very hard to grow up with wealthy snobs, so my mother made sure that we always had what we needed [crying]." Liza related, "My father was a good man. He was always there for us, working two jobs, so we just did it."

All of the caregivers who were motivated out of a sense of obligation or reciprocity were daughters. This is in contrast to earlier findings that intergenerational affection is the most important factor motivating daughters, while sons are most motivated by filial obligation and the legitimation of inheritance (Silverstein, Parrott, and Bengtson, 1995). These differences may arise from the fact that in this sample, daughters were providing regular ADL assistance, while in the study by Silverstein, Parrott, and Bengtson (1995), children were primarily providing social support. The findings in this study would suggest that it is daughters who are more responsive to filial obligation overall. It is also possible that a hierarchy of motivations is necessary to provide more difficult or intensive assistance, with affection being the base motivator and obligation being required for providing more difficult care for daughters. A hierarchy also exists for sons, but it is gauged at a higher level. That is, the base motivating factor (for providing social support) is obligation for sons and affection for daughters.

Walker (1996) argued that while reciprocity, affection, and obligation may affect the quality of the caring relationships, motivation to become a caregiver is based on external normative structures or expectations. That is, we have expectations of who is the appropriate caregiver based on gender roles and beliefs regarding the debt children owe to their parents. Thus, when asked why they provided care, people who were the appropriate caregivers (daughters) responded that it was their role, while others supplied additional explanations. In this study, those few daughters who stated that the motivating factor for caregiving was their role were more likely to state this as a secondary factor. In addition, while their role was what prompted them to become caregivers, it was the other factors (e.g., love, obligation) that motivated them to continue providing care.

Other researchers have focused on the norms of reciprocity, obligation, and attachment to parents (or affection) as motivating factors for providing care (Suitor, Pillemer, Keeton, and Robison, 1995). Additional factors were cited in the present study. For example, some children believed that their parents (in-law) would get better care at home than in a nursing home (four children or 8 percent). Others were granting a parent's wish to not be put into a nursing home (two caregivers or 4 percent), while two other children stated that what motivated them to be caregivers was that they were still trying to gain their parents' approval. Both caregivers in this situation said that this would be their last chance to do so.

Four of the caregivers (8 percent) felt that what motivated them to care for their parents was that they had seen their own parents caring for their grandparents. Brenda, one of the daughters-in-law, said that her mother had cared for her mother-in-law and that she had provided assistance for her grandmother, so she knew what was involved. Six other caregivers (12 percent) believed that caregiving was their role in the family. For one of the daughters-in-law, being a caregiver provided her with a long-awaited place in her husband's family. Others were daughters, often with nursing backgrounds.

In general, then, family members suggested reasons advantageous to both themselves and their parent for providing care. Only those two caregivers who cited gaining their father's approval appeared to provide care without regard for what was best for their parents. While few stated that they received something back from caregiving, they had no regrets because they were fulfilling important obligations, paying parents back, or providing care out of love. Thus, no matter how stressful or difficult caregiving was, there were beneficial reasons for providing that care.

On the surface, most of the adult children appeared to be providing care for the benefit of their parents rather than themselves. In considering what lay beneath their answers, nearly all of the caregivers wanted to avoid regretting foregone opportunities later on. That is, despite the difficulties, they provided care so that in later years they would not look back on this time and wish that they had done more for their parents. Similarly, all of the caregivers believed that the care they provided was superior to that provided in a nursing home and that their parents preferred to be cared for at home. All believed that they were doing the right thing for their parents, although in a few cases the interviewer questioned whether the parent would be safer in a nursing home.

IMPLICATIONS FOR THE FAMILY

In examining the implications of caregiving, researchers have focused primarily on the individual caregiver. The effects of caregiving, however, extend to the nuclear family as well. In this study at least, married children consistently spoke of the negative impact that being a caregiver had on time for their spouses. This included both leisure time and time for more necessary and serious discussions. In addition, disruptions in the relationship with a spouse took place just when family members needed one another more because of the unsettling changes in lifestyle, privacy, and family dynamics that usually accompanied caregiving. This issue became more problematic when emergencies arose in the family, such as when a spouse became seriously ill.

Caregiving also affected the lives of the caregivers' children, both young and old. Caregivers commented that they did not have the time to help their adult children with babysitting or to provide emotional support. Co-resident caregivers also felt guilty that children were no longer comfortable coming home; home was not a pleasant retreat. Younger children often had to adjust to the presence of their grandparents who imposed additional restrictions on their lives and to the loss of time with their parents. Grandchildren who provided care experienced new family obligations, often quite onerous and time consuming, and limitations on their time for school activities and friends.

We know very little, however, about the long-run effects on family relationships. Longitudinal studies are necessary to examine how caregiving affects family relationships over time. The questions to be addressed include: Does the diminished time with spouses lead to higher rates of divorce or separation? What effect does the stress itself have over the long run, five to ten years, for marital quality? And what of the children? Does the responsibility of being a caregiver at a young age lead to better relationships with older people? Do children who share their home end up resenting their grandparents in the long run?

IMPLICATIONS FOR LONG-TERM CARE

Earlier studies have documented the prevalence of emotional strain in providing family care (Abel, 1991; Brody, 1990; Kaye and Applegate, 1990; Montgomery, 1992). The strain can be reduced by social support, although more so by some types of support than others (Thompson, Futterman, Gallagher-Thompson, Rose, and Lovett, 1993). Engaging in social interaction for fun and recreation appears to be most important in diminishing the burden of caregiving. This finding is consistent with the results for middle class caregivers who perceived the loss of leisure-time activities with friends and colleagues as a hardship that contributed to the stress of caregiving. Working class caregivers also cited the loss of time spent visiting extended family and neighbors but did not describe it in stressful terms like the middle class. While researchers note the question of how to best target services such as respite care (Montgomery, 1995), these results suggest that allowing the caregiver continued access to leisure-time pursuits appears to be most important for those with higher expectations of leisure prior to caregiving.

Stress was also highest when adult children believed that they were all alone in providing care. In targeting services to relieve stress, we need to pay special attention to those who feel that there is no alternative to being a caregiver and those who have little or no assistance in providing care. Many of the caregivers who believed that they had no alternative saw nursing homes as a last resort to be pursued only when it was no longer "humanly" possible to provide care. In comparison, those who saw nursing homes as a more positive option experienced less stress. Perhaps case managers and those who coordinate community care need to pay greater attention to empowering caregivers and to delineating the positive aspects of alternative situations. Consistent with the findings from the section on Siblings and the Division of Labor, greater effort needs to be given to counseling families to share caregiving where possible. Family mediators and counselors could potentially reduce caregiver stress and delay institutionalization if they were successful in getting siblings to help one another. This, however, remains to be tested.

Adult children who cared for dementia patients or parents who displayed difficult behaviors also reported higher levels of stress. Where possible, these caregivers need to be monitored and given priority in receipt of services by community and elder outreach programs. Similarly, because the entire family, both nuclear and extended, is impacted by caregiving, the family as a single unit needs to be considered when developing support groups, educational programs, and even respite services for filial caregivers. Braithwaite (1996) also argues that it is important to focus on experience and comfort with degenerative conditions in reducing caregiver stress.

The stress that caregivers experience, in and of itself, is of concern to the gerontological and medical communities. The stress can lead to or create additional problems, such as the neglect and abuse of the elderly. Many of the caregivers reported at one time or another being on the brink of abuse, "walking a fine line" between what was abusive and what was necessary to preserve their sanity. Thus, it is with concern for the well-being of both the caregivers and their parents that we as a society need to continue to investigate the source of and solutions to caregiver stress.

CHAPTER 7

Daughters–in–Law as Caregivers

Relationships between in-laws, including daughters-in-law and their mothers-in-law, have been stereotyped as full of antagonism and tension. But, research in this area showed that most daughters-in-law actually "got along quite well" with their mothers-in-law (Fischer, 1986) and could be supportive of one another, although they were not always so (Cotterill, 1994). Yet the in-law relationship was different from that of comparable blood relations or mothers and daughters. In a study of forty-three daughters with surviving mothers, Fischer (1986) compared the relationships that young married daughters had with their mothers versus their mothers-in-law. She argued that while the lives of mothers and daughters were linked from the time of birth, in-law relationships had a shorter history and depended on the endurance of the marriage. Mothers-in-law and daughters-in-law lacked the familiarity and intimacy of mother-daughter relationships, and there was almost always less emotional involvement between them. Yet, daughters-in-law were still members of the family. In-laws were characterized as being both kinfolk and strangers simultaneously. Relationships varied from being minimally involved to being quasi-mother-daughter bonds.

In general, affinal kin (based primarily on marital ties) evoke lower levels of obligation to family than consanguineal kin (based on blood ties) in comparable positions. In their study of patterns of family obligation, Rossi and Rossi (1990) found that obligations to parents-in-law were ranked between those to grandparents (higher) and siblings (lower) but not as high as those to parents and children. In addition, daughters-in-law ranked kin higher in obligations than sons-in-law, while family members ranked obligations to children-in-law higher than those to parents-in-law.

Based on interviews with twenty-five daughters-in-law and ten mothers-in-law (not related to one another), Cotterill (1994) argued that there were no "real rules" for an appropriate relationship or social behaviors between mothers and daughters-in-law. Tension and conflict tended to be attributed to individual compatibilities rather than to the ambiguous structuring context. Because they determined the extent to which their mothers-in-law would be involved in their sons' and grandchildren's lives, daughters-in-law also held the balance of power in the relationship. Although mothers and daughters-in-law hoped to achieve something similar to the mother-daughter bond or aspired to be friends, often their relationships were neither.

Little is known about the mother–daughter-in-law relationship in later life families (Blieszner and Bedford, 1995; Burton, 1993; Mattessich and Hill, 1987). Lack of a lifelong history and an indirect linkage through another family member will continue into later life families. A longer period of shared history and the potential for assimilation into the family culture might solidify the relationship to resemble that of consanguineal or blood kin more closely. Based on an optimistic portrayal, one might expect intimacy and the depth and extent of obligation to increase across the family life course, perhaps with brief periods of interruption as mothers-in-law and daughters-in-law learn to adjust to one another and to family life events. Alternatively, relationships may remain unchanged or may worsen as new difficulties arise.

The differences in the in-law relationship that do persist into later life families may affect a daughter-in-law's likelihood of becoming a caregiver as well as the caregiver role itself. Merrill (1993) found that daughters-in-law were less likely to become caregivers and provided less overall care. Yet they assisted with as many tasks and were as likely to designate themselves as the primary caregiver. In a separate study, Cotterill (1994) found that daughters-in-law expected to be involved in the care of infirm parents-in-law only when no daughter was available and, in the case of long-term intensive care, when personal feelings in the past were good and the quality of the relationship was high. Nor did they believe that they would be willing to provide live-in care. Daughters-in-law were willing, however, to provide backup care for daughters. This would suggest that daughters-in-law then continue to assume a different role than daughters in later life families; they are involved in caregiving but not quite to the extent as daughters and only when a "more suitable" caregiver (i.e., a daughter) is not available. Mothers-in-law, too, had strong reservations about receiving support from female relatives and wanted to be instrumental in defining future support relationships (Cotterill, 1994).

The emotional distance afforded by in-laws providing care might also make daughters-in-law (or sons-in-law) superior caregivers. In their study of daughters providing care, Walker and Allen (1991) found that difficult or stressful family circumstances reduced the rewards and increased the costs of relationships with one's care-receiving parent. As such, daughters-in-law with less emotional involvement may be able to maintain a more positive caregiving relationship. Similarly, negative early family relationship histories recalled by adult children decreased concern for their parents' well-being and provision of emotional support (Whitbeck, Hoyt, and Huck, 1994). In addition, because of the emotional distance, daughters-in-law may be less affected by the visible loss in the elder's abilities, when present. Thus, the lack of an early history and the inherent distance in the in-law relationship might make daughters-in-law more effective caregivers.

This chapter continues to investigate the implications of the in-law relationship in later life families. Because the author was unable to locate sons-in-law who met all of the criteria for inclusion in the study, we will focus on daughters-in-law and their relationships with the elders whom they care for. Comparisons are made with daughters rather than sons to see what difference the in-law relationship makes, holding gender constant. This chapter focuses on the quality of relationships with in-laws, motivations and pathways to caregiving, and differences in the caregiving experience.

THE QUALITY OF THE RELATIONSHIP

All ten of the daughters-in-law in this study were providing care to mothers-in-law, although two of the women were also caring for their fathers-in-law at the time of the followup survey. The vast majority of the daughters-in-law (seven out of ten) described their mothers-in-law as being second mothers and referred to them in very loving terms. Billie, for example, described how her mother-in-law "took her in" while her husband, Steve, was in the service. She added that her mother-in-law always treated her as a daughter, not a daughter-in-law, which was important to Billie, particularly since her own mother died. Evelyn also consistently referred to her mother-in-law as her mother throughout the interview. Despite their feelings for their mothers-in-law, the daughters-in-law were still realistic in describing the challenges and burdens of providing care similar to the other caregivers.

Only one of the daughters-in-law had a difficult relationship with her mother-in-law. Celia's mother-in-law was a former alcoholic. Although Celia often described her mother-in-law as being manipulative and "hard to like," she argued that everyone in the family had a difficult time with Kay and that her feelings were not the result of being an in-law. Kay's own children, excluding Celia's husband, were unwilling even to visit Kay because of her history of alcoholism. Celia did add that it was her father-in-law whom she loved very much and that she cared for Kay "for Dad's sake."

All of the caregivers had worked out comfortable relationships with their mothers-in-law prior to caregiving. Edith, for example, had visited her mother-in-law everyday even before she became ill, to keep her company. Thus, by the time they became later life families, the barriers caused by the in-law relationship seemed to have weakened.

In contrast, daughters-in-law who did not provide care often had strained relationships with their mothers-in-law. Dominic suggested that his wife continued to work past retirement age so that she would not be home during the day with his co-resident mother. Although Dot sometimes laid out clothes for her mother-in-law to wear the next day, she avoided being in the room with her so that they would not fight. This supports Cotterill's (1994) argument that the "sentimental model" of the family is often inappropriate for women who have little affection for each other but are expected to form intimate, caring bonds.

Despite their closeness, even those caregivers who described their mothers-in-law as second mothers did not have a "child's prerogative." Billie, for example, stated:

> I don't make the decisions because it isn't my mother. I leave it up to Steve and his brothers. When she won't leave the laundry like I ask her to, I just tell Steve to talk to her. I don't feel comfortable. So, I just tell him when I need her to do something.

Although her mother-in-law treated her like a daughter, Billie still did not feel that she had a child's right to demand things of her mother-in-law. Similarly, Brenda asked her husband to tell her mother-in-law that she was becoming too dependent on her, although it was Brenda who was home with her all day. This is consistent with Cotterill's (1994) findings that in in-law relationships, anger had to be avoided because there was no emotional intimacy to sustain them and thus there was risk of rejection.

MOTIVATIONS TO BECOME A CAREGIVER

While adult children were motivated to provide care due to a variety of reasons, including obligation and a sense of reciprocity, daughters-in-law were motivated by a narrower set of circumstances. Most of the daughters-in-law said that they provided care because they had always been treated like daughters. These women felt like a part of the family, but they did not add that they felt obligated as part of the family. Instead, they said that they loved their mothers-in-law because they had been treated as family. They provided care out of love, not out of obligation.

Daughters-in-law who were motivated because they felt like daughters often had caregiving experiences similar to those of daughters. These daughters-in-law experienced high levels of stress and were emotionally involved. In addition, more similar to daughters than to the other daughters-in-law and sons, they were extremely reluctant even to think of placing their mothers-in-law in a nursing home despite the high levels of stress.

Other daughters-in-law were motivated to provide care in order to help out their husbands. Brenda, for example, said that her husband really wanted to keep his mother out of a nursing home. He could only do this if Brenda provided care during the day while he worked. Others believed that the care they provided at home was superior to what their in-laws would get elsewhere.

Caregivers from these last two categories seemed more detached from the caregiver role. These caregivers said that they would continue providing care only under certain circumstances (most often, if it did not interfere with their own families). These daughters-in-law were more likely to set and adhere to limits as to what they were willing to do as caregivers and to recognize the limitations of the caregiver role.

PATHWAYS TO CAREGIVING

In contrast to children who often became caregivers as a result of it "just happening" or being de facto caregivers, the pathway to caregiving was usually one of choice for daughters-in-law. Over half of the daughters-in-law (six out of ten) volunteered themselves for the role. Edith volunteered even though her husband, the care recipient's son, thought that it would be too much for her. Another daughter-in-law volunteered with her husband, suggesting that their in-laws come to live with them so that they could help their father (in-law) to care for their mother (in-law).

Two of the daughters-in-law were volunteered by their husbands. In both situations, the sons wanted to keep their mothers out of nursing homes, but their sisters were unwilling to be caregivers and the sons worked during the day. One of the daughters-in-law said that she did not mind being volunteered because her mother-in-law had been so good to her. It seemed that, although at her husband's suggestion, Billie actually volunteered herself. Brenda, however, felt that she could not say "no" once her husband volunteered her to his siblings. Only one of the daughters-in-law "just happened" to become a caregiver as her mother-in-law gradually required more and more assistance from her.

Daughters-in-law may be less likely to be caregivers but more likely to volunteer for the role when they do become caregivers because caregiving is not an expected part of the in-law role. Daughters-in-law understand that they are not obligated to provide care; nor do kin expect it of them even when they have very close relationships with their in-laws. Thus, daughters-in-law have a choice of becoming caregivers. Even in later life families, obligations for daughters-in-law differ from those of daughters, although they may be greater than during the early years of marriage. Although some daughters-in-law may volunteer out of a sense of obligation or responsibility as a daughter-in-law, in this sample they appeared to volunteer out of love.

THE TYPE AND EXTENT OF CARE

The daughters-in-law in this study provided as much care as any of the daughters. Caring for elders with some of the most extensive needs, all except one of the daughters-in-law cared for their mother-in-law in their home. All of the daughters-in-law had dealt with incontinence, lifting the elder, and at times, providing twenty-four hour care. Six of the caregivers said that they were willing to provide any type of care and as long as it was needed. Edith was even unwilling to let the adult day care provide the personal and medical care her mother-in-law needed if Edith could do it herself on weekends.

The daughters-in-law took pride in being able to care for their mothers-in-law. Billie and Laurie, in particular, were honored that they were the ones whom their mothers-in-law trusted. Nor did Edith or Billie complain about the long hours they spent caregiving. Although Edith spent two hours every morning and then another three hours every evening caring for her mother-in-law, she spoke of it as if it were nothing. Edith humbly added, "I am glad to help out, if I can." Disappointed that her mother-in-law would no longer get the best care, Billie was very angry when Pasquale went to live with another daughter-in-law rather than rejoicing that she no longer had to be a caregiver.

CONFLICT WITH SIBLINGS AND ASSISTANCE FROM OTHERS

Daughters-in-law were more likely than daughters and sons to complain when their husbands' siblings, especially their sisters, did not provide care. All of the daughters-in-law had at least one sister-in-law (their husband's sister) who lived nearby. Only Edith, however, was satisfied with the amount of assistance that she received from her sister-in-law. Consistent with the findings of Rossi and Rossi (1990) and Cotterill (1994), all of the other daughters-in-law, except for Edith, believed that their sisters-in-law should have been the primary caregivers. As one of the women stated, "I wouldn't let any sister-in-law take care of my mother." To the daughters-in-law, caregiving was not an expected part of their obligation as in-laws. This then further exacerbated their resentment when siblings, who clearly were obligated, did not even help them out.

In most cases, sons intervened with their siblings on behalf of their wives. As they did with their parents, sons assumed the prerogative of blood kin in negotiating the difficult issues with their siblings. Although daughters-in-law often voiced their opinions to their in-laws, they did not introduce substantive conversations that were intended to produce change. Only Edith, who had a good relationship with her sister-in-law, coordinated care herself.

Although daughters-in-law did not necessarily receive more assistance from their siblings-in-law than daughters did from their siblings, they did receive more assistance from their spouses. Their spouses would be the care receivers' sons. All of the daughters-in-law received at least some assistance from their spouses. The type and extent of assistance that sons provided in nearly all cases was greater than that provided by sons-in-law. Brenda's husband, Tom, provided all of the care himself when he was at home, while Celia and Patrick shared care equally. In contrast, daughters were often reluctant to ask their husbands for help, believing that the care of their parents was their responsibility.

Daughters-in-law often had the assistance of their own family in caregiving. Edith's mother, for example, cared for her mother-in-law while she went to church. More often, however, assistance from one's own family was more indirect, helping with housework or child care, to minimize the overall amount of work that needed to be done.

DETACHMENT

Daughters-in-law did seem more distant and detached in the caregiver role. They were able to maintain a better perspective and to set limits as to what they could and could not do as caregivers. Only one of the daughters-in-law mentioned that she was sometimes at the point where she could become abusive; it was more common for daughters to feel that they were driven to that point. Four of the daughters-in-law saw caregiving as an option that they could relinquish if they needed to. Daughters were more likely to feel that they had to continue providing care at whatever cost to their own health, work, and families.

Daughters-in-law were also more protective of the effect on their own families. All of the daughters-in-law had children who sometimes helped with caregiving, except for Brenda, whose children were very young. None of the daughters-in-law required their children to help. Instead, they had backup care for when their children had activities and were determined that their caregiving not "upset" their children's lives. While few of the daughters *required* their children to help out, they recognized that caregiving did upset their children's lives and were less vigilant in preventing it from doing so.

GENDER AND THE IN-LAW RELATIONSHIP

Why did sons-in-law not prevail as caregivers in the family? Although sons-in-law sometimes helped their wives with heavy lifting or running errands for their parents-in-law, assistance was minimal. In fact, no sons-in-law who fit the criteria for a caregiver could be located for the study. How do gender and the in-law relationship intersect so that sons-in-law are the least likely caregivers?

Sons-in-law were less likely to provide care owing in part to the gender appropriateness of caring tasks. Sons, too, are also less likely to provide care than daughters. But it is more than that. According to the research by Rossi and Rossi (1990), sons-in-law ranked lowest among children and children-in-law in their ratings of obligation to kin, including obligations of various types such as providing financial assistance, a gender-neutral activity. Compounded by the distance afforded by the in-law relationship is the greater distance men in general have as participants of family life. Thus, sons-in-law are not obligated in the same way that daughters-in-law are even for gender-neutral activities.

In addition to the scarcity of sons-in-law, why did daughters-in-law provide assistance instead of sons? One of the daughters-in-law explained that she did not work outside of the home, while her husband did; thus, she became the caregiver during the day, while her husband provided care at night. But for those who volunteered, why did they volunteer over their husbands? This suggests that gender is the master status when it comes to caretaking, over and above the distinction of affinal kin. The appropriateness of being a caregiver because of their role as women took precedence over the inappropriateness of caretaking because of their role as affinal kin. Daughters-in-law also liked to have a place in their husbands' families. One of the awkward issues of being an in-law is that you have no role in the family (Cotterill, 1994). This afforded them that role; they felt appreciated by their husbands' families. One of the daughters-in-law referred to herself as "the family caregiver" [referring to her husband's family].

Daughters-in-law rather than sons may also provide care because of the gender of the parent-in-law. Lee, Dwyer, and Coward (1993) found that adult children were more likely to provide care to a parent of the same gender and that infirm elders were more likely to receive care from a child of the same gender. Since most of the elders in this sample were women, normative expectations may have been that it was more appropriate for daughters-in-law to provide care over sons. While none of the daughters-in-law articulated this notion, one of the sons did say, "My mother needs to be bathed and dressed. I can't do that. That is women's work." Only two of the sons provided personal care for their mother in addition to what their wives provided, including assisting with dressing and toileting. However, daughters-in-law were not reluctant to care for their fathers-in-law. Three of the daughters-in-law cared for both during their caregiving careers. Although there may be something of a taboo in our society about sons providing personal care for their mothers, it does not appear to extend to female kin caring for male kin. This is likely to do with the overall appropriateness of women as family caregivers, which takes precedence over other improprieties.

It will be interesting to see whether the role of sons changes as the children of the baby bust become adults. As children become scarce resources, gender roles among adult children (and perhaps even children-in-law) may well become less differentiated. As couples have fewer or perhaps no available daughters, sons will be called upon to provide that assistance currently given primarily by women in the family.

POWER AND THE IN-LAW RELATIONSHIP

Cotterill (1994) argued that daughters-in-law were the ones who held power in their relationships with their mothers-in-law since they determined the extent to which mothers-in-law would be involved in their sons' lives. Whether or not daughters-in-law even recognize or exert that power is unclear. Clearly, in some situations daughters-in-law believe that their mothers-in-law determine their own role in the family, which the daughters-in-law must then follow. We must also ask the extent to which that power continues into later life families and into the caregiver role.

As caregivers, daughters-in-law clearly had some power. To the extent that they truly volunteered for the role or believed that they could quit caregiving, they had the power to be caregivers or not. Only one of the daughters-in-law "volunteered" unwillingly (being volunteered by her husband); she thus lacked power to determine her role in her mother-in-law's care. Once daughters-in-law decided to be caregivers, they also had some power in determining the quality of care that their mothers-in-law received. None of the daughters-in-law abused this power, however. Instead, they appeared to provide their mothers-in-law with the best care that they could, making extensive sacrifices to do what was best for the care receiver. In contrast, two of the daughters maintained their fathers in their homes for financial reasons but did not provide adequate care so that their fathers were "at risk."

Daughters-in-law lacked power among affinal kin in general. This is evidenced by the fact that it was their husbands who intervened with siblings and with their parents when difficult issues arose, such as pressuring their siblings to help more or asking mothers to change some aspect of their behavior for the daughters-in-law who were caregivers. One of the daughters-in-law said that she felt "uncomfortable getting after my mother-in-law." It is likely, however, that the daughters-in-law also did not feel that they had the power or authority to change their in-laws' behaviors.

In contrast to the findings of Cotterill (1994), daughters-in-law in this sample did not always have power in their relationships with affinal kin throughout the family life course. For example, both Billie and Laurie were dependent on their mothers-in-law financially when they were younger. Billie lived in her mother-in-law's home while her husband was in the service. Because she did not work, she was totally dependent on her in-laws. Perhaps the only power that she did have was that in the future she would have some influence in the extent to which her affinal kin were part of their son's life. In addition, Laurie and her husband had been dependent on her mother-in-law's financial contributions to the family for many years when their children were young.

In volunteering for the role of caregiver, daughters-in-law seemed to be thanking their mothers-in-law for not abusing that power. Daughters-in-law discussed how grateful they were that their mothers-in-law had been good to them. When asked what they meant by this, daughters-in-law said, "My mother-in-law didn't cause problems the way that some mothers-in-law do," or "She treated me like a daughter, not a daughter-in-law."

THE IN-LAW RELATIONSHIP IN LATER LIFE FAMILIES: MAIN DIFFERENCES

The in-law relationship does make a difference in the caregiving experience, at least for daughters-in-law. In comparison to daughters, caregiving was more often described as an option by daughters-in-law. Daughters-in-law were more likely to volunteer for the role or to believe that they could relinquish the role if it became too difficult. This optional quality was due to the fact that the affinal role does not include such an obligation. In contrast, daughters did not believe that they had a choice due to norms of filial obligation. This is consistent with Cotterill's (1994) findings that daughters-in-law expected to be involved in the care of infirm parents-in-law only if no daughter was available. They saw caregiving as optional for them, but not the daughters.

Daughters-in-law were also able to maintain a greater distance and better perspective in their role as caregivers. For example, several of the daughters, who seemed on the verge of collapse, said that they would continue to provide care for their mothers "no matter what, in order to keep them out of a nursing home." In contrast, daughters-in-law recognized their own limits and the limits of their families. They were watchful of when caregiving would become too much and thus become counterproductive for all involved. Daughters-in-law also showed a greater perspective in watching the interactions among siblings. As on-lookers, they could comment on the histories of the relationships and maintain a distance from the intense interactions.

Does this perspective make them superior caregivers? Clearly, the optional quality of caregiving reduced the pressure for daughters-in-law. In contrast to several of the daughters, none of the daughters-in-law seemed "at the end of their rope" or on the verge of abusive behavior. In addition, although they criticized their husbands' siblings for not being the primary caregivers, they were not caught up in feuding and bickering with siblings like several of the daughters and sons. Out of all of the caregivers, it was the daughters-in-law who were most likely to speak of what was best for the elder and to refer to the quality of care that they received. The greater effectiveness of daughters-in-law as caregivers was evidenced by the fact that of Kay's husband and children, it was her daughter-in-law Celia who was best able to manage her during hospital visits and to calm her at home.

These findings support earlier research that affinal kin do not operate at the same level as consanguineal kin or those related through blood ties. Obligations are not as great (Rossi and Rossi, 1990), and there is almost always less emotional involvement (Fischer, 1986). However, it furthers research by showing that even in later life families, the differences remain. Despite their extensive histories and (often) the sharing of resources, in-laws continue to remain quasi-kin at best, reflective of the formal nature of their bond.

The fact that daughters-in-law were even providing care, a highly burdensome task, as well as the amount and extent of care that they provided, implied that the differences were not as great as one would have expected. The comments made by these daughters-in-law suggested that in later life families, in-laws, too, had something to pay back, although the "debt" may not have been as great as that owed to a blood relation. It is likely that among those who did provide care, their shared histories also allowed them to work out any difficulties that arose in the in-law relationship early on in the marriage and to develop affectionate ties. Cotterill (1994) documented these difficulties as including how to address one's mother-in-law, juggling holiday arrangements between several families, and conflict over raising children. Not all daughters-in-law were able to work these difficulties through. Among those daughters-in-law who did not provide care, the sons often described the relationships between their mothers and wives as "always having problems."

It is also possible that daughters-in-law became more like blood kin over time. In another study, one woman even cared for her in-laws after she and her husband divorced (Merrill, 1993). The fact that she retained her obligation to her in-laws suggests that their relationship had become more of that of kin. Several of the daughters-in-law referred to their parents-in-law as "mom and dad." Such intimacy is likely to evolve, however. If one were to look at the development of the in-law relationship according to the different ages of the caregivers (i.e., younger caregivers being daughters-in-law for a shorter period of time), in this sample one could see a steady progression of increasingly close-knit, loving relationships developing. Daughters-in-law also spoke of their relationships with their mothers-in-law as developing over time. One of the daughters-in-law said,

> We weren't that close in the beginning. I had my own mother and she had her daughters. But then the kids were born, and she was good to them. She came over sometimes during the day when I was alone with them. I liked the company . . . and the help. I could see that she was being a good mother and mother-in-law. About six years ago I started to give her rides to places because she couldn't see. I could appreciate all that she had done for me and my family.

This is not to suggest that all later life families will proceed in a similar fashion. Some relationships may instead worsen over time. However, among those who provide care, we see such a development.

Cotterill (1994) argued that there were no rules for an appropriate relationship or social behaviors between mothers and daughters-in-law. Such rules, though family specific, may have developed as the in-law relationship entered its later life stage. All of the daughters-in-law had assimilated into the families and were aware of the appropriate behaviors. They also established their own rules, particularly if their mothers-in-law moved in with them. One of the daughters-in-law said, "My mother-in-law knows that she can't drink here. I lived with an alcoholic once, and I won't again." Rules reflected what could be asked of the caregiver (e.g., how often they could call for assistance) as well as general patterns of social behavior. Celia said, "We don't talk about it, but my father-in-law knows that we need some time alone to ourselves and to be with our kids. We had to make that clear." Expected patterns of behavior, however, were often relationship-specific. Mothers-in-law with several daughters-in-law found different expectations in each house. Billie stated, "My mother-in-law went to live with another daughter-in-law because she lets her get away with more. But she doesn't do as much for my mother-in-law; she doesn't care as much."

Although not by design, all of the daughters-in-law in this sample were working class. This is again consistent with the general ethos in the working class that family members provide direct care for one another. It is also likely that in the working class, daughters-in-law provided care as a way of thanking parents-in-law for the help given to them when the younger couple required financial assistance or other scarce resources.

FUTURE TRENDS

Future trends may alter the experience and likelihood of daughters-in-law providing care. In particular, the divorce revolution means that as couples age, there will be fewer sons who are currently married and more sons who are divorced. To what extent will ex-daughters-in-law be willing to provide extensive care? If the in-laws (usually mother and daughter-in-law) had a good prior relationship, the daughter-in-law was not remarried, and other caregivers were not available (including a new daughter-in-law), the daughter-in-law might be willing to provide some assistance. One would certainly expect, however, that it would be a rare occurrence. In Merrill's (1993) study of 100 daughters-in-law currently providing care, only one was an ex-daughter-in-law. In addition, since they are no longer formally part of the family (having dissolved their linkage to the family by dissolving the marital bond), daughters-in-law who do help may be willing to provide far less assistance, such as running errands versus providing personal care.

Sons may also be remarried, but the new daughters-in-law will not have as extensive a history with their parents-in-law. How will that then affect their willingness to provide care or to have their in-laws move in with them? To the extent that daughters-in-law provide care solely as a result of their marital status, there would be little difference. However, roles are acquired. In particular, among mothers and daughters-in-law for whom there are no rules for appropriate relationships and social behaviors, being an in-law would not automatically obligate one to provide care. Results of this study suggest that daughters-in-law provided care out of love and their shared history with their mothers-in-law. If this history is shortened due to divorce, there may be even fewer daughters-in-law providing extensive care in the future as a further consquence of the divorce revolution.

CHAPTER 8

The Caregiving Career

In addition to the personal accounts of individual caregiving careers (Koch, 1990; Starkman, 1993), researchers have begun to document the course of caregiving based on patterns of shared caregiving trajectories found in caregiver populations (Aneshensel, Pearlin, Mullan, Zarit, and Whitlatch, 1995; Given and Given, 1991; Lewis, 1987; Pearlin, 1992; Wilson, 1989). The experience of caregiving is referred to as a career because of the series of related positions through which the caregiver moves in an ordered sequence. That is, caregiving activities are connected to one another and there is a development of progressive accomplishment, thus making it a career (Aneshensel et al., 1995). The examination of caregiving as a career calls attention to the normative sequencing and structure of changes which, although patterns of diversity exist, are not ruled by happenstance.

Researchers have identified three basic stages of this career: role acquisition during which the caregiver recognizes the need for the role and assumes obligations; role enactment which includes the performance of role-related tasks within the home or long-term care facility; and role disengagement or the cessation of caregiving and the returning to other venues of life. During each stage, there is a major transitional event: illness onset occurs during role acquisition, nursing home admission sometimes happens during role enactment, and the death of the patient often occurs during role disengagement (Aneshensel et al., 1995).

In their discussion of the first stage, role acquisition, Aneshensel et al. (1995) referred to common patterns of sequencing for three events: symptom recognition, diagnosis, and assumption of the caregiving role. Their study, however, was of family members caring for dementia patients. It is expected that the caregiving career may vary when caring for an elder with a physical impairment. For example, according to the results of this study, the need for caregiving often occurred suddenly for elders with physical impairments (see chapter 3). As a result, symptom recognition and diagnosis played a less central role, replaced by the sudden need for care when a fall, for example, occurred. Similarly, elders with physical rather than cognitive impairments may be more likely to have some periods of improvement. As a result, greater change will take place over the course of caregiving. In addition, for all illnesses, the caregiving career is likely to vary tremendously according to family membership. This study focused exclusively on children and children-in-law, thus allowing for the examination of their careers in isolation.

Researchers have focused on two distinct phases of the second stage of caregiving, role enactment: in-home care and hands-on care following placement of a relative in a formal care facility (Aneshensel et al., 1995). Within each phase there are likely to be additional changes that prior researchers have not focused on, such as changes in the key individuals providing care, hospitalization, and changes due to oscillating care needs. In addition, it is expected that nursing home placement is not always common, particularly for working class families.

During the caregiving career, changes are likely to occur in the use of formal versus informal sources of care, although they may not be consistent for all caregivers. For example, researchers have noted racial differences regarding these changes. Although African Americans and whites were equally likely to use mixed sources of help at baseline, two years later African Americans were more likely to have shifted to strictly informal help. African Americans were also less likely to use nursing homes but had larger informal support networks (Miller, McFall, and Campbell, 1994). The authors stated that family structure may have had a deterring effect on the use of services for African Americans, depending on family members' level of awareness of services and ability to mediate formal organizations. It is expected that class differences also exist, given differences in the ability to pay privately for formal services, availability of siblings as helpers in informal care, access to information about formal care, and values regarding the appropriateness of use of formal care.

In the third stage, role disengagement, both grief and relief are common (Aneshensel et al., 1995). How one disengages, whether through death of a parent, nursing home placement, or transfer of the caregiver role to another family member will vary and will affect the process of readjustment. In addition, it is expected that there will be more consistent patterns of this stage when examining one set of caregivers, children, and children-in-law.

Although each stage of caregiving has its own unique challenges, researchers found that a process of adaptation occurred over the caregiving career (Ryff and Seltzer, 1995). In particular, caregiving effectiveness improved over time (Townsend, Noelker, Deimling, and Bass, 1989), as did the caregiver's ability to cope (Zarit, Todd, and Zarit, 1986). Nor was there an increase in depression during the course of caregiving (Townsend, Noelker, Deimling, and Bass, 1989).

While chapter 3 focuses on the first stage, the process of becoming a caregiver, this chapter examines the changes that occur across the career, emphasizing the stages of role enactment and role disengagement. Using the framework developed by Kahana et al. (1994), we will consider the experience of caregiving within changes in a spatial axis (i.e., the key individuals and groups), a temporal axis (i.e., the relevant time frames), and a transactional axis (i.e., the processes involved). The chapter begins by describing a "typical" caregiving career. Because caregiving is highly dependent on the elder's needs, this description is interwoven with details of the progression of "Hattie's" illness.

BETH AND HATTIE

Beth's mother, Hattie, was diagnosed with a polyp in 1989. While undergoing surgery for the polyp, physicians discovered that her stomach and pancreas were filled with cancer and so they had to postpone the surgery. Given only six months left to live, Beth brought Hattie home to live with her, thus beginning Beth's caregiving career. At the time, Beth was unmarried with one daughter still living at home. Beth had no siblings.

At that point in the caregiving career, Hattie needed help with all six of the activities of daily living and required full-time care. In addition to needing a special diet, Hattie wasn't able to control her bowels and choked on her food. When Hattie first came home to live with Beth, Beth did not have enough support to adequately care for her mother. During these early weeks, Beth cleaned her mother in the morning and fed her and then put her to bed for the remainder of the morning. She came home at lunchtime to feed her and again put her back to bed until she came home for the evening.

Beth knew, however, that Hattie should not be left alone. As a result, Beth hired a home health aide as well as a visiting nurse, each for a few hours a week, but it was still not enough to cover Beth while she worked full-time. So Beth hired someone to stay with her mother from 9:00 until 4:30 until she could switch to part-time work. In the meantime, she continued to use as many services as she could in order to give herself respite and to make her mother as well and comfortable as possible. For example, Beth had a priest come in to pray with her mother several times a week, thus freeing her for fifteen minutes or so a day. She would follow up on every suggestion that someone made, making phone call after phone call.

Trying to cover all of her mother's needs proved extremely stressful for Beth. A breaking point came for Beth when she returned home one day to find that Hattie had told her social worker that she did not want to be in the adult day care center that her social worker had found for her. Beth reported that she just snapped; she had worked so long to find a good center with an opening for her mother. She took a ruler and banged it on the table like you would for a child, saying "Don't you ever do that again." Beth was shaking and crying; at that point she knew that she needed more help. She enrolled Hattie in the adult day care that her social worker had found for three days a week. According to Beth, this was a turning point for Hattie. The visual and social stimulation encouraged her, and she began to get better.

After about four or five months, Hattie was independent enough that she wanted to go home to live. Beth was concerned, however, because her mother was forgetful and had difficulty walking up and down the stairs (she lived on the third floor). She sought the advice of the people at the adult day health center who suggested that Hattie try it several days a week, but stay at Beth's for the remainder of the week. So they tried this arrangement, again bringing changes to the caregiving career. Beth brought her mother cold cuts and other prepared food to have at home and spent more time arranging for her mother to be independent.

In the meantime, Beth was storing away information for the future. She attended seminars on reducing the cost of elder care, locating services, and providing in-home care. She kept Hattie's social worker informed of any changes in case she needed backup care and frequently asked the advice of people at the adult day health center regarding any changes or concerns.

This situation continued until Hattie fell and broke her elbow. Unable to feed or wipe herself, she moved back in with Beth who was working full-time again. Beth once again had to provide extensive personal care. She called upon every available resource, even taking her mother to work with her. (See the section on Work Accommodation in chapter 5.)

When Hattie was able to return home for the second time, new difficulties arose. Hattie's brother, who lived downstairs and had been a source of support, had died. Unable to get her mother into residential care due to their year-long waiting list, Beth sent a heartfelt letter to the director outlining her mother's needs. Her mother was bumped up to third on the list and moved into residential care two months later.

Beth, however, continued to provide care and support. Rather than giving personal assistance, caregiving now entailed coordinating services and assisting with instrumental activities of daily living. She did her mother's food shopping and prepared her meals on the days that she did not get Meals on Wheels. She arranged for her daughter to clean her mother's apartment and her aunt to take her mother out to dinner once a week. She did all of her mother's laundry, took her to doctors' appointments, and bathed her thoroughly once a week. Beth continued to seek every available social service and to keep her mother's social worker informed. She cut down to part-time work in case her mother needed her in the future.

This same situation continued but with minor medical interruptions. For example, Hattie developed a rash in December 1993 and required medication twice a day. With the help of home health aides and visiting nurses, Beth was able to manage on her own.

Then in February 1995 physicians discovered that Hattie's tumor had doubled in size. Beth was involved in her rehabilitation every day, helping her to practice in the walker. At that point, Hattie could no longer keep down food and was transferred from her nursing home to a hospital three times. Beth was ever vigilant, following up on tests and overseeing what Hattie's doctors were doing. Dissatisfied with the nursing homes, she had her mother transferred twice. She continued to encourage her mother to walk and to be as active as possible. Beth even smuggled her mother's dog into her hospital room as well as her two young grandchildren to lift her mother's spirits. At this point, Beth stayed with her mother sixteen to eighteen hours a day. This type of care continued until her mother died in March.

THE CARING CAREER

For many of the adult children, caring for their elderly parent was part of a lifetime of nurturing. That is, the caregiving career extended beyond the time frame for this one parent. Fourteen of the caregivers (28 percent) volunteered that they had cared for other family members as well. For example, Billie, one of the daughters-in-law, had also cared for her sister-in-law several years earlier when she was dying of cancer. Billie's husband confirmed, "Every one in my family knows what Billie does, that she is the caregiver. And they would do anything for her because they know what she did for my sister." At one point, Liza was caring for her father and husband, both of whom were dying of cancer, as well as her mother who was physically impaired. As if that were not enough, she later took her sister, who was also dying of cancer into her home, despite the fact that her sister had several available daughters living in the area. Liza said, "They all call me; I guess because I always come through for them." Four caregivers (8 percent) said that they had provided care to grandparents when they were very young and had always been taught to be responsible as such. Several other caregivers began by providing care to siblings as children. As the interview was nearing completion, Marie said,

> I have realized while sitting here talking to you that I have been a caregiver all of my life. It started when I was five. . . . I had to take care of all of my brothers and then my sisters too because I was the oldest girl. My mother would say, "Watch your brother, watch your sister. You can't go out to play. You have to help me." I didn't know that it was supposed to be any other way. . . .

Marie went on to lament that this early socialization into a caregiver role had been costly. That is, Marie grew up believing that she should sacrifice her needs for those of others. She explained that when her husband's mother became ill, her husband asked Marie if she would care for her in their home. Marie said that she felt that she had no choice, that she had to say "yes" even though she wanted to go back to school instead and even though her husband told her that she could say "no." So, she took her mother-in-law in and cared for her for sixteen years. She added,

> All of my life I have had to do for others. I could not go to school because I had to work so that my brothers could go to school. Then my kids were born. . . . It wasn't until my husband taught me that I am a person too that I went back to school. . . . I am lucky that I did not marry an Italian.

For a high proportion of adult children, the caregiver role extended into their professional lives as well. That is, sixteen of the caregivers were in the medical profession, while another four worked in social services (40 percent total). Several adult children said that it was easier to be a caregiver with the knowledge that they had from their work. As importantly, it suggests a predilection for a lifetime involvement in caring.

For others, although caregiving was not a paid profession, it consumed their lives. For example, Carrie cared for her mother in her home, an aunt who lived in the next town, and her teenage son who had spina bifida. Carrie's mother was manic depressive, diabetic, and in recent years had had a hip replacement, a double mastectomy, and cataract surgery on both eyes. Carrie provided care throughout each illness episode while also constantly caring for her son who was wheelchair-bound and incontinent and giving assistance with instrumental activities of daily living to her aunt.

THE CHANGING CAREGIVING CAREER

In almost all instances, the caregiving career could be best characterized as a series of changes. Consider the following example. In the first stage of caregiving, Minnie provided physical care to her father herself, first assisting with the instrumental activities of daily living and then with the activities of daily living. By the time that she was providing eight hours of care a day, Minnie found an Asian couple to stay with her father in exchange for rent. At this point in the caregiving career, she became a manager, overseeing that the couple met her father's needs. When her brother divorced and moved in with her father, Minnie then became part of a caregiving network and coordinated caregiving tasks with her brother. At this point, she provided some, but not all, of the care herself. When it became clear that her brother was not reliable, she then assumed her most recent stage of caregiving— coordinating care among formal providers. In this stage, Minnie pieced together her father's care among a myriad of formal services. In addition, there were also changes within each stage. For example, in the first stage, the amount and type of care that Minnie provided fluctuated greatly depending on her father's needs and changing health status. In furthering the analysis of Aneshensel et al. (1995), each of these changes occurred as stages or substages under the overall umbrella of role enactment.

The caregiving career changed in accordance with other roles and obligations in the caregiver's life. Lydia, for example, was able to switch from managing her mother's care to providing hands-on care herself when her job become less demanding owing to a reorganization of job responsibilities at her place of employment. Although she had not expected this change at work, it allowed her to pursue caregiving responsibilities that were more consistent with her expectations of appropriate filial care.

The caregiving career often oscillated in terms of the type and extent of care provided. Beth's mother, for example, improved to the point that she was able to live on her own (requiring mainly assistance with IADLs) but then relapsed and again required extensive personal care. In this example, care needs fluctuated. In other situations, caregiving careers changed as helpers exited and entered the caregiving network, often changing the type or extent of care to be provided.

The next sections further delineate specific changes in the key individuals, relevant time frames, and processes across the caregiving career.

CHANGES IN THE SPATIAL AXIS: KEY INDIVIDUALS

All of the fifty caregivers in this study were involved in providing care from the beginning. That is, none of the caregivers took over for siblings or in-laws who had been providing care, although Abby extended caregiving from one weekend per month to one week per month when she lost her job. However, eighteen of the children (36 percent) began providing care after the death or institutionalization of one parent, leaving the second parent requiring care. All said that they had not realized that their parent was so forgetful or frail, that the deceased parent had masked these changes, or that the parent had suddenly become ill after their spouse's death.

Changes occurred in the involvement of others, particularly for caregiving networks. When Liza began providing care, for example, she had the assistance of all five siblings. As so often happens, substitutions must be made as family members exit the network if the caregiving network is to continue. Thus, it becomes more difficult to sustain the network as time goes on. After five years into the caregiving career, one of Liza's sisters in the network had died and two others were too sick to provide help. Liza's daughter and two of her nieces substituted for the others, while Liza and her two brothers provided the bulk of the care.

Other changes included the addition of helpers. Brenda was a daughter-in-law. Her sister-in-law did provide more care over time, but only by a modest amount when Tom, Brenda's husband, insisted that she help more. The big change occurred when Gert, Brenda's mother-in-law, was well enough to return home. At that point, each of the siblings was assigned (by Tom) to stay with her for one day a week plus one weekend a month. Brenda said, "Now the visiting nurses get after them. If they find that one of them didn't come, they file charges of neglect. So, now they do it [provide help]." Several other caregivers asked for help from their children and spouses as their parents' needs increased. According to Leanne, "At first my husband wasn't involved in caregiving because I could do it myself. But my mother is a heavy woman, and when she couldn't walk on her own anymore, he had to help."

For the most part, amazingly little change took place. Only one of the daughters was able to get her sister to increase the amount of assistance that she gave by a substantial amount. Jody was providing all of her parents' care because the three lived together. When she explained to her sister that this was unfair, her sister agreed to help more and took on half of the care. This change occurred early on in the caregiving career.

Billie's caregiving situation changed the most in terms of the key individuals involved. Billie's mother-in-law lived with Billie and Steve for approximately five years in their basement apartment. Billie received some help from a second sister-in-law during times of crisis, such as when Pasquale was operated on. During the fifth year of caregiving, however, Steve discovered that his mother was sending away $30 to $40 every few days to a lottery. When he demanded that she stop doing this, Pasquale decided to move into her other son's home "to get her own way." At that point, the key individuals providing care were completely substituted.

The caregiving situations that changed the most were those with the daughters-in-law. When Brenda's mother-in-law returned to her own home, it was her husband Tom who then provided one day of care per week and who took his mother to doctors' appointments rather than Brenda. Billie was also relieved of caregiving when her mother-in-law went to live with another brother and sister-in-law. Daughters-in-law may be substituted as caregivers more frequently because they are not obligated to provide care as part of the affinal kin role (Cotterill, 1994). When a more appropriate caregiver becomes available, they are then substituted. As such, Brenda may have continued to provide care if it were her mother rather than her mother-in-law who moved back to her own home. Not only might she have felt more obligated to do so, but also other family members would have been more likely to expect her as the appropriate caregiver, including her mother.

There were changes in the spatial axis not only in terms of who provided help but also in terms of who required help. Sixteen (32 percent) of the caregivers found themselves providing care for additional family members, usually the second parent, during the course of caregiving. Two of the caregivers were caring for three people at once while also working full-time! However, only one of the caregivers temporarily placed her mother in a nursing home to care for her dying husband. The other caregivers did not decrease the time they spent caring for each person but instead increased their overall caregiving time. When caring for spouses or co-resident elders, time spent on the instrumental activities of daily living, such as cooking, did not have to be duplicated.

THE TEMPORAL AXIS: RELEVANT TIME FRAMES

Several time markers can be distinguished within the caregiving career. The most common time markers included the onset of assistance with both instrumental activities of daily living (IADLs) and activities of daily living (ADLs), hospitalization and rehabilitation, co-residence (where applicable), returning to one's home or to a state of wellness, nursing home placement, and death. Since chapter 3 focuses on the beginning of the caregiver career, including assisting with IADLs and ADLs, the next time marker to be considered is hospitalization and rehabilitation.

Hospitalization and Rehabilitation

For twelve of the adult children (24 percent), hospitalization and rehabilitation, due to a sudden fall or illness, preceded (and precipitated) the onset of caregiving. In fourteen other instances (28 percent), elders were hospitalized *during* the caregiving career. Six of the elders were hospitalized three or more times. Caregivers did not refer to the time that their parents were in the hospital as a respite, since they usually felt obligated to visit daily and continued to give care in the hospital (e.g., assisting with feeding and personal care). Three of the caregivers volunteered that caregiving was more time-consuming when their parents were in a hospital because they spent all of their free time with them.

Caregiving intensified when elders returned home after hospitalization, due often to the elder's frail condition and the need to continue rehabilitation. Several of the caregivers received more help from family during this time. Billie's sister-in-law, for example, moved in with her for two weeks after their mother-in-law's surgery. Similarly, Bebe's son and husband helped to bathe and medicate her father when he returned home from the hospital. When medically necessary, other elders had visiting nurses or therapists come to their home immediately following hospitalization.

In many cases, the period of rehabilitation afforded family members the time to work out a caregiving arrangement, which was particularly necessary in situations where the parent had previously been independent. With the urgency of the medical emergency behind them, they could focus on how they were then going to care for their parent. It was at this point that multiple family meetings would be called. Family members recalled that at this time they were surprised to learn that few social services were available to care for their parents and that they were not going to be able to leave their parents alone. The period of rehabilitation then was often a crisis period for families beginning the caregiving career.

Co-Residence

At some point in the caregiving career, 30 of the caregivers (60 percent) lived with their parents. Many of the caregivers referred to this as a relief since they no longer had to run to their parents' homes to provide care or to cook and clean in two homes. Other caregivers spoke of no longer having to worry whether or not their parents were alright. This was particularly important for children of Alzheimer's patients. There was, however, the cost of their privacy, for themselves and their own families. Sue stated, "When my parents weren't living with us, I could at least get away. I had an escape, but not anymore."

Excluding those caregivers who lived with their parents prior to caregiving (see chapter 3), children asked their parents to live with them when they could no longer be left alone. In all instances, this followed the initial diagnosis of a fatal illness, hospitalization, or the worsening of the parent's medical condition (most often with cases of dementia). The precipitating factor was the parent's need for assistance at night or the need for constant care or monitoring.

Returning Home

Six of the elders (12 percent) were well enough to return to their own homes during the course of caregiving. This number is likely an underestimation since the entire caregiving careers could not be followed. In all instances, the return of the parent to his or her own home required the continuation of care, at least for the short term. For example, Beth's mother, Hattie, eventually needed assistance with only the instrumental activities of daily living and weekly bathings after returning to her own home until again she had to return to her daughter's home when she broke an elbow. Hattie's health improved well enough to return to her own home twice during the caregiving career. Each time Hattie returned home, Beth's caregiving tasks changed, although gradually, from intensive personal care to more intermittent personal care and assistance with the IADLs.

Rarely did elders return to their own homes, not because they were well enough to do so, but because the caregiver wished to terminate their caregiving responsibilities. During the initial interview, Deborah stated that she did not want to be a caregiver. At the time of the followup interview, her father was living on his own and Deborah could not be located. Representatives of the adult day care center that he attended believed that Deborah's father should not be on his own.

Nursing Home Placement

The biggest change that occurred from the first interview to the followup interview was the institutionalization or death of the parent. Of the seventeen caregivers reinterviewed, eight of their parents (or 47 percent) had died. (Six had been in a nursing home for one to two months, while the remaining two had been in a nursing home for a little over a year.) Another eight (47 percent) had parents currently in nursing homes. (Remember that caregivers whose parents were institutionalized at the time of the original survey were not included in the study.) Thus, only one of the caregivers had not been institutionalized between the first and followup interviews. Nursing home placement was the result of the elder's inability to remain in the community or the caregiver's inability to continue providing care. As the elders' dementia continued, some could no longer remember how to walk up and down stairs. In other instances, children believed that their parents were a danger to themselves. Other elders lost all control of bowel movements, were bedridden, or needed around-the-clock care. Of the seventeen parents, twelve (or 71 percent) could no longer remain in the community by the time of the followup interview.

Coupled with these changes, a minority of the children felt that they could no longer provide care (four out of seventeen or 24 percent). Connie, for example, saw that her children were losing patience with their grandmother and believed that she could no longer ask them for assistance. Dominic did not want to have to clean his mother when she became incontinent. Although he could have provided the care, he added that it was more than he was willing to do. In contrast, the other twelve children wanted to continue to provide care, but the extent of their parents' frailty and degree of impairment made it impossible.

Although all of the adult children whose parents were institutionalized were originally reluctant even to consider nursing home placement, by the second interview all believed that they had done the right thing and seemed at peace with their decision. Connie stated, "It was time. I had to go through the process with her, and I did. We went from A to Z, but the time had come." Yet, nursing home placement was not an easy decision for those who had spent years keeping their parent out of a nursing home. Susan added,

It was the hardest thing I have ever done, leaving her there. She didn't know what was happening, but *I knew* that my real mother wouldn't want to be there. I did the right thing, but I let her down at the same time. How can that be? . . . I cried for days.

Death

Not only were they at peace with their decisions to institutionalize their parents, but caregivers whose parents had died also held positive attitudes toward their deaths. For example, with regard to her mother's death, Beth stated,

She died in the nicest way possible, it was really a wonderful experience. She told me on Friday that Monday was St. Joseph's day and that she was going to be with her husband and her brother on that day and she was. She never lost her sense of humor, she was making jokes and wisecracks to the end.

Family members may have been more likely to see their parents' deaths as positive because of the suffering they witnessed as caregivers.

All of the caregivers knew when their parents were in the final stages of life, and all except two out of the eight were with their parents when they died. All died in a nursing home. Caregivers whose parents were still alert made special allowances for their parents before they died. Beth, for example, convinced the nursing home staff to let her bring her mother's beloved dog in to see her. She said, "I knew that it would mean so much to Meme to give [the dog] a treat one more time, and she did. We put the treat in my mother's hand and the dog took it. Meme's whole face just lit up!"

As for their own involvement, caregivers whose parents had died felt that they had done the "right thing" to be caregivers. Kathy, for example, said that she only wished that she could have taken care of her mother longer before she had to put her into a nursing home. Even Dominic, who seemed most unhappy with the caregiving situation at the first interview, remarked after his mother's death that he had done the right thing to care for her at home. How caregivers readjusted to the loss of the caregiver role following death is discussed in greater detail below.

TRANSACTIONAL AXIS: PROCESSES INVOLVED

Processes involved in caregiving changed as elders' health changed, and often with that, their residence changed. For example, when elders returned to their own homes after living with their children, the caregivers' activities went from providing intensive personal care to monitoring their parents' health during the initial trial period to then helping their parents to maintain their independence. This last stage usually involved providing IADL care, particularly meal preparation, housekeeping, and taking parents to doctors' appointments, and oftentimes assisting with bathing.

Except for those elders who were well enough to return to their own homes, the majority showed a decline in health after the initial onset of illness but had brief periods of "good days." Declines in health status, often steady but sometimes precipitated by a worsening of the illness or the onset of another illness or accident, resulted in increased caregiving needs up to the point of institutionalization when caregivers could no longer meet those needs. These children found themselves providing more ADL assistance for longer periods, and when available, calling upon their own nuclear family members to provide more help. Siblings, however, were less reliable. For example, as her father's needs increased, Joan convinced her sister to provide more help, although it averaged only five hours a month. Although this seems scanty, six of the caregivers (12 percent) received no additional assistance as their parents' health worsened.

When parents went into nursing homes, caregivers found that they continued to provide as much care but that the content of the care had shifted. For example, when Susan's mother was institutionalized, she said that caregiving became more stressful. Earlier she had been able to care for her mother and father at the same time, but her mother's nursing home placement meant that she had to spend twice as much time caring for each separately. When asked what she did for her mother in the nursing home, she said that it was important that she see her mother every day to ensure that the nurses were caring for her properly and that she helped her mother to eat, read to her, took her for walks in her wheelchair, and brought her special items. This is consistent with earlier findings that family members of nursing home residents held themselves responsible for monitoring and evaluating the quality of care, teaching staff to deliver high-quality care, and providing direct care to preserve the resident's "self" (Bowers, 1988).

Other caregivers switched from caring for one family member to another after their parents' institutionalization or death, again an indication of a lifetime of caring. Consider the following examples. After his mother's death, Dominic switched focus and spent much more time meeting his father's needs in the nursing home. Both Nancy's father's and Sonia's father-in-law's physical impairments increased after their wives died, causing both to require care. Sonia's mother also became ill following her mother-in-law's death, requiring Sonia to make two-hour trips several times a week to her home. Beth began caring for her grandchildren after her mother died, while Liza cared first for her mother and then her sister after her husband and father died. Once Marie's husband and mother died, she began caring for her great-aunt.

ADAPTATION OVER TIME

Results from previous research showed that caregivers adapted to caregiving (that is, they adjusted to their role) over time (Townsend, Noelker, Deimling, and Bass, 1989). However, according to this study, the process of adaptation was not universal. That is, while some caregivers adapted, others did not. Dominic, for example, stated that the bitterness and stress from caregiving had increased over time and that caregiving had become substantially more difficult as the time period from his last vacation with his wife increased. Dominic did not believe that his mother's illness had worsened but that it had simply become harder for him to stay home with her. For Dominic, the point of institutionalizing both his mother and his father came early on in his caregiving career (i.e., when each became incontinent), while other caregivers continued to provide care until their parents could not walk, for example. These results suggest that Dominic, in fact, did not adapt over time. Deborah had also given up caregiving, even though her father still needed someone to live with him (according to personnel at the adult day health center). In contrast, Beth saw each new change as a challenge to make her mother's life as comfortable as possible and her mother as strong as she could be. Beth also accommodated the rest of her life in order to make caregiving easier. She gave up her job and installed equipment in her home, thus adapting to the circumstances as necessary. Beth saw caregiving as being easier to do as time passed and (in her words) as she learned to become an "effective" caregiver. These results indicate that Beth did adapt to her role.

Whether or not caregivers adapted to their circumstances thus depended on several things. Children who really wanted to provide care rather than doing it primarily out of obligation were better able to respond to each new challenge and thus to adjust to changing circumstances. Children who could make accommodations in their lives to ease the burden of caregiving and who had positive experiences in garnering support and assistance, whether from family members or the formal system, were also more likely to adjust to the role. Finally, children whose parents "got well," even if for the short term, found renewed energy in the positive changes that they made.

ROLE DISENGAGEMENT AND READJUSTMENT

Caregivers could disengage from the role of caregiver through one of three means: transference of the role to another family member, institution-alization of the parent with the cessation of caregiving, or death of the parent. Among the seventeen caregivers who were reinterviewed in a followup survey, only three (18 percent) had transferred the caregiving role to another family member during their caregiving careers. For Billie, however, it was her mother-in-law's choice to go and live with a second daughter-in-law although Billie was very concerned that her "mother" would not get proper care. In another instance, one of the daughters-in-law had transferred care of her mother-in-law to the other members of the family, including her husband, when her mother-in-law was well enough to live on her own and did not require full-time care. A third caregiver transferred the care of her father to her mother after her mother recovered from surgery.

In all three cases, caregivers had their own young children and jobs to focus on as they adjusted to the loss of the caregiver role. Only Billie, however, saw it as a loss, while the other two caregivers were relieved that their caregiving duties were over. When asked about the future, Billie was certain that she would care for additional family members, including other in-laws. Brenda hoped that she would be able to care for her *mother*, but added that it was too much to care for her *mother-in-law* while her children were young.

As was stated above, the majority of caregivers continued to provide care to their parents (in-law) even after they were placed in a nursing home, although the tasks of caregiving changed somewhat. Others, however, transferred caregiving to the nursing home staff and thus withdrew from the caregiving role. These caregivers continued to visit their parents but did not have regular responsibilities. For example, one of the sons stated, "Sometimes if a doctor won't come to the nursing home, I take my mother [to the doctor] so that someone she knows is with her. Other than that though, I just visit when I can."

Children were most likely to withdraw from caregiving if their parents no longer recognized them or if the caregiver was a son. Sons may have been more likely to believe that nursing home staff could adequately replace the care that they provided, while daughters were more likely to believe that parents were needy of the additional care that they gave. That is, since it was consistent with their gender ideology, daughters were less likely to relinquish the caregiver role. Of the two sons who were reinterviewed a second time, both had disengaged from caregiving after placing their parent in a nursing home. Of the fourteen daughters and daughters-in-law who had placed a parent in a nursing home before the second interview, only two daughters (14 percent) had disengaged from caregiving (chi-square (1) = 3.4, $p < .10$).

Daughters also had a more difficult time readjusting after the loss of the caregiver role through nursing home placement. Both daughters responded to the loss of the role as if they were in a state of limbo. One of the daughters said,

> I am not a caregiver anymore, but my mother hasn't passed away either. I haven't gone back to my old job yet, but there really isn't much for me to do at the nursing home either. I don't even visit as much as I used to because she doesn't recognize me and that hurts.

In contrast, the sons had refocused on the other venues of their lives, their families and jobs, and established a new routine.

Eleven of the caregivers had experienced the death of a parent. Three of the caregivers had parents who died just before the original interview, while eight experienced the death of a parent before the followup interview. Caregivers expressed a range of emotions, although there were consistent patterns. A common reaction among caregivers was to be relieved, not because they were freed from the burdens and difficulties of caregiving, but because their parents were no longer suffering. Celia stated in the original interview that "If there were a God and there were a kind world, He would take Kay. That would be the best thing for her." This was due to the mental agony that Celia saw her mother-in-law suffer from her advanced stage of Alzheimer's. In the second interview, Celia said that she was happy for Kay that she was no longer being tormented, not knowing where she was or who she was with. Liza, too, could not bear to see her father in pain and encouraged him to "let go." She said, "I used to tell him, "Pa, St. Peter is moving over for you. Are you sure that you do not want to get off on cloud nine? . . . I told him that it was alright for him to die, that we would take care of Mom." Liza added that when her father finally did die, she breathed a sigh of relief that he would no longer be hooked up to machines.

Caregivers who were relieved by the death of a parent were also more likely to see their parent's death from a positive point of view. Beth mentioned that her mother was looking forward to her death to be reunited with her husband and brother, that she was not in pain, and that she died on the day that she wanted to die (i.e., St. Joseph's Day). It is also likely that

Beth could see her mother's death positively because she knew that she had done all that she could for her mother, quitting her job and caring for her mother in her home.

For other caregivers, the overwhelming reaction to their parent's death was one of grief. Often that grief was an extension of additional circumstances. One of the caregivers, for example, was grieving not only for the loss of her mother but also for the premature loss of her husband and the financial repercussions of his illness. Paula, who was single, had lived alone with her mother her entire adult life. Paula grieved not only for the loss of her mother's companionship and the termination of three years of caregiving, but also for the lack of her own family. The death of Paula's mother emphasized to her that she had entered a new stage of life (no longer the middle generation but instead the eldest generation in her family), still unmarried, and reinforced the increasing likeliness that she would end up "a maiden aunt" like her own aunt.

Caregivers entered the final stage of caregiving when they readjusted to the loss of their parent. Several of the caregivers made this adjustment by becoming the caregiver for another member of the family. Two of the caregivers who continued to attend caregiver support groups provided respite care for other members of the group. At some level, the role of caregiver became important to them, providing significant intrinsic rewards. Not wanting to lose that role, they substituted one elder for another. In addition, they may have been willing to help other caregivers since they recognized the importance of respite.

Other caregivers readjusted to the loss of their parent and of the caregiving role by changing other aspects of their lives. Two of the caregivers quit their jobs after their parents died. One of the caregivers said that the stress of her job compounded the difficulties of losing her parent, but both said that they "wanted a change to look forward to."

A minority of caregivers attended counseling sessions to adjust to their parents' deaths. Two of the caregivers continued to attend caregiver support groups, while two others were undergoing private counseling. All four of the caregivers described themselves as being in a state of depression.

Thus, with the death or institutionalization of the parent or the reassignment of caregiving duties, many adult children and children-in-law ended the provision of care to their parents. It is likely, however, that the overall caregiving career will extend across multiple elderly family members. Particularly for working class families who emphasize the direct provision of care, the caregiving career (for elders) may extend across several decades.

THE CAREGIVING CAREER

Results of this research confirm that caregiving was a career. That is, caregiving was a series of related positions through which the caregiver moved in an ordered sequence (Aneshensel et al., 1995). Yet, there was diversity within that career. This diversity was dictated by the direction and changing circumstances of the elder's health needs, by the family's perceptions of the appropriateness of nursing home and other formal care usage, and by the changing circumstances of (potential and actual) helpers. Thus, the caregiving career was often a mixture of providing hands-on care alone, managing others, and coordinating care within a network of formal or informal providers.

The caregiving career often spanned beyond care for just one parent. The caregiving career instead was part of a lifetime of caring. While some of the adult children had become caregivers as children caring for siblings or grandparents, others cared for additional elders (the second parent, aunts, etc.) as adults. Caregivers frequently cared for several persons at once, including spouses.

What was striking was the extent to which caregiving occurred as a series of many changes. There were multiple substages under the time frame of role enactment, an elaboration of Aneshensel et al.'s (1995) model. These changes were due, in part, to the fact that elders with physical impairments had periods of improvement and to the changing health care needs of the elder. Thus, in considering elders with physical impairments as well as cognitive impairments, one finds the caregiving career to be one of greater diversity and change.

Although all of the caregivers provided in-home care for most of their caregiving careers, nursing home placement was also common. By the time of the followup interview, only one out of the seventeen caregivers had not institutionalized their parent (6 percent). In contrast to prior research, nursing home placement did not necessarily include hands-on care (Bowers, 1988). Of the sixteen children who had institutionalized a parent by the time of the second interview, four (25 percent) had disengaged from caregiving. Disengagement from caregiving was more common when the parents no longer recognized their children and when the caregiver was a son. In contrast, caregivers often remained engaged in caregiving even after the death of their parent, transferring the role to another family member. This, again, suggests the existence of a caregiving career that spans across care recipients as well as an attachment to the caregiving role.

Because of the debilitating condition of their parents, nursing home placement was common in both classes. That is, when elders became severely disabled and unable to function in the home, class differences in attitudes toward nursing home placement were of secondary concern. Caregivers who institutionalized their parents because they were no longer able to provide care themselves (as opposed to those who provided care as long as was humanly possible) were more likely to come from the middle class. In fact, all four were middle class. In contrast, in the working class, caregivers were more likely to see themselves as able to provide care until elders had to be institutionalized because of their physical conditions. This confirms earlier findings from this study that working class caregivers were less likely to utilize formal services overall.

We would all like to believe that caregivers are able to adapt to caregiving over time and that family members readjust after they disengage from caregiving. Believing these things would make us all feel more comfortable in acknowledging the burdens of caregiving that we know exist in the community and perhaps in our own homes. Adaptation to the caregiving role was not universal, evidenced in part by those caregivers who disengaged from the role prematurely or for whom the stress of caregiving became more difficult over time, all else constant. In addition, at least some caregivers required counseling in readjusting to the loss of their parent, while others chose not to disengage from the role, instead replacing one care recipient with another. These are the groups of caregivers who need our help the most and who cannot be dismissed with euphemisms of adaptation.

How one disengaged from caregiving did not appear to affect the process of readjustment. Instead, those who had difficulty readjusting after disengagement showed the greatest stress at the loss of the role and were daughters who had always been extremely close to (and perhaps dependent on) their mothers. These results suggest that it may be at the time of loss of the caregiver role rather than at the loss of the parent that intervention is most necessary. Overall, results suggest the need to target caregiver support services to caregivers who provide care primarily out of obligation rather than desire, those who are unable to make accommodations or garner support from others, and caregivers who do not experience at least brief periods of their parents getting well. Without these supports, caregivers do not adapt to the role, and the caregiving career, an integral part of the life span, may be ended prematurely.

CHAPTER 9

Just Plain Folk: Class, Ethnicity, and Gender

Class differences in family values and structure, especially for working class or blue collar families, have been a particular focus of family sociologists and practitioners (Langman, 1987; Rubin, 1976, 1994). Many researchers have found that working class families demonstrate more intergenerational contact and supportive relationships (particularly between parents and adult children) in comparison to families of higher class status. For example, working class adult children are more likely to provide direct care to their elderly parents versus managing care (Archbold, 1983; Cantor, 1975; Hill, 1970; Horowitz, 1985a; Sussman, 1988), in part because of economic restriction (Abel, 1990; Glazer, 1993; Walker, 1983) and in part because they are likely to reside in close proximity (Hoyert, 1991). Others have found no class differences with regard to more general contact with family or support received from others (Krause and Borawski-Clark, 1995; Pyke and Bengtson, 1996). This suggests that class differences, including norms of interdependence and assistance, become salient with regard to particular relations, that is, the parent-child relationship.

It is expected that these class differences will continue and affect other aspects of parent-adult child relationships, including the caregiver role that adult children perform. As such, this study examines whether the likelihood of greater contact and assistance from working class children means that when they become caregivers they will also provide more hours of care and for longer periods before institutionalizing their parents. Also, how does the expectation of family cohesiveness affect the likelihood of receiving assistance from others? Are working class adult children more likely to help one another and form caregiving networks? What are the implications for caregiving of the financial strain common in working class families?

Ethnic variations in caregiving have received little attention, although there has been some research on expectations for care. Indeed, C. Johnson (1995) found that Italian daughters and daughters-in-law placed a strong emphasis on caring for elderly parents. Previous research has also found that, in general, members of ethnic groups rely more on one another in help-seeking than Anglo-Saxon families (T. Johnson 1995). McAdoo (1993) and Markides and Mindel (1987) argued that many aspects of ethnic culture were mediated through the family and family interaction. One would therefore expect ethnic differences in family support and subsequent caregiving.

In contrast, Rosenthal (1986) projected that there would be more differences in cultural norms and beliefs than in actual behaviors across ethnic groups. Others agreed that the pressures of daily activities in providing care were more important than cultural norms (Lawton, Rajagopal, Brody, and Kleban, 1992). In accordance, one would expect little difference in caregiving behaviors. The effect of ethnicity is examined in this study using caregivers from Italian, French, French Canadian, and Irish backgrounds.

Much more attention has been given to gender differences in caregiving. Overall, results suggest that daughters are more involved in caregiving. For example, they are more likely to be caregivers, provide more hours of care per week, and are more likely to assist with personal care tasks (Coward and Dwyer, 1990; Dwyer and Coward, 1991; Montgomery, 1992; Montgomery and Kamo, 1989; Spitze and Logan, 1990; Stoller, 1990). But do the differences persist for sons who are committed to caregiving, those who provide assistance with activities of daily living? This study also examines gender differences in unexplored areas such as the different pathways that sons versus daughters take to becoming caregivers, how sons versus daughters negotiate work and caregiving, and whether there are gender differences in the formation of caregiving networks.

CLASS DIFFERENCES

The Extent of Care Provision

It was expected that the tendency toward greater contact and the direct provision of assistance among working class families (Archbold, 1983;

Cantor, 1975; Glazer, 1993; Hill, 1970; Hoyert, 1991) would continue into the caregiver role. Taking into account the severity of the parent's illness and the amount of help that the caregiver received from others, little difference was found between working class and middle class caregivers in the number of hours of care provided. Caregivers from both groups provided the amount of care that was necessary for their parents, which often increased as their parent's impairments worsened.

Although middle class children provided as many hours of care, there were class differences in the extent of impairment that they were willing to care for. That is, middle class caregivers were more likely to place a parent in a nursing home as his or her impairments worsened. Whether because parents were incontinent, unable to walk on their own, or were disoriented, middle class children institutionalized their parents at earlier points than working class children. For example, Abby, Marie, and Liza, all working class, were caring for parents at home who were well beyond the criteria for institutionalization. In contrast, Dominic, Kathy, and Judy, all middle class, sent their parents to nursing homes as soon as their parents became incontinent. Not all middle class caregivers gave up early, however. Beth and Sally cared for their mothers at home until medical requirements necessitated otherwise.

In addition to institutionalizing their parents faster, middle class caregivers used adult day care more often. This, however, was not due solely to ability to pay, since Medicaid and Elder Home Care reimbursed on a sliding scale. (This issue is discussed further below.) Of the middle class caregivers, twenty-four out of twenty-six (92 percent) used adult day care, while sixteen out of twenty-four (67 percent) working class caregivers did so at some point during the course of caregiving (chi-square $(1) = 4.5$, $p < .05$). Although working class caregivers used adult day care nearly exclusively while they worked, middle class caregivers also used it to provide their parents with social contact or to give the caregiver a break. This would suggest that working class families use formal services more out of necessity relative to middle class caregivers, whereas middle class caregivers are more liberal in their use of formal services.

Since adult children from the working class are more likely to provide direct care versus managed care (Abel, 1990; Archbold, 1983; Glazer, 1993; Hoyert, 1991; Walker, 1983), this orientation was expected to translate into their greater likelihood of volunteering for the role of caregiver (as the pathway to caregiving). Class differences in rates of volunteering, however, were not found. Instead, working class children were more likely to be *chosen* by their parents as caregivers relative to middle class caregivers.

(Four out of five caregivers chosen by their parents were working class.) It may be that in the working class, the expectation of filial care and the proximity of more than one child mean that elderly parents believe that they have a choice as to who will care for them. In fact, several adult children from the working class said that their parents had several adult children (or children-in-law) to select from as caregiver.

Sibling Networks

Given cultural prescriptions for family interdependence (Myers and Dickerson, 1990), it was expected that adult children would be more likely to form caregiving networks in the working class. Indeed, these results were found, but they were not due to a larger family size in the working class (see chapter 4 for further information). While the results may, in part, be explained by greater proximity among working class siblings (both a cause and a result of family interdependence), in several instances siblings in the working class relocated or traveled lengthy distances to be part of the caregiving network. Thus, it was more than convenience that accounted for sibling networks.

In instances in which siblings did not form caregiving networks, adult children from the working class were more likely to acknowledge conflict with siblings. Although an inability to purchase formal assistance may have exacerbated their annoyance with the lack of assistance from siblings, cultural prescriptions that siblings should provide help likely contributed to the conflict as well. Thus, it would appear that as part of the family interdependence common in the working class, a strong expectation of filial care was evidenced in both the greater likelihood of forming caregiving networks and in the conflict that ensued when assistance was not provided.

Given a strict gender division of labor in the working class and greater status given to men than women (Langman, 1987; Rubin, 1976, 1994), it was expected that (1) male members of the family would be more involved in caregiving in the middle class than in the working class and that (2) caregivers would have a more difficult time involving male members than female members of the family in providing assistance in the working class. But just the opposite was found on both accounts. Brothers helped more in the working class than in the middle class. For example, it was Liza's two brothers, rather than her sisters, who continued providing care throughout her father's illness. In addition, among the daughters-in-law in the working class, husbands (as sons) provided more assistance than in the middle class (taking into account differences in extent of care needed). Brenda's husband,

Tom, took over caring for his mother when her care needs were reduced to one day a week. In the middle class, sons-in-law were more willing to assist their wives who were caregivers. Their wives interpreted it as assistance to them rather than to their parents, suggesting the relative importance of the conjugal unit in the middle class.

Middle class caregivers seemed more resigned to the fact that brothers did not help. While it may in part be explained by a lack of expectation of filial assistance in general, middle class caregivers did expect more from their sisters than from their brothers. An additional explanation may be that in the middle class, brothers' earning powers were accepted as cause for not providing assistance, particularly for tasks that we often think of as menial, that is, unpaid.

Were there then different motivations for working class versus middle class caregivers? Consistent with values of family interdependence, working class caregivers were motivated more often by a desire to pay parents back or a belief that family, and children in particular, are obligated to provide care. That is, fifteen out of twenty-four (63 percent) of the working class caregivers cited these reasons versus six out of twenty-six (23 percent) of the middle class caregivers (chi-square (1) = 8.2, $p < .005$). Sheila, for example, wanted to pay her mother back for the financial struggles that she endured on Sheila's behalf. Another working class caregiver focused more on family obligation as the motivating factor for providing care. He said, "I think that family should take care of their own. Who else have you got; what else have you got? I don't want some stranger taking care of my own mother."

In contrast, in the middle class, caregivers were more often motivated by additional reasons to provide care. One of the middle class daughters said that she was still trying to gain her perfectionist father's approval. Several middle class children in the medical profession reported that they just liked taking care of people, whereas others stated that they did it out of love for the second parent.

Financial Implications

Although there was a strong ethos to provide care, working class caregivers were constrained by financial limitations. It was expected that this constraint might limit their ability to invite parents to live with them (if resources were tight or homes required remodification) or to afford necessary services. These limitations would, in turn, increase the amount of stress that caregivers were under.

We know, already, that working class caregivers were less likely to use adult day care. Given the reimbursement by Medicaid and Elder Home Care, this difference was not likely due to the cost. Previous findings show that while lower incomes restrict the ability to hire formal helpers, subsidization for home health care (or in this case, adult day care) compensates for the difference in ability to pay (Soldo, Agree, and Wolfe, 1989). Of the fourteen caregivers whose parents paid for their own day care, only one was working class.

Caregivers were more likely to give cultural reasons rather than financial reasons for not using formal services. For example, when asked why they did not use adult day care, working class caregivers often seemed insulted and stated proudly that they could care for their parents themselves. Two of the caregivers said that they did not want strangers taking care of their mothers, that their parents deserved better. Others said that family should care for its own. Working class children who chose not to use it seemed to perceive of adult day care as a "handout" or an indication that they could not or did not want to care for their parents, that they were a "bad" family. Perhaps those children who saw it as a "handout" would have been more likely to use the service if they could have afforded to *pay* for it in full.

Working class children also objected to having nonfamily in their homes. Seventeen percent of the working class caregivers (four out of twenty-four) stated that having visiting nurses in their homes made them uncomfortable. Brenda, for example, referred to them as "strangers" whose presence interfered with their normal family interactions. Middle class caregivers did not see service workers' presence as disruptive or intrusive.

Those working class children who used adult day care, however, seemed to be satisfied with it and wanted to be able to send their parents more often. Of the eight caregivers in this situation, all were working class. In the middle class, parents were more likely to pay for their own day care if they wanted to go more often. (More specifically, in most cases, *children* used their parents' money to pay for the services they wanted their parents to use.) This suggests that working class children who are willing to try formal services realize the benefits of these services. An additional explanation is that working class caregivers who are desperate for assistance will turn to formal services despite norms to do otherwise.

Consistent with their orientation to manage care, middle class caregivers were also more likely to hire help to assist with caregiving. Of the eight caregivers who hired assistance, only two (25 percent) were working class. In both instances, children hired someone to care for their mothers while they worked (when parents were not in adult day care). Working class caregivers hired help for short periods of time but could not afford care for long. In contrast, in the middle class, children hired assistance for as long as they needed it. Middle class caregivers may be more likely to hire help not only because of cultural values of what is appropriate assistance but also because they are not eligible for other community services. Kayla, for example, applied for elder care services but was told that she was not eligible because she "made too much money."

In contrast to what was expected, financial constraints did not prevent working class families from sharing their homes with their parents. Of the working class caregivers, sixteen out of twenty-four (67 percent) were co-resident in comparison to fourteen out of twenty-six (54 percent) of the middle class caregivers (chi-square $(1) = 1.33$, not statistically significant). Working class caregivers were more likely to already live with their parents before they began caregiving. Several of the caregivers already had in-law apartments in their basements or had been sharing the cost of housing with their parents. In one instance, it was the parent who had taken the child in following divorce. Thus, lack of resources encouraged rather than discouraged intergenerational co-residence.

In several working class families, adult children shared the financial responsibility of caring for their parents. Jan and her four siblings each contributed to the support of their parents who were on a very limited income. Only Jan, however, provided personal care. Perhaps siblings believed that in contributing scarce financial resources, they were not obligated to provide additional assistance in the form of hands-on care.

Did these differences result in greater stress among working class caregivers? Clearly, those children under the most stress were those who provided extensive amounts of personal care with little assistance from siblings or other family members and who had not been able to reduce their work hours. To the extent that financial constraints made it difficult, if not impossible, to hire help for extensive periods of time or to switch from full-time to part-time work, working class caregivers were under additional stress. Cultural prescriptions that mandate filial care as long as possible before institutionalization also contributed to this stress. That is, working class caregivers were more likely to believe that they were obligated to maintain their role even when they were under enormous amounts of strain.

Work and Leisure

Class differences were also expected to operate in the matter of whether and how adult children accommodated their work. Given the lack of flexibility or autonomy in working class jobs (Archbold, 1983), working class caregivers were expected to be less able to accommodate their work. In terms of altering their hours, results suggested that both working and middle class caregivers rearranged their work schedules and took time off during the day. As was expected, these arrangements, on the whole, were more constricted for working class caregivers. For example, one of the daughters from the working class made arrangements with her boss to come in fifteen minutes late every day and stay fifteen minutes after closing time. In comparison, middle class caregivers sometimes had the option of leaving work one or two hours early. This was due to the fact that middle class caregivers could take work home with them, which was usually not an option in the working class.

The class differences that did exist were in terms of more substantial changes in work. While differences in work accommodation (e.g., rearranging one's work schedule) were not extensive, middle class caregivers were more likely than working class caregivers to quit their jobs or reduce their work to part-time. Of the six caregivers who switched from full-time to part-time work, five were from the middle class (83 percent). In addition, both caregivers who quit their jobs were middle class. In all likelihood, working part-time or not at all was more feasible for middle class caregivers whose spouses had higher incomes. Middle class caregivers may have found it more difficult to combine work and caregiving if middle class jobs required working late hours or entailed additional commitments and stresses. Working class caregivers were more likely to already work part-time, to be on disability, or to have retired early.

Class differences in leisure and leisure expectations were also found. Prior to caregiving, middle class caregivers had higher expectations of going out to dinner and belonging to organizations and clubs, both of which were much more difficult to do as caregivers. Shirley, for example, had been very active in the Daughters of the Nile and volunteered at a children's hospital as part of a club organization. In contrast, working class caregivers pursued activities that could be combined with caregiving, such as working in the garden and having children and relatives over to their homes. As a result, working class caregivers were less likely to say that caring for their parents interfered with leisure-time activities.

ETHNICITY

According to Sokolovsky (1990), ethnicity is defined as "social differentiation derived from cultural criteria such as a common place of origin

. . . and values that engender a sense of exclusiveness. " The urban areas in which the data were collected included a high concentration of ethnic groups. In this sample, fourteen out of fifty (or 28 percent) of the caregivers were first and second generation (born in the United States) from Italian (eight), Irish (two), and French or French-Canadian (four) backgrounds. Of these, eight (57 percent) were working class.

Earlier researchers have argued that the family transmits ethnic culture (Markides and Mindel, 1987). Ethnic culture also affects family processes. As such, ethnic variations in how family roles and responsibilities were defined and distributed were expected to affect caregiving. In fact, nearly all of the caregivers mentioned on their own how their ethnic backgrounds affected their desire to provide care themselves. Liza, for example, stated,

> We are a big French family. My parents were born in Canada, and they taught us the old ways. If we put my mother into a nursing home, well, before we had to anyway, my father would have rolled over in his grave. . . . It is just our way. We take care of our own.

This is consistent with the findings of both Woolfson (1996) and Johnson (1985) in their studies of Franco-American and Italian-American families. Members of both ethnic groups felt strongly about the responsibility to care for elderly family members and emphasized respect for the elderly in general. Woolfson (1996) argued that although practices (of providing care one's self) had eroded somewhat, there was still an avoidance of nursing homes to care for the elderly. Similarly, in Irish-American families, the wishes of any one individual were less important than the overall welfare of the family (Markides and Mindel, 1987).

The provision of care by more than one member of the family was relatively common among the ethnic families, suggesting the pervasiveness of this value throughout the family. Eight of the caregivers (57 percent) shared care with a sibling, including four who were part of a sibling network of caregivers. This is in comparison to five out of the twenty-six caregivers (19 percent) of Anglo-Saxon descent who shared at least some caregiving tasks with siblings (chi-square (1) = 5.52, p < .025; based on forty caregivers with at least one sibling). These results are consistent with T. Johnson's (1995) findings that while Anglo-Saxon families operated with a tradition of self-sufficiency and hyper-individualism, other ethnic groups were more likely to rely on one another in help-seeking. Hughes (1963) referred to this as "individualism of the family"; that is, the individual is expected to subordinate his or her interests for the good of the family.

As part of their family interdependence, male members of the family also shared in caregiving. Only four of the ethnic families (28 percent) did not include a brother/son as one of the caregivers. Dominic (who was Italian) himself was the caregiver, with little or no assistance from the female members of his family.

Consistent with the findings of C. Johnson (1985, 1995), Italian daughters, in particular, placed a strong emphasis on caring for their elderly parents. Marie, for example, pointed to her upbringing in a large Italian family for her strong belief that it was her responsibility to care for others. She stated that it was "drummed into her" from the time that she was five that it was her job as the oldest girl. Later she went on to add,

> I feel like I am trapped in my ethnic background. This is what I am supposed to do, take care of others. I didn't know that it was supposed to be any other way. . . .

Johnson (1985) argued that adult children internalized the values of caring for their parents out of a lifelong socialization pattern of implicit expectations of duty. For example, elderly parents told their adult children how their friends had been "abandoned" by children who did not provide care, implying that the provision of care was expected. In this study, too, children spoke of ethnic parents telling them their whole lives that they were expected to "take care of their own."

There was some cultural variation in help-seeking. While all of the caregivers from Anglo-Saxon backgrounds used some form of formal service, four of the ethnic families (29 percent), all working class, had not sought any outside services such as adult day care. This is with the exception of visiting nurses who were "prescribed" by the doctor. One of the Italian daughters fired a visiting nurse because she felt that the nurse was not taking good care of her mother. She pointed out that the nurse came to bathe her mother after 2:00 P.M. and socialized with her rather than "working."

These findings are consistent with prior research that members of ethnic groups (at least Italian Americans and Franco Americans) are loath to go outside of the extended family for help and feel uncomfortable in dealing with social service agencies, similar to findings for the working class (Johnson, 1985; Woolfson, 1996). T. Johnson (1995) argued that this was due to cultural paranoia resulting from prior stigmatization and exclusion of the minority group members from mainstream society. In addition, the need for organizational contacts signified that the elder had no family or that adult children were not living up to their responsibilities, and so outside help was negatively sanctioned (Johnson, 1985). In addition, because the elderly were so used to relying on their children, they had no prior contact with social service agencies and had not banded together (Johnson, 1985). In contrast, Stull (1993) found that *Hispanics* used health, social, and long-term care services *more* often than whites and African Americans. Together, these results suggest the importance of recognizing individual differences among ethnic groups.

Intergenerational conflict was common as children strove to meet the cultural expectations of their parents while having assimilated to the American culture. Rose, for example, was frustrated with her mother's "Italian ways." According to Rose, Gert did not understand that Rose needed to work outside of the home to support herself since Gert believed that Rose should marry or depend on her brothers. Both Rose and Marie pointed out that their mothers did not understand how difficult caregiving was since their parents had been cared for and died in Italy. Rose stated, "My mother just sent my aunt money in Italy. If I could just do that, it would be great." This is consistent with the intergenerational strain that results when the demands of both worlds become incompatible as adult children assimilate to the dominant culture (T. Johnson, 1995). While T. Johnson (1995) argued that immigrant parents may feel at a loss due to the incompatibility between generations, results of this research show that adult children also feel this strain, perhaps even more so.

GENDER

Along with class and ethnicity, gender played an important role in the caregiving experience, although the differences between sons and daughters were not as drastic as is portrayed in the literature. In this study, it was more difficult to locate caregiving sons than daughters. Perhaps male caregivers did not make themselves as visible to the rest of society as female caregivers, or perhaps there were simply fewer male caregivers overall (Stone, Cafferata, and Sangl, 1987). In a national survey of informal caregivers, Stone et al. (1987) estimated that 28.5 percent of all caregivers were male, including husbands. Similarly, in this sample, 16 percent (eight out of fifty) of the adult children were sons and 84 percent (forty-two out of fifty) were daughters and daughters-in-law. There were no sons-in-law who could be located who provided care with at least one activity of daily living four or more times a week.

Even though there were fewer sons than daughters and daughters-in-law, many of the sons provided extensive amounts of care. This is in sharp contrast to representations of sons' involvement in the literature (Matthews and Rosner, 1988). As with the daughters, there was great variation among the sons. Dominic, Frank, and Peter provided all of their mothers' care, without help from relatives (although all three were married) but with the assistance of adult day care. That is, they provided as much care as any of the daughters. Peter, for example, fed his mother, administered her medications and colostomy bag, and helped her to dress (she received baths at the adult day care) every day of the week. Peter said that he could leave his mother once she had been cared for, but that he usually did not go very far. He had been providing care for approximately one year.

Other sons provided less assistance. In most instances, they relied heavily on female relatives to "share" the care (often shifting it). Mark provided the least amount of care and assumed the least responsibility. Although he helped his mother to dress every morning and gave her her evening medication, his sister-in-law cared for his mother during the day in her own home. It was his sister-in-law who bathed his mother, fed her an evening meal, took her to doctors' appointments, and so on. Often Mark did not pick his mother up until late into the evening.

For several of the daughters-in-law who were caregivers, their husbands provided substantial amounts of care. Although Brenda cared for her mother-in-law during the day, Tom took over her care when he returned home from work. Later, when Gert returned to her own home, it was Tom who provided care one day a week with each of his siblings and who took time off from work to take his mother to doctors' appointments. While daughters-in-law were providing substantial amounts of care, it was not always as a substitute for their husbands, but as a supplement to what husbands could not provide on their own. In many instances, this was because daughters-in-law accommodated their work, allowing for greater availability.

Overall, sons were more likely to receive assistance, though from other family members. That is, four out of six (67 percent) sons with siblings received at least some help from them compared to nine out of thirty-four daughters and daughters-in-law (26 percent) (chi-square $(1) = 3.54, p < .10$). This is in contrast to Kaye and Applegate's (1990) findings that the majority of male caregivers rarely or seldom received help from family. Kaye and Applegate's study included mainly retired men and the husbands of the care recipients. Family members may not have seen them as being needy of assistance in comparison to sons who had their own families and jobs. In addition, the gender differences in this study may arise from the sons' greater likelihood of pushing or demanding that siblings help out while daughters were more likely to expect siblings to help out without being cajoled. Six out of eight (75 percent) of the sons demanded help compared to one out of thirty-two (3 percent) of the daughters. The findings could also be due to our cultural perceptions that men need help with such nurturant tasks.

In contrast to expectations based on prior findings (Matthews and Rosner, 1988), sisters were as difficult to involve as brothers in the caregiving network. Among those caregivers who had at least one brother and one sister in the area and who had been able to involve a sibling in caregiving, half received help primarily from a brother, while the other half received help primarily from a sister. When sons were part of the caregiving network, they often provided high levels of care, assuming as much responsibility as their sisters, as in the case of Liza and her brothers. This is in sharp contrast to the portrait painted by Matthews and Rosner (1988) of brothers as peripheral helpers who provide primarily sporadic and circumscribed assistance.

As was discussed in chapter 3, sons and daughters became caregivers vis-à-vis different pathways. Sons were less likely to be selected by their parents, both mothers and fathers, and did not volunteer for the role. That is, caregiving by sons was usually not a choice, whether it be the adult child or parent's choice. Instead, sons were more likely to be the de facto caregivers or to be caregivers because "it just happened." Sons became caregivers when there was no one else to do it or it was an extension of prior roles.

Overall, sons were less likely to accommodate their work than daughters. Only one son who provided extensive amounts of care accommodated his work to do so. Dominic's mother required supervision all day long, which, in part, prompted him to retire early. Only daughters, however, quit their work well before retirement or reduced their work from full-time to part-time. Two other sons occasionally missed work to take their mothers to doctors' appointments, although it was not frequent. The other five sons depended on female relatives to provide such services while they worked. As such, sons usually provided care only up to the point that it interfered with their paid employment. Kaye and Applegate (1990) also found the requirements of the job to be one of the least important barriers to caregiving for men.

Daughters were also more likely to describe caregiving as being very stressful. This may have been because they received less assistance with caregiving or because they cared for parents with greater physical impairments and more extensive dementia. Sons who provided similar levels of care with no help also described caregiving in stressful terms. Dominic, for example, stated,

> I don't know how much more my wife and I can go on like this. This is no life, it has to end. Some day I will just snap and that will be the end. I will have to put my mother into a nursing home because I just can't take it anymore.

An additional reason for sons being less stressed by their role was that they were more likely to believe that there were alternatives to caregiving. Daughters often said that they would care for their mothers as long as was humanly possible. In contrast, sons said that they would provide care until "it got to be too much," whether caregiving became too difficult or interfered with their work and other commitments. Sons sent their mothers into nursing homes at earlier stages in the progression of their illness than did daughters.

The differences between sons and daughters as caregivers were not as great as one might expect from the literature (that is, sons assuming a much more peripheral role). But gender ideology, or our perceptions of what is appropriate for our gender as well as the opposite gender, likely played a role in differentiating some behavior. The main difference between sons and daughters was the rarity of sons in the sample. This suggests that sons were less likely to recognize caregiving as being an appropriate part of their life course. Several of the sons saw it as more appropriate for their wives. Tom did not provide care at first because it interfered with his work role which was more consistent with the male life course. Several of the male caregivers provided assistance only up to the point that it conflicted with their work roles, while daughters were more willing to accommodate their work. More sons might be willing to provide care if it could effectively be combined with paid employment. Yet once sons became caregivers, many provided extensive amounts of care.

Gender ideology also affected family members' perceptions of what was appropriate for sons and daughters, brothers and sisters. Lee, Dwyer, and Coward (1993) found that infirm elders were more likely to receive care from a child of the same gender. This study found that fathers who had both a daughter and a son living in the area all *chose* their *daughters* over their sons to provide care. In addition, sons were more likely to receive assistance from their siblings than daughters. This suggests that what is more important than having a same-sex caregiver are our cultural notions of the appropriateness of women as family caregivers. Regardless of whether we believe that women are naturally more nurturant or that men's work should not be compromised, mothers and fathers looked to daughters rather than sons for care and siblings helped their brothers more frequently than their sisters. This finding is consistent with Kaye and Applegate's (1990) report that a significant barrier to caregiving by male members of the family is their own and others' opinions of what is appropriate male behavior.

Results of the present study suggest that sons play a more important role in caregiving than has previously been assumed. In many of the sibling networks, assistance by brothers was seen as invaluable, in contrast to prior findings that assistance by brothers was perceived as less important than that provided by sisters (Matthews, 1995). Matthews (1995) argued that the various indices of help to parents are biased toward daughters, for they focus on the services that daughters are more likely to provide. As such, assistance by sons is undermined. Unfortunately, our perceptions of sons as helpers to their sisters or as dissociated from caregiving also undermine the significant roles that many sons are playing and, more importantly, perpetuate our cultural assumptions that caregiving should be and is a gendered activity.

According to the life course perspective, the aging experience will differ between successive cohorts (Riley and Riley, 1993). If so, future cohorts of caregivers may be less influenced by such stringent gender ideology. Although assumptions of what is appropriate for men versus women have been slow to change, progress is likely among younger and more educated cohorts. Thus, it may be that in future generations, gender ideology will play a less important role in the caregiver process among professional and middle class than among working class caregivers.

THE INTERSECTION OF CLASS, ETHNICITY, AND GENDER

I began this chapter by asking whether class differences in the greater tendency for higher socioeconomic adult children to be care managers versus providers of direct care would continue and result in class differences in the caregiver role itself. According to research findings, the greater family interdependence expected in the working class has resulted in working class siblings being more willing to assist one another in caregiving. Working class children were also found to be more likely to co-reside with their parents and to have shared housing prior to caregiving. Such interdependence is the result of a greater scarcity of financial resources and a belief that family should care for itself. Working class caregivers more often cited wanting to pay parents back or feeling that family is obligated to provide care as their motivating factors.

Once they took on the caregiver role, middle class caregivers did not provide less care, thus showing a greater commitment to the role than just being a care manager. They did, however, institutionalize their parents earlier on in the progression of their parents' illness. Results also showed that while middle class caregivers used adult day care more often, some working class caregivers wanted more day care but could not afford it. In contrast, other working class caregivers thought that using formal care showed a lack of respect for their parents. In addition, although a minority of working class caregivers hired help for awhile, they could not afford to extend it as long as middle class caregivers. As such, working class caregivers again depended more on siblings and other family members for assistance.

The working class ethnic families placed even greater reliance on family members and showed a greater reluctance to use formal services. All of the caregivers within this group shared care with siblings and with their own adult children, including their sons. They emphasized among one another that they could care for their parents themselves and that they did not have to have strangers (i.e., formal services) caring for them. Mary was so embarrassed that she had to send her father to adult day care for a short period that she did not even tell the rest of her family. In like manner, Rose took a leave of absence from work before she would seek assistance from formal services.

The intersection of gender and class was also significant. Male caregivers from the working class were more persistent that siblings help them and appeared to be more determined to keep their parents out of nursing homes. Doug, for example, was the only one in his family who wanted to keep his mother at home. When his mother was in rehabilitation, his sisters insisted that they send her to a nursing home. According to Doug,

> So I asked my mother, in front of my sisters, if she wanted to go into a nursing home and she said "no." So I said to my sisters, "Are you going to make her go against her will?" They couldn't, so now one of my sisters comes in the morning and late at night to bathe and dress her.

Sons from the working class were also quick to enter into conflict with family members when they would not provide help. For example, while Dominic, a middle class son, was very bitter that his siblings did not assist him, neither did he push or cajole them to help. In contrast, Frank claimed that he called his brothers and sisters on the phone regularly "ranting and raving when they would not do for my mother." One of the male caregivers from the working class spoke of his mother's dignity being at stake when his brothers and sisters did not show their respect by caring for her.

Thus, class, ethnic, and gender differences must be considered in describing the caregiving process. Gender ideology as well as cultural and class differences in family roles and responsibilities, family interdependence, and financial constraints each play a central role in shaping the caregiving experience. The intersection of any of the three emphasizes overlapping characteristics as well as offers distinct configurations.

Among the important distinctions considered is ethnic variation. There is a commonly held stereotype that long-term care is less of an issue in ethnic minority populations because of strong family and community supports (Barresi and Stull, 1993; Markides, 1995). According to results of this and other research, the importance placed on the family as the source of care for the elderly by working class and ethnic families does not mean that ethnic and working class elders need no formal assistance. For one thing, not all ethnic (or working class) elders receive help from their families (Rosenthal, 1986). Weeks and Cuellar (1981) found that despite the continuing *ideal* of intergenerational family concern and the availability of a large kin network, obligations and expectations of kin support were declining among ethnic families. Accordingly, there was substantial variation in familial and nonfamilial support systems.

Even when they do exist, informal support networks are not enough. Sokolovsky (1990) found that among African-American elders, informal support networks were effective in handling short-term difficulties, but he believed that they would not be adequate for long-term needs. He argued that our view of ethnicity as a resource has been overly optimistic. Instead, ethnic compensation can be effective when coupled with nonfamily systems of support such as respite and day care programs.

This research supports the view that ethnic and working class families also need formal support, despite their desire to provide care on their own. Except for those few families who could provide twenty-four hour care vis-à-vis a caregiving network, Italian, French-Canadian, and Irish families needed (at a minimum) adult day care to provide care while they worked and as a source of respite when they retired. Although some of the families insisted that they could provide all of the care on their own, others stated that it would be "a godsend" to have at least visiting nurse or homemaker services since they felt that they had "all that they could do" to meet their parents' minimal needs.

Results of the present study contradict the expectations of prior researchers. Based on earlier findings, Rosenthal (1986) predicted that greater differences would be seen among ethnic groups in cultural norms and beliefs than in actual supportive behaviors. In contrast, the present work suggests that although the differences were not extensive, there were differences among ethnic groups (compared to those from Anglo-Saxon backgrounds) in actual supportive behaviors as well as in cultural norms and beliefs. Perhaps the most illustrative example is that of sibling networks. Not only did children from ethnic backgrounds espouse the importance of family interdependence, but also siblings were more likely to act on that norm and help one another in caring for elderly parents.

Rosenthal (1986) further argued that socioeconomic, rather than cultural, factors would be more important in predicting supportive behavior. When adult children from ethnic backgrounds were reluctant to use formal services, they explained their reluctance in terms of cultural rather than socioeconomic terms. That is, they cited the importance of family providing for itself rather than cost in their decision to avoid formal help. Thus, while it is important to conceptualize dimensions of ethnic culture from socioeconomic status, the salience of culture and its effect on behavior need not be minimized.

In conclusion, these findings suggest that class differences found in the earlier stages of the family life cycle (Langman, 1987; Rubin, 1976, 1994) continue into later life families. If anything, the differences become more pronounced as needs increase and resources dwindle among working class elders. Such differences are likely due to norms of family interdependence (expressed in caregiving networks), filial obligation (resulting in the motivation to be a caregiver), financial constraints (expressed in co-residence), and a belief that family is the best provider of care (resulting in a reluctance to use formal care). In future research, one may wish to tease out the pathways for each of these effects and to consider the implications for other dimensions of later life families and intergenerational relationships. In the next chapter, the policy implications of these differences are also considered. Further discussion of the theoretical implications for class and ethnicity is included in Conclusions, chapter 11.

CHAPTER 10

Policy Implications

THE NEED TO RESTRUCTURE LONG-TERM CARE POLICY

Analysts forecast that by the year 2000, there will be 9 million elders requiring long-term care and that this number will increase to 12 million by the year 2020 (Brubaker and Brubaker, 1995). At approximately the same time, the children of the baby bust will reach middle age, providing elderly parents with fewer potential caregivers than in recent decades. In addition, the aging revolution, divorce revolution, and gender revolution will mean that elderly parents will live longer but will not have daughters readily available to provide care (Cantor, 1993). Middle-aged daughters are more likely to be working full-time out of the home, whether due to divorce or seeking the intrinsic rewards of a paid career (Boyd and Treas, 1996). These changes in society, both demographic and social, offer new challenges to long-term care policy.

As the needs of the elderly have changed, so too has the availability of health services changed. The fiscal conservatism of the 1980s along with rising health care costs has resulted in limiting basic health services for the elderly, including both hospitalization and community services (Wallace and Estes, 1989). For example, elders are limited in the number of hospital days allotted to them under Medicare. Under the current system of Diagnostic Related Groups (DRGs), elders are allocated a hospital stay based on the average length of illness for someone in their diagnostic group but are not given further hospital coverage in cases of greater severity or compounding illnesses. As a result, elders are released from the hospital "quicker and sicker" (Gaumer and Stavins, 1992; Shaughnessy and Kramer, 1990) and families are expected to care for them with fewer and fewer community services (Wallace and Estes, 1989).

Elders overwhelmingly wish to remain in their homes or in the community, regarding residential care as a last resort (Qureshi and Walker, 1989). Only a very small proportion of our long-term funds are spent in helping families to maintain their elders in the home. Medicaid, for example, spends less than 10 percent of its long-term care funds on home health care. In the state in which this study was done, however, it covered 75 percent of nursing home care (Central Massachusetts Agency on Aging). Medicare Part B (which is optional) will pay for a home health aide following a hospital stay of three days for a maximum of six months (Atchley, 1994). Therefore, family members are left on their own to provide personal and medical care for frail and disabled parents.

The predominant long-term care policy in this country has been to leave the organization and delivery of the care of the elderly to the family. Social policies reinforce the ideology of familism by assuming that the family is the right location for the care of elders and that female kin are the most appropriate carers. Walker (1996) referred to this position as "compulsory altruism" and pointed out that female kin are under enormous pressures to provide care. The author argued that we need a policy of shared care that does not put female kin under any obligation. Such a policy would support caring services rather than exploiting them (Walker, 1996).

Others agree that family care cannot be considered a panacea for long-term care. After examining family care for the elderly in sixteen different countries, Kosberg (1992) emphasized the importance of communal responsibility in caring for the elderly not just in the United States but worldwide. The author discovered a trend of greater publicly sponsored resources for the elderly by those countries with greater proportions of elders. While this may be related in part to the stage of development, it also suggests a recognition of the need for government support as families become overwhelmed by increasing proportions of elders.

Before we begin to consider restructuring the long-term care system, we need to clarify the precise goals of a publicly funded program. To date in the United States, community care has been focused on the government providing only what it cannot get families to provide for free (Rivlin and Wiener, 1988). In other words, community care has been used to fill in the gaps of what the family does not provide. This may not be the most appropriate objective. According to the Older Americans Act, long-term care services should include those that support family members providing voluntary care. This would suggest that long-term care policy be focused on protecting families from the difficulties of caregiving. This approach would help to support the services that caregivers currently provide rather than the government providing substitute care. Others would argue that policy should be directed to support families, but the goal is not to improve their well-being. Instead, the goal of long-term care policy should be to delay institutionalization of the elderly. Although some espouse such a goal claiming that the elderly prefer community care, often it is espoused to conserve government spending.

The goal of long-term care policy should be to support the family in order to improve their well-being *and* to delay institutionalization since that is what the elderly and their families prefer (Qureshi and Walker, 1989). First, supporting the family (in its myriad forms) rather than exploiting their altruism and sense of obligation should be the goal of any social policy. Throughout this study, family members have cried out for assistance from other family members and from social services. In almost all cases, they did not want others to replace them but to help them to provide care. Without that support, all too often caregivers themselves became the victims of high levels of stress and strain, with negative effects on their work and family lives as well.

Second, supporting family members to provide care will delay institutionalization, improve the quality of care that elders receive, and in the end be less costly to the government. Caregivers who received help were more likely to keep the dependent person at home, and nonintervention was more likely to put caring relationships under strain (Walker, 1996). Home care is also substantially less costly than nursing home care even if you include the implicit costs of informal services (Anderson, Patten, and Greenberg, 1980). Elders also prefer to live in the community (Qureshi and Walker, 1989). To the extent that support to the families makes this possible, a long-term care policy that takes into account caregiving needs will improve the well-being of elders as well.

As part of the long-term care policy, we need a "caregiver policy" that will focus on supporting the well-being of the caregiver and the family as the first priority. This policy will help the caregiver to provide care instead of substituting for the family but will do more than just fill in the gaps, which is the intent of our current policy. A caregiver policy will recognize the undercurrents of familism or an idealized vision of family life which informs current policy and will instead respond to the realities of the family.

Such a policy will encourage the "right" balance and types of both family care and formal care.

RECENT CONTROVERSIES AND QUESTIONS IN LONG-TERM CARE POLICY

In deciding the future of long-term care policy, particularly that which affects caregivers and their families, policymakers and analysts have asked a number of questions and voiced a number of concerns. In keeping with the status quo that the family is the best provider of care, conservatives have expressed concern that the family will withdraw its efforts if community or formal care is available. They have also asked for evidence of the effectiveness of programs that currently support the family before continuing or furthering such programs. In addition, there is the question of whether family caregivers should be financially compensated for the care they provide. Each of these issues is addressed in the next section.

The Substitution Effect

For years, fiscal and social conservatives have been concerned that families will withdraw their efforts to provide support if community services are available. Evidence suggested, though, that while there was some substitution, it was limited and transitory (Tennstedt, Crawford, and McKinlay, 1993). For example, in the Channeling Demonstration Program, family members receiving community services provided slightly less care but reallocated their care from more medically oriented and intimate personal care services to more instrumental care (Tennstedt, Crawford, and McKinlay, 1993).

In Oregon's client-employed home care program, clients were assessed for need and authorized a specific number of hours of reimbursed care. They then hired the caregiver directly. While this program has grown in terms of both number of clients served and total costs, the costs of community care have been kept low. In addition, participants (both the elders and the family caregivers) have expressed overwhelming preference for the program (Kane and Penrod, 1995).

Other studies report that substitution does not exist. Perlman (1983), for example, found that families sought less paid help than professionals recommended. Community services can also be targeted to support but not replace family help. In the Family Support Program of the Community Service Society of New York, modest benefits were given to complement but not substitute for family help. Family members said that the services helped them to sustain their efforts, and they agreed to continue to provide support as a condition of eligibility (Frankfather, Smith, and Caro, 1983).

These findings then suggest that the goal of policy analysts and researchers should be to find that threshold where assistance to the family is welcome and allows them to sustain their caregiving and improve their well-being but is not an unwelcome intrusion or substitute for the family. Such a threshold may differ from family to family. It should then be the task of case managers to determine the eligibility level for community services for each individual family based on the needs of the family, their desired level of assistance, and the availability of community services.

Given the evidence that very little of a substitution or "woodwork" effect exists, why then do some politicians and analysts continue to be concerned? According to Clark (1993), the government is able to create the impression that nonintervention is justified and acceptable by viewing the private domain of families as natural or normal. However, the real reason for withholding support is to limit public expenditures on health care for the elderly as much as possible and to reinforce a traditional ideology of the family.

Programs That Support Family Caregivers

A related question is just how effective programs that support family caregivers have been in the past. A wide range of caregiver support programs exists, including respite care, educational programs, and counseling. According to Montgomery (1995) and Greene and Coleman (1995), scientific evidence has shown little benefit from such programs. However, those who used the programs extensively were highly satisfied. According to Kane and Penrod (1995) and Montgomery (1995), the overall success of the programs may have been blunted by the large numbers of people who used them sparingly or not at all and the tendency to group programs together. In addition, caregiver support programs may have been serving their function without showing overall improved well-being, such as providing respite care when the caregiver was sick.

In this section, we examine the effectiveness of one benefit, respite care. Respite care includes all subsidized, formal services designed to augment rather than supplant families (Montgomery, 1995). Often respite services are provided in-home, but they can include short-term institutional care and day care as well.

As one example of a respite program, in 1984 California set up a statewide system of eleven Caregiver Resource Centers that offered a wide range of respite services to unpaid family caregivers living with the patient. The respite program was intended to provide flexibility, choice, and consumer control. Caregivers received an average of nine hours of respite care per week and paid a copayment fee based on a sliding scale, averaging approximately $27 per month. In terms of outcome, family caregivers reported high satisfaction and were grateful for the financial help, perceived relief, and break in the routine (Feinberg and Kelly, 1995).

According to Montgomery (1995), there is insufficient evidence to argue for or against respite services. However, there is certainly enough evidence of its effectiveness and low cost that we should not simply abandon the service. For example, Barresi and Stull (1993) maintained that although respite and other family supports do not reduce the likelihood of nursing home placement, they do improve the quality of life for the elder and family. The challenge then remains to more effectively target and deliver the service to the "right" people.

Family support programs in general help families to sustain their caregiving efforts (Frankfather, Smith, and Caro, 1983; Walker, 1996). In addition, to the extent that educational and counseling services helped caregivers to feel more competent, caregiver mastery had a direct negative effect on depression. Feeling competent as a caregiver also moderated the effects of stressors on both depression and role strain (Miller, Campbell, Farran, Kaufman, and Davis, 1995).

Should Family Caregivers Be Paid?

To go a step further (a much larger step at that) is to ask whether family caregivers should be paid for their caregiving services. Financial compensation to family caregivers has been tried as a means of easing the burden on family caregivers as well as ensuring the delay of institutionalization and thus decreasing the cost of long-term care. Compensating family caregivers is also an important step in recognizing the otherwise unpaid labor that has long been provided in the home. Those who argue along these lines emphasize that it is exploitative to not pay a relative what one would pay an unrelated caregiver.

As of 1990, thirty-seven out of fifty-four jurisdictions in the United States allowed for family payments, although forty out of fifty-four jurisdictions had at least one agency citing program prohibitions. Although federal Medicaid regulations prohibit the payment of relatives through the definition of personal care services, states use other resources, such as state cash grants, to pay for family care. Payments are extremely low however. In 1985 in Alabama, elders received a supplementary payment (SSP) to their supplemental security income (SSI) benefits to pay a caregiver, related or nonrelated, a maximum of $60 per month for personal care services. In 1983, in California the SSP level was $794 per month but that was $259 more than in any other state. As can be seen, there is also wide variation between states. Only about 5.9 percent of the elderly nationwide receive SSI/SSP (Linsk, Keigher, England, and Simon-Rusinowitz, 1995).

The use of payments to relatives is restricted to particular circumstances, such as when the elder is at high risk of institutionalization. In addition, as of 1990, fifteen states allowing payment to relatives excluded spouses, while four jurisdictions excluded adult children. Other states have imposed one or more of the following restrictions: the caregiver and elder cannot co-reside, the caregiver must meet welfare income guidelines, family care must be a last resort (that is, other caregivers cannot be found), and the caregiver must be employed by a county or Area Agency on Aging. Another common requirement is that the caregiver must give up employment to be compensated (Linsk et al., 1995).

Whitfield and Krompholz (1981) studied the Maryland Family Support Demonstration Project which offered payment to family caregivers. The average grant at that time was $1,824 yearly or $152 monthly. Clients hired their own caregivers and did not use home care agencies. Although the program did not reduce rates of institutionalization, it did significantly lower mortality in subsidized families.

The extent to which family compensation saves money will depend on both the eligibility criteria and the level of allowances. However, the greater the savings in cost, the less beneficial the program is to families. Although the low wages currently offered provide protection against family members flocking to quit their jobs, they also offer less than adequate compensation. In addition, because of means testing and other criteria, most families do not even have access to these programs.

The benefit of such a program may be more symbolic than instrumental. By compensating family caregivers, we recognize, at a minimum, the costs that they bear and the importance of caring for our elderly. Compensating caregivers also sets a precedent for social policies that value the family.

RECOMMENDATIONS FROM PRIOR RESEARCH

A Caregiver's Policy

Although long-term care policy has received considerable attention, few analysts have discussed an explicit caregiver's policy. Most often, those who have written on the subject have argued that greater support needs to be given to family caregivers (Rivlin and Wiener, 1988). Kane and Penrod (1995), for example, suggested that family caregivers should be compensated at the market rate for care by a long-term care benefit, paid directly by the elder. Some uncompensated help would undoubtedly continue since not all family members could be fully paid. In addition, they and others argued for provisions for education, support groups, counseling, teaching about procedures, and technical backup for family caregivers (Toseland, Smith, and McCallion, 1995). Perlman (1983) contended that families be compensated only for out-of-pocket expenses but that elders have access to institutional settings for respite.

Long-Term Care Policy

The Older Americans Act (legislation that identifies objectives aimed at improving the lives of older Americans and is reauthorized by Congress every four years) states that older persons who cannot care for themselves or function in their homes are entitled to a modest set of long-term care benefits. Kane and Penrod (1995) argued that these benefits should be considered separate from any health benefits and should be dependent on the income of the person receiving care. Consumers would use the benefit to purchase care from a family member if they chose to but would not be forced to. A case manager would be responsible for establishing the initial eligibility and level of services, for approving the caregivers chosen by the client, and for providing the ongoing technical information and advice that the consumer needed. According to Kane and Penrod (1995), funding would come from progressive taxation.

Perlman (1983) maintained that elders must have as much discretion in this process as possible. He suggested that in order to increase self-esteem and reduce feelings of helplessness, the elderly client determine the type, quantities, and providers of in-home services. Perlman favored bringing professional services into the home as needed and providing paraprofessional aid to supplement or substitute for family aid (e.g., homemaking chores). Such proposals are likely to be very costly and contested by fiscal and social conservatives.

There is also a need for greater coordination throughout the long-term care system. This system is currently being run in a piecemeal fashion with little or no coordination between community services, providers of home care, and other formal care services (Harrington, Newcomer, Estes, and Associates, 1985). Hollingsworth and Hollingsworth (1994) espoused integrating the management of resources such as through a central authority. They argued for coordination not only within institutional and community-based care, but also between them.

IMPLICATIONS OF THE STUDY: A CAREGIVER'S POLICY

Results of this study suggested that family members primarily wanted help with the assistance that they provided, but that they did not want or expect formal services to substitute for them. Adult children took pride in caring for their parents themselves, but they expressed the need for some help in doing so. While family members were most interested in help from siblings, some also expressed a desire for more formal respite and assistance that would give them a break.

Among adult children from the working and middle classes, there was little evidence of a possible woodwork effect. When support was available to them, it did not stop family members from providing care. A minority of the caregivers even refused assistance! Edith, for example, told her mother-in-law's adult day health center that it was not necessary to give her mother-in-law a bath because she could do it herself on weekends. Although the vast majority of the elders appeared to meet the criteria for institution-alization, caregivers continued to provide care on their own for as long as they could.

Work and Caregiving

Caregivers stressed the importance of having someone to look after their parents while they worked. Nearly half (44 percent) of the caregivers depended on day care as the source of care (at least in part) for their parents while they worked. However, eight of the caregivers (16 percent) wanted to send their parents to day care more often but could not afford to do so. They suggested that Medicaid and Elder Home Care fund adult day health care more extensively, in part to make work and caregiving more compatible.

Caregivers who used adult day health as the source of care for their parents while they worked also pointed out that they needed day care to extend throughout the afternoon. Elders often returned home as early as 2:30 in the afternoon, long before their adult children were home from work. Caregivers then had to locate a second source of assistance. They pointed out that it would be easier for them if their parents could stay in the adult day health center until they returned home from work. Children of very frail elders, however, realized that this would be very taxing on their parents.

Caregivers also needed respite care for their parents while they were sick or when the adult day health center was closed due to snow. Four of the caregivers had other family members who were available to provide care during such occasions, while the others said that they had to take the day off from work. Only two caregivers suggested a need for more flexibile hours for van drivers picking their parents up for day care so that they could get to work on time.

Caregivers suggested policy initiatives for employers to make work and caregiving more compatible. Although only two of the caregivers (4 percent) had ever taken extended leaves of absence from their jobs for caregiving purposes, caregivers recognized that at some point such an option might be necessary. Those caregivers who were working said that it would be a substantial hardship to take an extended leave unless they continued to be paid and were assured that their jobs would be protected. Of those caregivers working, half (eighteen out of thirty-seven) worked for small companies with fewer than fifty employees. Thus, the Family and Medical Leave Act of 1993 (with regard to care of frail elders) could be much more useful to adult children providing care if it included pay and were extended to small companies (Ferber and O'Farrell, 1991).

The financing of such a program would clearly be a hardship for any company. However, the cost could be more effectively shared by state and federal government if paid leave reduced rates of institutionalization and the spending down of savings, which then resulted in the need for nursing home reimbursement. Such benefits could also be phased in to minimize economic disruptions (Ferber and O'Farrell, 1991) and could be offered as one of several benefits (Wagner, 1991). Funds would be available in a dependent care account to be used as necessary by employees. Remington, for example, has established a spending account to assist employees in the cost of needed services (Wagner, 1991). In addition, companies might find extended leaves of absence no more costly than high rates of absenteeism and low worker productivity or retraining of employees (Ferber and O'Farrell, 1991; Scharlach and Boyd, 1989). Such a question merits further investigation (see also chapter 5 on work and caregiving).

Respite and Other Caregiver Programs

The most commonly requested assistance was respite. When referring to respite services, caregivers often stated that they would like other family members to either come and stay with their parents occasionally or take them to their own homes (twenty out of fifty caregivers or 40 percent).

However, seventeen other caregivers (34 percent) referred to acquiring formal respite (nonrelative). Caregivers who requested professional respite were as likely to be working class as middle class, but all believed that respite services should be at least partially subsidized for them (two caregivers specifically mentioned by Medicare). Rose wanted someone to stay with her mother three nights a week so that she could get a good night's sleep. Sally wanted a companion for her mother to give her a break, but it did not have to be a medical professional. Caregivers wanted respite care on a regular basis to spend time with their own families and to give them a break, occasionally for the weekend, and for annual vacations. Few companies currently offer respite services. Remington, however, does have a fund for accessing in-home respite services for its employees (Wagner, 1991).

Less frequently, caregivers mentioned needing assistance with homemaker chores to reduce the overall amount of work they had to do. This was mentioned most frequently by caregivers who had very young children in the home or who worked extensive hours outside of the home. Elders who did not live with their adult children were more likely to have received homemaker services for themselves in the last year compared to those who lived with their children (approximately two-thirds versus zero).

Other caregiver programs were infrequently mentioned as being needed. Although one-third of the sample were selected from caregiver support groups, none mentioned needing additional support. Three of the caregivers, however, continued attending caregiver support groups even after their parents died, suggesting the importance of the groups to at least some caregivers. Two of the nurses mentioned how crucial it was to have educational programs (although they did not believe that they themselves needed additional education). Several families were in situations where they could have benefited from educational programs, but they did not recognize the need. Marie, for example, might have found information in a pain management course useful to lessen her mother's tendency to scream all night (in pain). Given the stress universally reported, counseling would also have been helpful. Caregivers mentioned that although they had considered counseling, the thought of having yet another "requirement" in their day prevented them from seeking support.

Currently, many companies offer such services to their employees. Pepsico distributes a guide that covers normal aging, health, and consumer-oriented information on health and social services. They also have a caregivers' fair and noontime seminars. Travelers offers support groups and counseling, while IBM contracts with a consultant group to offer access to information and services. Other companies have Employee Assistance Professionals who provide counseling and referrals to community agencies (Wagner, 1991).

Assistance from Siblings

Caregivers most frequently mentioned that assistance from siblings would make caregiving easier. Twenty (40 percent) of the caregivers suggested that siblings provide respite. An additional seven caregivers (54 percent total) said that siblings needed to share care (more or less equally) in order to make a difference.

Getting siblings to help was not an easy task, particularly if one person was already providing all of the care. When Brenda's mother-in-law returned to her own home, a case manager divided the caregiving tasks equally among the siblings, taking into account as much as possible the availability of each sibling. Brenda said, "Now they help. They have to or the case manager files charges of neglect." Thus, rather than caregivers themselves trying to get their siblings to help, a third party, such as a case manager trained in family mediation, should divide care as equally as possible. For this arrangement to work, the availability of siblings needs to be taken into account as does the history of the family.

Such a proposal, of course, presents difficult issues. At a minimum, it would require counseling the entire family to coordinate care. In situations where a sibling refused to provide care, he or she might be required instead to provide financial compensation to those who did provide care so that they might hire additional formal care to substitute for the sibling or to meet some of their caregiving expenses. Siblings who lived far away would be expected to provide respite services, the frequency depending on their distance. In addition, the case manager would assess whether or not family members were adequate caregivers. As part of the ongoing counseling efforts, brothers would be educated in caring for their mothers and encouraged to see these tasks as appropriate for their gender.

Direct Payment

None of the caregivers were being paid as personal care attendants for their parents. In addition, all except for two of the caregivers had continued to work outside of the home, and none expressed a desire to quit their jobs at the time of the initial survey, a common requirement in family compensation. It is unlikely that the caregivers would have been willing to give up their employment for the low wages offered by most state programs even if means testing did not exist.

Rather than being paid themselves, caregivers would be happy to use additional financing to purchase assistance, either respite care or regular assistance. Those caregivers who had a preference for family help might be able to get more assistance if they could provide financial compensation to family members. Caregivers who did not mind (or even preferred) formal assistance could also hire a personal care attendant. This would allow the caregivers to continue providing care but would ease some of the constraints on their time. In fact, Quadagno, Sims, Squier, and Walker (1987) found that nonmedical attendants made it possible for caregivers to continue to care for their relatives at home and improved overall family relationships.

IMPLICATIONS OF THE STUDY: LONG-TERM CARE POLICY

Several changes to long-term care policy for the elderly could improve the well-being of elders as well as make caregiving much easier for family members. To begin with, the general trend of deinstitutionalization has resulted in a more rapid discharge of the very ill (Gaumer and Stavins, 1992; Shaughnessy and Kramer, 1990). As a result, family members of the elderly must now provide care (including medical care) that was once provided in a hospital. While Medicare's prospective payment system was intended to save money, it has been very costly for caregivers. A long-term care policy that took into account multiple illnesses, the severity of the illness, and older people's particular health care needs in determining length of hospital stay would permit the provision of significant medical care in a hospital rather than at home by family members.

Caregivers in this study did not want to see their parents institutionalized and went to great lengths to prevent nursing home placement. Assistance in caring for elders at the point that they are discharged from the hospital or rehabilitation center or at the point where personal care begins would ease the transition into caregiving and assuage the extensive demands of early illness. Caregivers stated that visiting nurses and home health aids were crucial during that initial phase of caregiving but that they were available only for short periods of time.

Several caregivers stated that few resources were available to help their parents stay in their own homes prior to co-residence. Beth, for example, had a hard time finding an independent living facility for her mother when Hattie could no longer stay in her apartment. Although Hattie qualified for admission, there were extensive waiting lines in all the facilities. One caregiver tried a companion program so that her mother would not be lonely in her apartment, but the companion started to require as much care as her mother. Few caregivers were able to purchase personal care attendants or visiting nurses so that their parents could stay in their homes. Caregivers did point out, however, that the Meals on Wheels program made it possible for their parents to remain independent when they could no longer cook.

Extensive levels of assistance in the home could also become intrusive when parents and children co-resided. Two of the working class caregivers said that they did not want strangers in their homes. Four others (12 percent total) stated that having visiting nurses around when they were at home sometimes made them feel uncomfortable despite the fact that they liked the assistance. It would then become imperative for a case manager, based on family input, to determine the optimum level of assistance.

ISSUES OF CLASS AND ETHNICITY

Case managers working with families must take into account their class status and ethnicity. Working class caregivers were less likely to use adult day care. Of the eighteen caregivers who did not use adult day care, all were working class. When asked why they did not use adult day care, working class caregivers seemed insulted and stated proudly that they could care for their parents themselves. Working class children who chose not to use it seemed to perceive of adult day care as a "handout" or an indication that they could not or did not want to care for their parents, that they were a bad family. Two working class caregivers said that they did not want a stranger taking care of their parents, that they deserved better. Case managers who are trying to introduce formal assistance should be aware of such barriers in some, but not all, working class families.

Working class caregivers who see formal assistance as a handout might be more willing to use it if it were part of a social security benefit that they (or their husbands) earned through employment or a Medicare benefit that they were entitled to through old age. This matter needs to be investigated further to determine the extent to which the general public, and older generations in particular, distinguish Medicare versus Medicaid and its criteria for entitlement. Alternatively, we need to work on delivering the message that elder assistance is an entitlement in our society in accordance with the Older Americans Act versus a handout for the poor.

Families from ethnic backgrounds, both working and middle class, were also loath to use community services. Although they used adult day care, they accepted it as necessary given their need to work. In contrast, many believed that using services that would substitute for the care they provide would be disrespectful to their parents. This included providing personal care, preparing meals, and the like.

It is important to note the differences between ethnic groups. The Irish Americans, for example, did not emphasize the importance of family providing care to the extent that the Italian-American and Franco-American families did. Stull (1993) found very different results for yet another ethnic group. He found that Hispanics used social and long-term care services (such as senior centers and group meals) *more* often than whites or blacks. Thus, in managing long-term services it is important to acknowledge and act on differences between ethnic groups. Although there were also differences within ethnic groups, they were most often in terms of degree.

CONCLUDING REMARKS

Results of this study cry out for the need to support family caregivers. This is not because family caregivers wish to relinquish their caregiving duties but because support allows them to fulfill what they see as their filial responsibilities and because supporting the family should be the goal of any social policy. Support needs to be given beyond filling in the gaps of what families do not provide. Instead, the goal of a caregiver's policy should be to promote the well-being of family caregivers.

A caregiver's policy can be beneficial to more than the caregiver. By delaying institutionalization, taxpayers will likely save on the high cost of nursing home care. A caregiver's policy also allows elders to remain in the community as they wish (Qureshi and Walker, 1989). In addition, support to employees providing care would likely reduce the interference to work activities such as quitting work, being tired on the job, absenteeism, and declining promotions (Scharlach and Boyd, 1989).

Not all families, however, would need full subsidization for caregiving assistance. Families that could afford co-payments (based on a sliding scale) would be expected to provide them, thus making it more feasible for the many families that have already spent down their savings already on long-term care to receive greater subsidization. The ability of both the elderly to pay for their own care and the caregiver (to a lesser extent) to purchase his or her own assistance would be taken into account.

A second criterion for receiving assistance would be based on need for various services as determined by a case manager. After assessing the availability of additional family members, the elder's needs, and the needs of the caregiver in question for respite and other forms of caregiver support, the case manager would determine the type and levels of support that the caregiver was qualified for.

A caregiver's policy would be costly. Institutional care is also costly for both the elderly as they pay out-of-pocket and for society as we support Medicaid. There have also been tremendous costs to the family (and their employers) that often go unrecognized. The funds for a caregiver's policy would be financed out of a progressive tax as well as through savings by delaying institutionalization. Employers would also be expected, in part, to fund a caregiver's policy by providing paid leaves of absence for caregivers of the very frail.

A caregiver's policy would be aimed at the entire later life family. The goal of the case manager/family mediator would be to try to promote siblings working together. Getting siblings to share care may not work in all situations. When successful, the benefits would extend beyond caregiving to improve relationships overall. This would be especially advantageous given the importance of sibling bonds in the latter stages of the family life cycle (Bedford, 1995, for review; Brubaker, 1985; Cicirelli, 1991).

A caregiver's policy aimed at helping adult children to care for their elderly parents would also promote intergenerational linkages. At some point, many from the currently younger generations will need to call upon these resources as their parents become frail. While we share the cost of educating one another's children, why not share the cost of caring for one another's parents? After all, the goal of social policy should be to improve the quality of life for all generations.

A policy such as the one described here goes against the grain of our notions of family privacy and fiscal conservatism. Although a few families did not want strangers coming into their homes, that does not mean that they wanted no assistance or support programs at all. In fact, most of the families did want formal assistance. Our assumptions that they do not want outside help are based on outdated notions of the family that are unrealistic but are encouraged to promote the traditional family. To those social conservatives who maintain that we no longer have family values, I would say that rather than promoting values that no longer fit the family, we should promote policy that values the family, that improves the well-being of the family, rather than exploiting it.

CHAPTER 11

Conclusions

I first began this study in order to ask family members to explain, in their own words, just how they managed to be caregivers and work outside of the home at the same time. After beginning my pilot interviews, I realized that caregiving was actually part of the caregivers' overall life course and that there were important class distinctions in how families negotiated work versus caregiving. In other words, I began to see the theoretical implications of my work. In this last chapter, I will summarize the theoretical implications and conclusions that can be drawn from this study. These conclusions are specific to families who care for elders and may not be generalized to all later life families.

LIFE COURSE PERSPECTIVE

According to the results of this study, family caregiving fits within the expectations of a life course perspective. For example, caregiving can be thought of as an extension of prior nurturing experiences. In addition, to some extent, the choice of who ultimately provides care and assistance is also the product of prior family relationships. In other words, family caregiving is not an isolated event in an individual's or a family's life course history.

A life course perspective emphasizes the interrelatedness of role trajectories across the life span. According to this study, the caregiving role had important implications for the work trajectory. Fully 30 percent of the caregivers were not working (whether due partially or fully to caregiving demands), while another 8 percent had reduced their work from full-time to part-time. Changing to part-time work often resulted in actually changing jobs. Beth, for example, went from being a full-time dental hygienist to a part-time receptionist. Thus, 38 percent of the caregivers' work trajectories were drastically altered by their caregiving careers.

Family caregiving affected the work trajectory in other ways beyond quitting work. For example, caregivers reported being unable to concentrate at work, leaving work frequently to help their parent, and cutting back on hours at work. Thus, the caregivers did not feel they were doing well at their jobs or would be able to progress in their careers even if they had not quit their jobs.

The current caregiving role will likely continue to have important implications for the future of the work trajectory. As caregivers try to go back to work, to reclaim their careers, as middle-aged and older adults, they may find it very difficult to reestablish themselves in their careers. The caregivers who were looking for work after they had ceased providing care were having difficulty finding new jobs. Although none of the caregivers had been out of the workforce for more than a couple of years, none had found new positions. This may, in part, be due to their age (despite the fact that age discrimination is illegal in hiring practices according to the Age Discrimination Employment Act of 1967). Caregivers may have also had difficulty finding work because they had recently quit another job, sending signals to potential employers that they might do so again.

Work and family may be so intertwined for women that they choose jobs when they are younger that will allow them to fulfill expected family obligations later in the life course. For example, earlier research has shown that expectations of childrearing and working outside of the home are related. Over the long run, expectations of employment reduce fertility, while expectations of higher fertility reduce the likelihood of employment (Cramer, 1980; Smith-Lovin and Tickamyer, 1978; Stolzenberg and Waite, 1977; and Waite and Stolzenberg, 1976). While younger women may not choose careers with the expectations of caring for elderly parents, middle-aged women may make career changes (maybe even unconsciously) with such expectations in mind. Beth, for example, chose a different line of work and did not return to full-time employment when her mother's health improved so that she would be available if her mother needed her again in the future. Women may be making career choices throughout their lives based on the needs of family members.

Work affects caregiving as well but mainly in terms of preventing family members from being full-time caregivers. Although it could not be ascertained from this study, family members with jobs that cannot be accommodated may not become caregivers. Some of the caregivers said that their siblings did not help more because of the constraints of their jobs. For the most part family members who did take on the caregiver role said that their work did not prevent them from taking parents to doctors' appointments or leaving work during emergencies (although it was more constricted for working class caregivers), but it did require them to find substitute care while they worked. That is, their work prevented them from being full-time caregivers.

Caregivers also mentioned that constraints at work prevented them from spending more time with their elderly family members. Connie, for example, said that she felt guilty when her mother was lonely because she had to work such long hours. Still, Connie was able to provide assistance with her mother's immediate medical and personal needs.

In accordance with the life course perspective, transitions in and out of the workforce were also heavily dependent on the health career of the aging parent. Not only were role trajectories or careers interrelated across one's own life span, but also they were interrelated with the role trajectories of other family members. Beth's labor force status was highly contingent upon her mother's health. Beth first accommodated her work and then switched to another part-time job when her mother was diagnosed with cancer. It was not until Hattie died several years later that Beth began to look for another job.

Repeated transitions in and out of the labor force were more limited than a life course perspective assumes. As was discussed earlier, many caregivers could not afford to be out of the labor force and remained in their jobs even when their parents' health care needs increased. Other caregivers who quit their jobs had a difficult time getting back into the workforce when their parents' health improved or they were institutionalized. Thus, in later life, transitions in and out of the labor force may not be as common as those in earlier life.

Transitions in parents' health status can also be quite sudden. Thus, unless one is going to quit a job abruptly, planning for career changes may be difficult. Adult children had to find a way to meet new caregiving requirements quite suddenly. If a parent was hospitalized or in a rehabilitation center, caregivers had some time to plan for their parents' new needs. Those caregivers who did not change their work trajectory sometimes enlisted additional help from family members, were allocated visiting nurses or home health aid services, or institutionalized their parents.

Life courses were interrelated with other family members' life trajectories as well, although it was not as common as a life course perspective suggests. For some family members, assistance with caregiving was dependent on the availability of siblings and nuclear family members, dictated by their own life trajectories. For example, one of the daughters, Abby, joined a network of caregiving siblings when she retired. Thus, the amount of time that her sister spent caregiving decreased when Abby's work trajectory ended. In like manner, Connie received less overall assistance when her own daughter started college and was no longer available to help with caregiving. Other family members would not provide assistance regardless of their other role trajectories. (In these situations, siblings usually preferred that their parents be institutionalized.)

The interrelatedness of family members' life trajectories was most noticeable in caregiving networks. Liza's brother became an active member of the caregiving network when he switched his work and home to be near his parents. Liza's sisters became unavailable members of the network as their health trajectory worsened. As the availability of family members changed due to their own role trajectories, additional members of the family had to be substituted into the network.

The caregiving trajectory was the result of one's own history or life course. Prior nurturing experiences, including caring for grandparents or siblings as children, were important motivations to become a caregiver. In addition, caregivers often had careers in medical and social services (primarily nursing) which predisposed them to becoming caregivers.

One's history with other family members also affected the caregiving trajectory. Some of the caregivers were selected by their parents to be caregiver because of their prior relationships. One of the sons said, "My mother wants Laurie [the daughter-in-law] to care for her because they have always been close. . . . [Laurie is] like a daughter. She has always been my mother's favorite." Sometimes one child became the caregiver because of the parent's history with the other children in the family. One of the daughters who was adopted thought that her sister should be the caregiver but said that she wasn't because her sister and mother had such a poor relationship over their lives.

Whether adult children received help from siblings seemed to depend more on the siblings' attitudes toward family obligations rather than the histories between the siblings. Several of the caregivers, for example, said that they were surprised that their siblings did not help out more because they had always been so close. Thus, it is important to distinguish between family expectations of interdependence (or lack thereof) and family history as separate concepts.

A life course perspective also emphasizes the interdependence of successive generations. Several of the caregivers from ethnic backgrounds pointed out that their parents did not realize how difficult caregiving was because they had immigrated from other countries before their own parents required care. Other relatives in their home countries then cared for their parents. They thought that their own parents would not expect them to be caregivers if they had made similar sacrifices themselves. Thus, events in the lives of three generations were bound together.

According to the life course perspective, social change affects individual life patterns. Although many changes in society could affect caregiving, women's labor force participation and gender ideology seem to offer the most significant impact. Because of increases in women's labor force participation since the 1950s (Ferber and O'Farrell, 1991), fewer middle-aged women are exclusively in the home. Thus, middle-aged women cannot readily incorporate daily caregiving into their lives unlike many women in the cohorts before them. As a result, this broader social change has had important implications for individual women's lives as they battle to combine work and caregiving.

Other social changes have not kept pace with the need for caregiving. The number of elderly persons requiring care has increased at the same time that the number of daughters available to provide care has decreased owing to increases in women's labor force participation and divorce (Boyd and Treas, 1996; Brubaker and Brubaker, 1995). As a result, sons and other male members of the family have had to assume some of the caregiving responsibilities. At the same time, changes in gender ideology have not kept pace with the need for greater male participation in the home. In this study, sons had to be purposively oversampled due to their rarity. Daughters were also more likely to receive assistance from female members of the family than from male members. Assistance from male members of the family was more common in working class families than in middle class families. Male members were often seen as inappropriate caregivers and so were "let off the hook" more easily than their sisters. Changes in gender ideology which recognized not only the appropriateness of men as caregivers but also the need for men to be caregivers would ease the burden on women's lives and establish a more equitable distribution of labor in the family.

This inability of societal norms and practices to keep pace with the realities of contemporary life is referred to as structural lag (Riley, Kahn, and Foner, 1994). Other social institutions that have not kept pace with the growing demands of caregivers include workplace initiatives for employed caregivers, long-term care policy that recognizes the need for greater resources for home care and a caregiver's policy, and social services that support elders in remaining independent in the community. While a life course perspective emphasizes the interdependence of social institutions, it should also be pointed out that change often does not keep pace with the *need* for change in social norms, practices, and institutions.

In conclusion, the life course perspective is a useful framework for examining the caregiving career. This perspective can be used to emphasize the interrelatedness of caregiving and other roles in the caregiver's life as well as the interrelatedness of the caregiver's life course with the life courses of other family members. With a life course perspective, one can also recognize cumulative patterns and role trajectories across the caregiver's life as well as the effect of social change on individual life patterns.

The life course perspective does have some limitations in explaining or predicting caregiving. Based on a life course perspective, one might expect that receiving assistance from siblings was dependent on the siblings' history or relationship. However, even in families in which siblings were close, brothers and sisters often did not provide needed assistance. Nor was assistance from siblings dependent on life course trajectories in the siblings' lives; instead it was based on the siblings' attitudes toward their own obligations (versus that of other siblings) and the appropriateness of nursing home placement.

Based on a life course perspective, one would expect that transitions in and out of the workforce would be heavily dependent on the health career of the aging parent. Although many caregivers did quit their jobs, at least partially because of caregiving, certainly not all caregivers could do so no matter what their parents' health status. In addition, caregivers who did exit the labor force had a very difficult time reentering when their parents' health status changed (for better or worse). Transitions back into the labor force were more dependent on other societal structures, possibly age bias in the workplace.

Overall, a life course perspective is effective in recognizing that caregiving takes place within the context of the caregiver's entire life. As such, caregiving is affected by prior events and is likely to affect subsequent events as well. Caregiving then is part of an overall life pattern woven into a series of nurturing activities across women's lives.

CLASS AND FAMILY

According to earlier research, distinct differences exist between working class and middle class families. Working class women were found to express a stronger family ideology vis-à-vis work roles than professional and middle class women (Burris, 1991). Working class families have also been found to engage in more intergenerational contact and helping activity (Cantor, 1975; Hill, 1970) and to provide direct care to elders versus managing care (Archbold, 1983). Are the results of this study consistent with the findings? Do class differences persist into later life?

The working class women in this study did express a stronger family (versus work) ideology, although the differences were not substantial. For the most part, all of the caregivers in this study expressed a high level of familial obligation given their willingness to be caregivers. On the surface it might appear that middle class women had higher family ideology since they were more likely to quit their jobs or reduce their work substantially to provide care. This would suggest the greater importance that they place on family versus work. However, it was also more feasible for middle class women to quit their jobs or reduce their work because their spouses had a higher income. In addition, working class women may have been less likely to quit their jobs to provide care because they were more likely already to work part-time, to be on disability, or to have retired early rather than due to a lack of family ideology. In fact, several of the working class women on disability leave said that even if they could go back to work, they would not want to so that they could care for their parents themselves.

The strength of family ideology was also expressed in the caregivers' tendency to use formal services versus relying on other family members and providing care one's self. As would be expected, working class women used formal services less frequently, relying more on siblings, spouses and children, and themselves to provide additional care. Some of the working class women were uncomfortable with strangers in their homes. For the most part, working class women were more likely to say that family, not strangers, should care for their parents.

Although working class families expressed only a somewhat stronger family ideology than middle class families, they did exhibit higher rates of family interaction and helping activity. Clearly, all of the caregivers were involved in helping their parents. Working class caregivers, however, were more likely to form caregiving networks with their siblings. In addition, adult children from the working class were more likely to acknowledge conflict with siblings when they did not form caregiving networks. Thus, there was a greater expectation and realization of family interdependence and helping among siblings in the working class. There was also an emphasis on family versus individual achievement in the working class. Particularly in caregiving networks, siblings were expected to put the good of their parents and helping one another above their own needs. Liza's brother, for example, quit his job and moved to be near his parents in order to participate in the caregiving network. Finally, although middle class caregivers did not provide fewer hours of care to their parents, they were more likely to place a parent in a nursing home as their impairments worsened. Together, these issues suggest higher rates of family interaction and helping activity in the working class.

Evidence of a more traditional emphasis on masculine ideology in the working class was mixed. Brothers helped more in the working class than in the middle class, participating as integral parts of the caregiving network. In being taught to be responsible to the family, caregiving activities were regarded as appropriate for working class men. Less frequently, working class men avoided participating in caregiving activities because it was "women's work," instead pointing to a traditional masculine ideology.

Strong family bonds in the working class may be threatened as women, in particular, are pressed for time. Unable to quit their jobs because of financial constraints and the difficulty of finding new jobs, working class women struggled to meet the demands of both work and caregiving. In this study, many sons also struggled as they tried to care for parents, "help" their working wives around the house, and spend time with their children. In the future, as parents live longer and there are fewer siblings to help out, working class children may not be able to make the level of commitment that they make now.

What accounts for the differences between working class and middle class caregivers? In part, financial restrictions made working class family members more dependent on one another. For example, working class caregivers were less able to hire assistance with caregiving for long periods of time and thus had to provide more care themselves or rely on other family members. Norms of both family interdependence and filial obligation also played a part in the higher rates of family interaction and helping activity displayed in the working class. Each of these three factors needs to be teased out further in examining the separate effects of class differences in later life families.

ETHNICITY

Several of the caregivers from ethnic backgrounds spoke of the incompatibility in the expectations from their ethnic backgrounds versus the realities of their lives in America. An example would be the conflict inherent in a daughter's desire to care for her parent versus her need to work outside of the home. This is consistent with the "intergenerational strain" found by C. Johnson (1985, 1995). Caregivers who spoke most frequently about these incompatibilities defined themselves as Italian. One of the caregivers explained that in Italian families, the eldest daughter and son were expected to care for their parents, no matter what that entailed. However, the assumption was that the daughter and the son's wife were available in the home to provide care and that they had an extended kin network to assist with that care (i.e., their own children, siblings, and younger aunts and uncles). Parents expected that children in America should provide care even without these resources. Daughters, in particular, pointed out that they had to work all day to make ends meet while their aunts and grandmothers in Italy had not worked outside of the home. Their own children, now adults, did not live nearby, and their siblings also worked outside of the home or did not possess the filial obligation that was expected of them. This latter finding suggests a process of acculturation with regard to intergenerational relations for at least some first-generation children.

Adult children who were not from ethnic backgrounds also pointed to generational differences in their abilities to provide care. Daughters observed that their mothers did not realize how difficult it was for them to be caregivers because they had not worked outside of the home when caring for their own mothers. Daughters from ethnic backgrounds argued that the expectation of providing care was stronger in their families. As one of the daughters said, "Not only was I taught to care for my parents when they got old, but my mother said that it would be an honor, a joy. It would be a slap in the face to her if she knew how unhappy I am." Caregivers from ethnic backgrounds mentioned that according to their heritage, family was supposed to come first. According to previous research (C. Johnson, 1985), these internalized values are the result of a lifelong socialization pattern of implicit expectations of filial obligation.

Caregivers noted that it was hard to reconcile caring for one's parents with working to further one's nuclear family. Thus, a cultural conflict was involved in meeting the obligations of family interdependence versus pursuing individual interests. Woolfson (1996) and C. Johnson (1985) also found that the expected allegiance to the family competed with current mainstream values of social independence for Franco Americans and Italian Americans.

Caregivers who expressed this incompatibility in role expectations due to their ethnic origins stated that they did not expect their own children to care for them when they were older. Caregivers from Italian backgrounds were more likely than all other caregivers to have adult children living far away. They said that, unlike their own parents, they encouraged their children to be independent and to pursue individual pursuits. Like many of the caregivers from nonethnic backgrounds, they said that when they grew old, they would prefer to be in a nursing home rather than be cared for by their children. It is not clear whether these adult children will change their minds when they themselves grow old or whether this is a generational difference in filial expectations among ethnic families. This desire to not burden one's own children was found in the population in general, which may indicate a process of acculturation with regard to intergenerational relations. In the population in general, older parents express lower levels of norms of filial responsibility to the elderly than do their adult children (Hamon and Blieszner, 1990). Lawton et al. (1994) found that parents of adult children endorsed norms of filial responsibility less often than the childless, again, because they wished to avoid being a burden on their own children.

According to prior research, elders from ethnic backgrounds believed that materialism was weakening family loyalties (Johnson, 1985). That is, they saw the conflict that adult children experienced between making sacrifices for the family versus pursuing individual gain as being due to the materialism of American society. As a result, Italian Americans saw non-family influences in America as undesirable and a threat to the family.

THE STATE OF THE FAMILY

What does this study then tell us about the state of the family among "just plain folk"? Despite admonitions that the family is falling apart and that we as a society no longer have family values, the adult children and children-in-law in this study were examples of just the opposite. The caregivers in this study provided high levels of very difficult, burdensome care for long periods of time despite significant barriers. Children provided this tremendous service often in the name of love and family obligation, indications of the strength of their family values.

Not all members of the family were as committed to caring for elderly parents. This may have been as much of a "free rider" problem as it was an indication of the breakdown of the family. That is, these same siblings might be willing to provide care if others were not available to do so. However, many of these siblings did suggest that the caregiver place the parent in a nursing home. This suggests not that adult children lack strong family values but that a shift has taken place in what it means to be a responsible family member. We have come to see nursing homes as appropriate places for older members of society. Adult children who institutionalize their parents may feel that they are living up to their responsibilities when they find a "good" nursing home for their parent. That is, adult children who care for their parents themselves may not necessarily have stronger family values as much as poorer opinions of nursing homes.

To suggest that the family is stronger than assumed does not imply that we should discontinue support. Instead, we need to provide greater assistance so that family members can uphold their family values. Current policy offers little support for family members to give care on their own but does offer incentives to place a parent in a nursing home. As was discussed in chapter 10, we need to offer greater home assistance in our long-term care policy so that family members can fulfill their filial obligations when that implies providing care in their homes. Such an emphasis would switch away from the current institutionalization of long-term care.

ELDER CARE AS A SOCIAL PROBLEM

Although family care for the elderly is most often presented as a social crisis, results of this study instead reveal that families are able to cope effectively with the potential conflict between their work and caregiving responsibilities. Few of the caregivers quit their jobs outright, owing in part to the accommodations made by their employers. As was stated earlier, this does not mean that families do not need continued support. Without government-subsidized adult day care or assistance from their employers, the majority of the caregivers in this study would have been forced to choose between providing care for their parents and employment.

This study further shows that those caregivers who do quit their jobs may do so because they would prefer to provide care for their parents directly. Particularly among the working class caregivers, there was a strong motivation to provide care to parents directly. Working class caregivers, often intimating that they were uncomfortable with "strangers" caring for their parents, were most likely to be nonemployed while caregiving or to rely on siblings to provide care when they did work.

ELDERS AT RISK

The positive value placed on family care for the elderly in our society assumes that home care is always best. Just as adult children may institutionalize their parents without malice or lack of family values, informal family care is not always the most appropriate care for elders. Some elders in this study, though exceptions, seemed to be "at risk" in the home.

The parent who was most at risk for injury in the home, either to himself or to a family member, was William, who lived with his daughter and her family. William had to be locked in the basement at night because he wandered. He had also "attacked" his daughter several times. When other family members were around, they then had to "pin him down." On one occasion, William remained on top of his daughter for several hours before his granddaughter came home. These incidents suggest potential harm to both William and the other members of the family.

Whether or not William was better off in his daughter's home (despite the risks) versus a nursing home may be an individual judgment. Nonetheless, nursing homes are set up and staff are trained to handle at-risk elders (Burgio and Burgio, 1990; Linn, Linn, and Stein, 1989; Smyer, Brannon, and Cohn, 1992). Adult children often felt guilty for institutionalizing a parent because of an assumption that family care is superior care. As such, many family members were providing care under great stress and "at the end of [their] rope." In these situations, their parents may have been better off in a nursing home. It is incumbent upon us as a society to recognize the appropriateness of institutionalization in these cases and to provide support (rather than criticism) to families when they recognize the risks of maintaining an elder at home. In short, home care is not always the best care.

THE FUTURE OF THE FAMILY

Given the difficulties with which working and middle class families currently provide care, the expected increase in need for care, and the deinstitutionalization of all but the most medically needy, the future of family caregiving is ominous. Although more families may find themselves having to provide care, it may also be done with greater hardship. Families who would prefer to provide home care may be forced to institutionalize at least some of their elderly family members. Others will continue to provide care but at what costs? Working class women may be further constrained by an inability to purchase additional assistance. Results of this study suggest that given the importance they place on the family, many women will continue to provide care, despite the sacrifices.

Yet, steps can be taken to improve the situation of family caregivers. To begin with, we need to strive for greater gender equity in the family. Women in this study frequently pointed to the lack of assistance from brothers and husbands, citing the inappropriateness of men as caregivers. However, it is the social construction of masculinity which prevents more men from assuming caregiving roles. By socializing our sons to be nurturant and active members of family caregiving at all stages, we will relieve women of the total responsibility and offer men the opportunity to participate more fully in family life.

In addition to socializing our children to raise their own families with a more equitable distribution of labor and responsibility, we need to reconsider social policy which unfairly places much of the burden of family responsibility on women. By assuming that women are the appropriate caregivers for the elderly, fiscal conservatives justify not paying for long-term care. Such a policy, however, further exacerbates the gender inequities of the home. Women are unduly burdened, and men lose out on participation in the family. By compensating caregivers for the work that they do, we recognize the value of that work and the need to reimburse for it. By challenging the notion that only women are the appropriate caregivers for their parents, we offer deliverance to those women who feel trapped by the belief that only they can care for their elders and those men who fear that they would be incompetent caregivers. Caregiving should be a choice for both sons and daughters and not based on compulsory altruism.

As citizens, we need to lobby for improved long-term care. Most of us do not want to pay higher taxes or to pay for the long-term care of others. Improving the health care of our elderly will benefit us all directly in the long run as we become elderly and indirectly in the short run as our own parents become elderly. In general, working together across the generations rather than pitting generations against one another is the best way to solve social problems (Kingson, 1988). Members of Congress and state and local representatives need to be urged to see that these issues are important to all of us and that we want to improve the availability of long-term care services to the elders of our society.

This study also suggests concern regarding the future of sibling relationships in later life. Many of the caregivers thought that conflict with siblings would have long-lasting implications. But previous researchers have found that siblings offer important sources of social support in later life (Cicirelli, 1991). If conflict is left unchecked, the overall social support of the elderly is likely to be reduced in the future. Those professionals working with families need to find ways to resolve that conflict in order to improve later life relationships. Policy initiatives to involve the whole family would not only reduce the burden for the caregiver at present but also improve their chances for social support in the future.

In the future, working and middle class family members will probably find it more difficult to maintain their roles as caregivers due to expected demographic and social change as well as recent trends in health care. Accordingly, families will need more support to maintain the family values that we espouse in our society. Since family caregiving is interconnected with other events and transitions in the life course, it is essential that the ramifications for other role trajectories and family members be considered to maximize the well-being of elders and later life families over the life course.

Appendix: Methodology

PARTICIPANTS

The fifty caregivers selected for this study were chosen on the basis of several criteria. Only adult children and children-in-law who were providing care for noninstitutionalized parents were considered. Only caregivers who had worked outside of the home at some point during the course of caregiving were included in the analysis. Based on a combination of family income, lifestyle, education, and relative position within the occupational hierarchy (Kerbo, 1991), only working class and middle class caregivers were included. Finally, each of the caregivers had to provide assistance with at least one activity of daily living four or more times a week. This insured that the caregiver was truly involved in providing personal assistance on a regular basis.

Three of the caregivers' parents had died within the last six months prior to data collection. As the caregiver support groups made clear, the conflict they underwent in balancing work and caregiving was still fresh in their minds. Furthermore, they had a perspective on how being a caregiver affected their lives, which seemed richer and more thoughtfully considered than the information provided by other caregivers. As such, these caregivers were included in the analysis.

Although there is no clear-cut definition of the middle and working classes (Rubin, 1994), the concept was operationalized as follows. Respondents had to satisfy two out of the three criteria that defined class: family income, relative position in the institutional structures of one's occupation, and education. Yet no one had to be dropped from the study because they met only two of the criteria. Working class was defined as (1) having an annual income of between $20,000 and $40,000; (2) being low in bureaucratic authority and in a low position in the occupational hierarchy (Kerbo, 1991); and (3) having low levels of education (up to and including completion of high school). Middle class was defined as (1) family income up to $55,000 (Newman, 1993); (2) midlevel bureaucratic authority and a midlevel position in the occupational hierarchy (Kerbo, 1991); and (3) higher levels of education (up to and including a bachelor's degree). Relative position in the institutional hierarchy of one's occupation was measured by asking respondents to describe the workers to whom they "reported" and who "reported" to them (referred to as bureaucratic authority) and the various positions within their occupations which were both above and below them (referred to as their occupational position). The cutoff point for middle class was that the respondents had to have at least as many people reporting to them as the respondents reported to (bureaucratic authority) and at least as many positions below their position as above it (occupational position).

Table 1 presents a description of the sample and a comparison to other representative samples. The other samples include Abel's (1991) study based on interviews with fifty-one daughters in Los Angeles and a nationally representative sample of informal caregivers from the National Long Term Care Survey (Stone et al., 1987). While the youngest caregiver in this study was in her late 20s, Stone et al. (1987) included family members as young as 14 years of age.

This sample is similar to other representative samples with a few minor exceptions (see Table 1). It included a somewhat higher proportion of women in this sample than the National Long Term Care Survey (NLTCS)—84 percent versus 72 percent. The NLTCS included husbands as well as sons, thus increasing the proportion of males. In addition, fewer of the caregivers in this study and in the Abel study were 65 years of age and older because both studies focused exclusively on adult children. Because of convenience sampling, this study included only whites. In addition, in comparison to the Abel study, this study and the NLTCS contained a higher proportion of caregivers with minor children in the home (22 percent and 21 percent compared to 4 percent) and a higher proportion of those who co-resided with the elder (60 percent and 61 percent versus 25 percent). Finally, because all of the caregivers must have worked outside of the home

Table 1
Description of the Sample of Caregivers (percentage)
(N=50)

	Study Sample	Abel Study	National Long-Term Care Survey
Class			
Middle class	52	n.a.	n.a.
Working class	48	n.a.	n.a.
Gender			
Female	84	100	72
(Daughters	64)		
(Daughters-in-Law	20)		
Male	16	0	28
Age (in years)			
14–44	18	18	22
45–64	76	78	42
65–74	6	4	26
75+	0	0	10
Marital status			
Married	58	67	70
Nonmarried	42	33	30
Race			
White	100	94	80
Other	0	6	20
Presence of minor children in home			
Yes	22	4	21
No	78	96	79
Employment status			
Currently working	74	53	31
Not currently working	26	47	69
Living arrangement			
Lives with parent	60	25	61
Lives separately	40	75	39

Table 1 (continued)

	Study Sample	Abel Study	National Long-Term Care Survey
Length of caregiving			
Less than 1 year	14	6	18
1–4 years	60	49	44
5 years or more	20	39	20
Parent died less than one year ago	6	n.a.	n.a.
No longer giving care	0	6	16
Number of ADLs elder needs help with			
0	0	19	3
1–2	44	41	32
3–4	24	21	23
5–6	32	20	42

at some point during caregiving, this sample contained a higher percentage of employed caregivers (74 percent versus 53 percent and 31 percent). (The status of those not working is discussed in chapter 5.) These similarities to existing data sets suggest the relative representativeness of this study, despite the small sample size.

Slightly more than half of the caregivers (52 percent) in this study were middle class; the remaining 48 percent were working class. The majority were female, 64 percent daughters and 20 percent daughters-in-law. The remaining 16 percent were sons. The sons were not married to the daughters-in-law in this study; they are distinct families. Over half (60 percent) lived with their parent; in all cases, the parent lived with the child rather than vice versa, although two of the sons bought their parents' homes. The majority of the caregivers were not novices. While over half had provided care for one to four years, only 14 percent had provided care for less than a year. Although not included in Table 1, all of the caregivers lived in close proximity to their parent (i.e., within a twenty-minute drive). Where it is relevant to individual cases, the proximity of siblings is included in the text.

PROCEDURES

Once the criteria for selection were decided on, I began the process of recruiting participants. I attended four series of caregiver support group meetings in two metropolitan areas in central New England. The purpose of attending the sessions was explained to the group leaders beforehand, and their permission was secured. These support groups were advertised in local newspapers and on the bulletin boards in the Geriatric Centers of local hospitals. While two of the support groups were intended to be informational (e.g., bringing in speakers to lecture on such topics as caring for Alzheimer's patients, navigating local social service agencies, and protecting parents' assets) as well as a forum for discussion, the other two support groups were exclusively for discussion.

After attending several sessions, I explained the nature of the study to the caregivers and asked for volunteers. Between 16 and 83 percent of the caregivers agreed to participate. The lower rates of participation correspond to the informational support groups where caregivers went to gather information on available resources and on the necessary procedures to access those resources. Caregivers were then contacted from the list of volunteers to verify criteria selection.

Another method used to recruit participants required the assistance of two local adult day health centers. I asked the directors at each center to phone the caregivers of their clients (adult children and children-in-law only) and inquire whether they would willing to be interviewed. The directors provided a list of caregivers who had both worked and not worked while caregiving since some of the caregivers could have worked before sending their parent to the adult day health center. In one center, 83 percent of the adult children contacted agreed to participate. In the second center, the comparable figure was 80 percent. It is quite likely that the initial contact made by center staff, those with whom the caregiver had a working relationship, increased the degree of compliance.

Finally, I asked the caregivers themselves, local clergy, colleagues, and friends and neighbors to provide the names of people who might be willing to participate. These "informants" were also asked to contact the person and to explain to them that they would be called. This method resulted in 100 percent compliance. This confirms earlier suspicions that asking persons known to the participant to make the initial contact would increase their willingness to participate in the study.

Data were collected in two metropolitan areas in central New England. Caregivers were recruited equally through the three sources: caregiver support groups, adult day health centers, and word-of-mouth. That is, one-third of the caregivers came from each of the three sources (N = 16, 18, and 16, respectively). I varied the method by which participants were recruited to increase the generalizability of the results. A convenience sample such as this one is not intended to be representative of the nation, but it can be used to describe processes and patterns that are likely to occur. Sons and daughters-in-law were oversampled in order to achieve a sufficient number of respondents. Sons-in-law providing regular assistance, however, could not be located. Ten additional family members were interviewed when they were available (including two parents, five spouses, and three children) to supplement information from the caregiver.

Once the participants had been selected, I contacted them and arranged a meeting time at the caregivers' convenience. I conducted forty open-ended interviews; ten interviews were conducted by a research assistant after training to ensure consistency in the recording of information and the delivery of questions. All except three interviews, which took place at a local restaurant or at the caregiver's workplace, were conducted at the caregiver's home. In only one instance was another family member present. However, this caregiver and her husband argued so extensively that his presence did not shape her responses; she was clear in her own personal view. In a second instance, a family member was present for part of the interview; questions that were asked of the caregiver during that period were asked a second time to make sure there was no additional information or clarification.

Based on feminist interviewing methodology (Reinharz, 1992), participants were asked a series of open-ended questions and were allowed to explain their answers in their own words rather than using externally imposed categories and questions that potentially limit information. Careful listening also allowed me to probe more effectively by introducing additional questions as the interview proceeded. Such interviewing is at least partially "interviewee-guided." Other researchers have noted the need for such studies in caregiving (Abel, 1991; Brody, 1990) and in social science research in general (Patton, 1990; Reinharz, 1992).

Topics for the questionnaire came from definitive hypotheses based on issues raised during the caregiver support group meetings (which served as in-situ focus groups) and my own prior research using secondary data analysis (Merrill, 1990, 1993). The key constructs focused on included how caregivers were selected, conflict among siblings, effect on work and leisure, and how the caregiving career had changed over time. Also examined were the elderly parent's medical history and the tasks and amount of time that each member of the family provided. The following are sample questions: (1) Have you continued to ask your siblings for assistance? If so, how have they responded? (2) Does there continue to be conflict between you and your siblings? What do you think is the cause of the conflict?

A followup interview was conducted approximately eighteen to twenty-four months after the original survey for a subsample of the caregivers in order to examine the caregiving career. Twenty out of the original fifty caregivers were randomly selected to examine whether and how the following had changed over time: parent's health status, caregiving tasks provided by the respondent, division of labor with siblings, conflict with siblings, effect on work and work accommodation, effect on family, and general well-being. Only a subsample of caregivers were interviewed due to time constraints.

Of those randomly selected, seventeen were interviewed a second time. Two of the caregivers could not be located. Among those, Deborah's father was still at the adult day health center, although he was no longer living with Deborah. The contact person at the center stated that Alfred had improved since his fall two years ago, but that he probably should not be living alone. Another caregiver reported that she did not have the time after having to cancel several appointments.

Approximately three-quarters of the interviews were audiotaped. In situations where the respondent showed any hesitancy in being taped, I wrote down the answers word-for-word as closely as possible and then immediately transcribed the interview with as much detail as possible. In analyzing the results, these cases did not appear to have any less detail than those that were recorded.

DATA ANALYSIS

Content analysis was used to examine the data. After reading all of the responses for a particular question, themes were identified. Cases were divided according to the presence or absence of that theme or placed into multiple categories derived from the theme. Often this was a multileveled process resulting in increasingly fine distinctions across cases.

The following is an example of this procedure. The caregivers were asked, "What about your brothers and sisters? What task(s) or form of help does each sibling provide? Let's start with your brother (or sister) _____ ." After reading all of the responses, categories were formed based on the type and frequency of the tasks performed and whether they were intended to occasionally substitute for or regularly complement the work of the primary caregiver. One group of caregivers, defined as "being in a network," had at least one sibling who provided hands-on assistance on a regular basis and usually other siblings who complemented the primary caregiver by providing more circumscribed help such as taking a parent for doctors' appointments. Other caregivers in this category had siblings who rotated care, taking alternate shifts for the same care. The second category included children whose siblings provided "some care," although it was a substitute for what the primary caregiver occasionally could not do. Siblings might help with the laundry or substitute for the primary caregiver when he or she was unavailable, but they were seen as "helpers" to the primary caregiver. The third category consisted of siblings who provided "little or no help," including those who had furnished some service in the past, such as staying with the parent during a special event that the caregiver wanted to attend (e.g., a wedding). Such care was infrequent, usually not more than once a year.

There was some evidence that the results of this study were both valid and reliable. The second wave of data collection began by requesting a description of the caregiving situation at the time of the first interview. Similar descriptions were collected during the followup, suggesting that the measuring instruments were reliable. In addition, in the original survey, five or six of the more central questions were asked several ways to ensure validity. For example, caregivers were asked, "If you could think of it as a series of steps, please describe the process by which you became a caregiver." As a check, they were again asked, "*How* were you selected to be the caregiver?" Results were consistent across questions.

LIMITATIONS OF THE SAMPLE

The sample had several scientific limitations. The first was its uniqueness. For example, 67 percent of the sample had a parent in adult day health one or more days a week. This sample was unusual in that a large proportion had access to these services, which were not common in all areas of the country. Other caregivers had family members, in-laws, or the other parent, who could provide care at least partially while they were at work. What this suggests though is that these features are necessary for caregivers to be able to combine work and caregiving. Many of the caregivers intimated that without access to adult day health, for example, they would have to put their parent into a nursing home.

Another potential bias of this sample is that all of the caregivers agreed to take the time to be interviewed. Thus, those caregivers who were having more difficulty combining work and caregiving might be less likely to volunteer because they did not have the time. However, all of the caregivers were extremely busy and mentioned having little or no free time. The interviews were possible because they were done at the sole convenience of the caregiver.

Bibliography

Abel, Emily K. (1990). "Family Care of the Frail Elderly." In E. Abel and M. Nelson (eds.), *Circles of Care* (pp. 63– 91). Albany, NY: SUNY Press.

Abel, Emily K. (1991). *Who Cares for the Elderly? Public Policy and the Experience of Adult Daughters*. Philadelphia: Temple University Press.

Aging in America. (1991). Prepared by the U.S. Senate Special Committee on Aging, American Association of Retired Persons, Federal Council on the Aging, and the U.S. Administration on Aging.

Albert, Steven M., Moss, Miriam, and Lawton, M. Powell. (1993). "The Significance of the Self-Perceived Start of Caregiving." Paper presented to the Gerontological Society of America, November, New Orleans.

Aldous, Joan. (1994). "Someone to Watch over Me: Family Responsibilities and Their Realization Across Family Lives." In Eva Kahana, David Biegel, and May Wykle (eds.), *Family Caregiving Across the Lifespan* (pp. 42– 68). Thousand Oaks, CA: Sage Publications.

Allan, Graham. (1979). *A Sociology of Friendship and Kinship*. Boston: George Allen and Unwin.

Allan, Graham. (1989). *Friendship: Developing a Sociological Perspective*. Boulder, CO: Westview Press.

Altschuler, Joanne, Jacobs, Susan, and Shiode, Deena. (1985). "Psychodynamic Time-limited Groups for Adult Children of Aging Parents." *American Journal of Orthopsychiatry* 53: 397–403.

Anderson, Nancy N., Patten, Sharon, and Greenberg, Jay N. (1980). *A Comparison of Home Care and Nursing Home Care for Older Persons in Minnesota, Vol. III Summary.* University of Minnesota.

Aneshensel, Carol S., Pearlin, Leonard I., Mullan, Joseph T., Zarit, Steven H., and Whitlatch, Carol J. (1995). *Profiles in Caregiving: The Unexpected Career.* San Diego, CA: Academic Press.

Archbold, Patricia G. (1983). "Impact of Parent-caring on Women." *Family Relations* 32: 39–45.

Atchley, Robert C. (1994). *Social Forces and Aging* (7th ed.). Belmont, CA: Wadsworth Publishing Co.

Barresi, Charles M., and Stull, Donald E. (1993). "Ethnicity and Long-Term Care: An Overview." In *Ethnic Elderly and Long-Term Care* (pp. 3–21). New York: Springer Publishing Co.

Bedford, Victoria H. (1989). "A Comparison of Thematic Apperceptions of Sibling Affiliation, Conflict, and Separation at Two Periods of Adulthood." *International Journal of Aging and Human Development* 28: 53–65.

Bedford, Victoria H. (1992). "Memories of Parental Favoritism and the Quality of Parent-Child Ties in Adulthood." *The Journals of Gerontology: Social Sciences* 47: S149–S155.

Bedford, Victoria H. (1995). "Sibling Relationships in Middle and Old Age." In Rosemary Blieszner and Victoria H. Bedford (eds.), *Handbook of Aging and the Family* (pp. 201–222). Westport, CT: Greenwood Press.

Bedford, Victoria H., and Gold, Deborah T. (1989). "Siblings in Old Age: A Forgotten Relationship." *The American Behavioral Scientist* 33: 19–32.

Blieszner, Rosemary, and Bedford, Victoria H. (eds.). (1995). *Handbook of Aging and the Family.* Westport, CT: Greenwood Press.

Bowers, Barbara. (1988). "Family Perceptions of Care in a Nursing Home." *The Gerontologist* 28(3): 361–368.

Boyd, Sandra L., and Treas, Judith. (1996). "Family Care of the Frail Elderly: A New Look at Women in the Middle." In Jill Quadagno and Debra Street (eds.), *Aging for the Twenty-First Century* (pp. 262–268). New York: St. Martin's Press.

Brady, E. M., and Noberini, M. R. (1987). "Sibling Support in the Context of a Model of Sibling Solidarity." Presented at the 95th Annual Meeting of the American Psychological Association, New York, August.

Braithwaite, Valerie. (1996). "Understanding Stress in Informal Caregiving." *Research on Aging* 18(2): 139–174.

Brody, Elaine M. (1981). " 'Women in the Middle' and Family Help to Older People." *The Gerontologist* 21(5): 471–479.

Brody, Elaine M. (1985). "Parent Care as a Normative Family Stress." *The Gerontologist* 25: 19–29.

Brody, Elaine M. (1990). *Women in the Middle: Their Parent-Care Years.* New York: Springer Publishing Co.

Brody, Elaine M. (1995). "Prospects for Family Caregiving: Response to Change, Continuity, and Diversity." In Rosalie A. Kane and Joan D. Penrod (eds.), *Family Caregiving in an Aging Society: Policy Perspectives* (pp. 15–28). Thousand Oaks, CA: Sage Publications.

Brody, Elaine M., Kleban, Morton, Johnsen, Pauline, Hoffman, Christine, and Schoonover, Claire. (1987). "Work Status and Parent Care: A Comparison of Four Groups of Women." *The Gerontologist* 27: 201–208

Brody, Elaine M., Litvin, Sandra J., Albert, Steven M., and Hoffman, Christine J. (1994). "Marital Status of Daughters and Patterns of Parent Care." *The Journals of Gerontology: Social Sciences* 49(2): S95–S103.

Brody, Elaine M., Litvin, Sandra J., Hoffman, Christine, and Kleban, Morton H. (1992). "Differential Effects of Daughters' Marital Status on Their Parent Care Experiences." *The Gerontologist* 32(1): 58–67.

Brody, Elaine M., and Schoonover, Claire B. (1986). "Patterns of Parent Care When Adult Daughters Work and When They Do Not." *The Gerontologist* 26(4): 372–381.

Brubaker, Ellie, and Brubaker, Timothy H. (1995). "Critical Policy Issues." In Gregory C. Smith, Sheldon S. Tobin, Elizabeth Anne Robertson-Tchabo, and Paul W. Power (eds.), *Strengthening Aging Families: Diversity in Practice and Policy* (pp. 235–247). Thousand Oaks, CA: Sage Publications.

Brubaker, Timothy H. (1985). *Later Life Families.* Newbury Park, CA: Sage Publications.

Burgio, Louis D., and Burgio, Kathryn L. (1990). "Institutional Staff Training and Management: A Review of the Literature and a Model for Geriatric, Long-term Care Facilities." *International Journal of Aging and Human Development* 30(4): 287–302.

Burris, Beverly H. (1991). "Employed Mothers: The Impact of Class and Marital Status on the Prioritizing of Family and Work." *Social Science Quarterly* 72(1): 50–66.

Burton, Linda (ed.). (1993). *Families and Aging.* Amityville, NY: Baywood Publishing Co.

Cantor, Marjorie. (1975). "Life Space and the Social Support System of the Inner City Elderly of New York City." *The Gerontologist* 15: 23–27.

Cantor, Marjorie. (1979). "Neighbors and Friends: An Overlooked Resource in the Informal Support System." *Research on Aging* 1: 434–463.

Cantor, Marjorie. (1983). "Strain Among Caregivers: A Study of Experience in the United States." *The Gerontologist* 23(6): 597–604.

Cantor, Marjorie. (1993). "Families and Caregiving in an Aging Society." In Linda Burton (ed.), *Families and Aging* (pp. 135–144). Amityville, NY: Baywood Publishing Co.

Cantor, Marjorie, and Little, Virginia. (1985). "Aging and Social Care." In Robert Binstock and Ethel Shanas (eds.), *Handbook of Aging and the Social Sciences* (pp. 745–781). New York: Van Nostrand Reinhold Co.

Chappell, Neena L. (1991). "Living Arrangements and Sources of Caregiving." *The Journals of Gerontology: Social Sciences* 46(1): S1–S8.

Cicirelli, Victor G. (1983). "Adult Children's Attachment and Helping Behavior to Elderly Parents: A Path Model." *Journal of Marriage and the Family* 45: 815–824.

Cicirelli, Victor G. (1985). "The Role of Siblings as Family Caregivers." In William Sauer and Raymond Coward (eds.), *Social Support Networks and the Care of the Elderly* (pp. 93–107). New York: Springer Publishing Co.

Cicirelli, Victor G. (1991). "Sibling Relationships in Adulthood." *Marriage and Family Review* 16(3–4): 291–310.

Cicirelli, Victor G. (1992). *Family Caregiving: Autonomous and Paternalistic Decision Making*. Newbury Park, CA: Sage Publications.

Clark, Phillip G. (1993). "Public Policy in the United States and Canada: Individualism, Familial Obligation, and Collective Responsibility in the Care of the Elderly." In Jon Hendricks and Carolyn Rosenthal (eds.), *The Remainder of Their Days: Domestic Policy and Older Families in the United States and Canada* (pp. 13–48). New York: Garland Publishing.

Clipp, Elizabeth C., and George, Linda K. (1990). "Caregiver Needs and Patterns of Social Support." *The Journals of Gerontology: Social Sciences* 45: 102–111.

Cohler, Bertram J., and Altergott, Karen. (1995). "The Family of the Second Half of Life: Connecting Theories and Findings." In Rosemary Blieszner and Victoria Hilkevitch Bedford (eds.), *Handbook of Aging and the Family* (pp. 59–94). Westport, CT: Greenwood Press.

Connidis, Ingrid Arnet. (1994). "Sibling Support in Older Age." *The Journals of Gerontology: Social Sciences* 49(6): S309–S317.

Cotterill, Pamela. (1994). *Friendly Relations? Mothers and Their Daughters-in-Law*. London: Taylor-Francis.

Coward, Raymond T. (1987). "Factors Associated with the Configuration of the Helping Networks of Noninstitutionalized Elders." *Gerontological Social Work* 10: 113–132.

Coward, Raymond T., and Dwyer, Jeffrey W. (1990). "The Association of Gender, Sibling Network Composition, and Patterns of Parent Care by Adult Children." *Research on Aging* 12: 158–181.

Coward, Raymond T., Horne, Claydell, and Dwyer, Jeffrey W. (1992). "Demographic Perspectives on Gender and Family Caregiving." In Jeffrey W. Dwyer and Raymond T. Coward (eds.), *Gender, Families, and Elder Care* (pp. 18–33). Newbury Park, CA: Sage Publications.

Cramer, James. (1980). "Fertility and Female Employment: Problems of Causal Direction." *American Sociological Review* 45: 167–190.

Day, Alice. (1985). "Who Cares? Demographic Trends Challenge Family Care for the Elderly." *Population Trends and Public Policy* No. 9, Population Reference Bureau.

Deimling, Gary, and Bass, David. (1986). "Symptoms of Mental Impairment Among Elderly Adults and Their Effects on Family Caregivers." *The Journals of Gerontology: Social Sciences* 41: 778–785.

Dwyer, Jeffrey W., and Coward, Raymond T. (1991). "A Multivariate Comparison of the Involvement of Adult Sons Versus Daughters in the Care of Impaired Parents." *The Journals of Gerontology: Social Sciences* 46(5): S259– 269.

Dwyer, Jeffrey W., and Henretta, John C. (1994). "The Impact of Early Life Course Transitions on Long-Term Care Outcomes." Paper presented at the annual meeting of the American Sociological Association, August, Los Angeles, California.

Dwyer, Jeffrey W., Henretta, John C., Coward, Raymond T., and Barton, Amy J. (1992). "Changes in the Helping Behaviors of Adult Children as Caregivers." *Research on Aging* 14: 351–375.

Elder, Glen. (1992). "The Life Course." In E.Borgatta and M. Borgatta (eds.), *Encyclopedia of Sociology* (pp. 1120– 1130). New York: Macmillan.

Eshleman, J. Ross. (1994). *The Family: An Introduction* (7th ed.). Boston: Allyn and Bacon.

Esman, Marjorie R. (1985). *Henderson, Louisiana: Cultural Adaptation in a Cajun Community*. New York: Holt, Rinehart, and Winston.

Feinberg, Lynn Friss, and Kelly, Kathleen A. (1995). "A Well-Deserved Break: Respite Programs Offered by California's Statewide System of Caregiver Resource Centers." *The Gerontologist* 35(5): 701–706.

Ferber, Marianne A., and O'Farrell, Brigid (with La Rue Allen). (1991). *Work and Family: Policies for a Changing Work Force*. Washington, D.C.: National Academy Press.

Fischer, Claude S. (1982). *To Dwell Among Friends: Personal Networks in Town and City*. Chicago: University of Chicago Press.

Fischer, Lucy Rose. (1986). *Linked Lives: Adult Daughters and Their Mothers*. New York: Harper and Row.

Frankfather, Dwight L., Smith, Michael J., and Caro, Francis G. (1983). "Designs for Home-Care Entitlements." In Robert Perlman (ed.), *Family Home Care: Critical Issues for Services and Policies* (pp. 264–279). New York: Haworth Press.

Franklin, Susan T., Ames, Barbara D., and King, Sharon. (1994). "Acquiring the Family Eldercare Role: Influence on Female Employment Adaptation." *Research on Aging* 16(1): 27–42.

Franks, Melissa M., and Stephens, Mary Ann Parris. (1996). "Social Support in the Context of Caregiving: Husbands' Provision of Support to Wives Involved in Parent Care." *The Journals of Gerontology: Psychological Sciences* 51B(1): P43–P52.

Gallagher, Sally. (1994). "Doing Their Share: Comparing Patterns of Help Given by Older and Younger Adults." *Journal of Marriage and the Family* 56: 567–578.

Gardner, Saundra. (1991). "Exploring the Family Album: Social Class Differences in Images of Family Life." *Sociological Inquiry* 61(2): 242–251.

Gaumer, G. L., and Stavins, J. (1992). "Medicare Use in the Last Ninety Days of Life." *Health Services Research* 26(6): 725–742.

George, Linda K., and Gwyther, Lisa P. (1986). "A Multi-Dimensional Examination of Family Caregivers of Demented Adults." *The Gerontologist* 26: 253–259.

Gibeau, Janice (1986). *Breadwinners and Caregivers: Working Patterns of Women Working Full-Time and Caring for Dependent Elderly Family Members*. Waltham, MA: Brandeis University.

Given, Barbara A., and Given, Charles W. (1991). "Family Caregiving for the Elderly." *Annual Review of Nursing Research* 9: 77–101.

Glazer, Nona Y. (1993). *Women's Paid and Unpaid Labor: The Work Transfer in Health Care and Retailing*. Philadelphia: Temple University Press.

Goetting, Ann. (1986). "The Developmental Tasks of Siblingship over the Life Cycle." *Journal of Marriage and the Family* 48(4): 703–714.

Gold, Deborah T. (1989a). "Sibling Relationships in Old Age: A Typology." *International Journal of Aging and Human Development* 28: 37–51.

Gold, Deborah T. (1989b). "Generational Solidarity: Conceptual Antecedents and Consequences." *American Behavioral Scientist* 33: 19–32.

Gottlieb, Benjamin, Kelloway, Kevin, and Fraboni, Maryann. (1994). "Aspects of Eldercare That Place Employees at Risk." *The Gerontologist* 34(6): 815–821.

Greene, Vernon L. and Coleman, Patricia D. (1995). "Direct Service for Family Caregivers: Next Steps for Public Policy." In Rosalie A. Kane and Joan D. Penrod (eds.), *Family Caregiving in an Aging Society: Policy Perspectives* (pp. 46–63). Thousand Oaks, CA: Sage Publications.

Hagestad, Gunhild O., and Neugarten, Bernice L. (1985). "Age and the Life Course." In Robert Binstock and Ethel Shanas (eds.), *Handbook of Aging and the Social Sciences* (2nd ed.) (pp. 35–61). New York: Van Nostrand Reinhold Co.

Hamon, Raeann R., and Blieszner, Rosemary. (1990). "Filial Responsibility Expectations Among Adult Child-Older Parent Pairs." *Journal of Gerontology* 45(3): 110–112.

Harrington, Charlene, Newcomer, Robert J., Estes, Carroll L., and Associates. (1985). *Long Term Care of the Elderly: Public Policy Issues.* Beverly Hills, CA: Sage Publications.

Hill, Reuben. (1970). *Family Development in Three Generations.* Cambridge, MA: Schenkman.

Himes, Christine L. (1994). "Parental Caregiving by Adult Women: A Demographic Perspective." *Research on Aging* 16(2): 191–211.

Hochschild, Arlie R. (1989). *The Second Shift: Working Parents and the Revolution at Home.* New York: Viking Press.

Hollingsworth, J. Rogers, and Hollingsworth, Ellen Jane (eds). (1994). *Care of the Chronically and Severely Ill: Comparative Social Policies.* New York: Aldine de Gruyter.

Horowitz, Amy. (1985a). "Family Caregiving to the Frail Elderly." In M. Powell Lawton and George Maddox (eds.), *Annual Review of Gerontology and Geriatrics* (pp. 194–246). New York: Springer Publishing Co.

Horowitz, Amy. (1985b). "Sons and Daughters as Caregivers to Older Parents: Differences in Role Performance and Consequences." *The Gerontologist* 25(6): 612–617.

Horowitz, Amy, and Dobrof, Rose. (1982). *The Role of Families in Providing Long Term Care to the Frail and Chronically Ill Elderly Living in the Community.* Final report submitted to the Health Care Financing Administration (Grant no. 18–P–9754/2–02). Washington, DC.

Horowitz, Amy, and Shindleman, L. W. (1983). "Reciprocity and Affection: Past Influences on Current Caregiving." *Journal of Gerontological Social Work* 5: 5–20.

Hoyert, Donna L. (1991). "Financial and Household Exchanges Between Generations." *Research on Aging* 13: 205–225.

Hughes, Everett C. (1963). *French Canada in Transition.* Chicago: University of Chicago Press.

Ikels, Charlotte. (1983). "The Process of Caretaker Selection." *Research on Aging* 5: 491–509.

Johnson, Colleen L. (1983). "Dyadic Family Relations and Social Support." *The Gerontologist* 23: 377–383.

Johnson, Colleen L. (1985). *Growing Up and Growing Old in Italian-American Families.* New Brunswick, NJ: Rutgers University Press.

Johnson, Colleen L. (1995). "Cultural Diversity in the Late-Life Family." In Rosemary Blieszner and Victoria Hilkevitch Bedford (eds.), *Handbook of Aging and the Family* (pp. 307–331). Westport, CT: Greenwood Press.

Johnson, Colleen L., and Catalano, Donald J. (1983). "A Longitudinal Study of Family Supports to the Impaired Elderly." *The Gerontologist* 23: 612–618.

Johnson, Thomas. (1995). "Utilizing Culture in Work with Aging Families." In Gregory C. Smith, Sheldon S. Tobin, Elizabeth Anne Robertson-Tchabo, and Paul W. Power (eds.), *Strengthening Aging Families: Diversity in Practice and Policy* (pp. 175–201). Thousand Oaks, CA: Sage Publications.

Kahana, Eva, Biegel, David E., and Wykle, May L. (1994). *Family Caregiving Across the Lifespan*. Thousand Oaks, CA: Sage Publications.

Kahana, Eva, Kahana, Boaz, Johnson, J. Randal, Hammond, Ronald J., and Kercher, Kyle. (1994). "Developmental Challenges and Family Caregiving: Bridging Concepts and Research." In Eva Kahana, David E. Biegel, and May L. Wykle (eds.), *Family Caregiving Across the Lifespan* (pp. 3–41). Thousand Oaks, CA: Sage Publications.

Kane, Rosalie A., and Penrod, Joan D. (eds.). (1995). *Family Caregiving in an Aging Society: Policy Perspectives*. Thousand Oaks, CA: Sage Publications.

Kaye, Lenard W., and Applegate, Jeffrey S. (1990). *Men as Caregivers to the Elderly*. Lexington, MA: Lexington Books.

Kemper, Peter. (1988). "The Evaluation of the National Long Term Care Demonstration." *Health Services Research*. 23(1): 161–173.

Kerbo, Harold. (1991). "Social Stratification in the United States." In *Social Stratification and Inequality: Class Conflict in Historical and Comparative Perspective* (2nd ed.) (pp. 177–193). New York: McGraw Hill.

Kingson, Eric R. (1988). "Generational Equity: An Unexpected Opportunity to Broaden the Politics of Aging." *The Gerontologist* 28: 765–772.

Kinnear, D., and Graycar, A. (1984). "Aging and Family Dependency." *Australian Journal of Social Issues* 19: 13–25.

Kinsella, Kevin. (1995). "Aging and the Family: Present and Future Demographic Issues." In Rosemary Blieszner and Victoria Hilkevitch Bedford (eds.), *Handbook of Aging and the Family* (pp. 32–56). Westport, CT: Greenwood Press.

Kleban, Morton H., Brody, Elaine M., Schoonover, Claire B., and Hoffman, Christine. (1989). "Family Help to the Elderly: Perceptions of Sons-in-Law Regarding Parent Care." *Journal of Marriage and the Family* 51: 303–312.

Koch, Tom. (1990). *Mirrored Lives: Aging Children and Elderly Parents*. New York: Praeger Publishers.

Kosberg, Jordan I. (1992). *Family Care of the Elderly: Social and Cultural Changes*. Thousand Oaks, CA: Sage Publications.

Kramer, Betty, and Kipnis, Stuart. (1995). "Eldercare and Work-Role Conflict: Toward an Understanding of Gender Differences in Caregiver Burden." *The Gerontologist* 35(3): 340–348.

Krause, Neal. (1991). "Stress and Isolation from Close Ties in Later Life." *The Journals of Gerontology: Social Sciences* 46: S183–S194.

Krause, Neal. (1994). "Stressors in Salient Social Roles and Well-Being in Later Life." *The Journals of Gerontology: Psychological Sciences* 49: P137–P148.

Krause, Neal, and Borawski-Clark, Elaine. (1995). "Social Class Differences in Social Support Among Older Adults." *The Gerontologist* 35(4): 498–508.

Lang, Abigail, and Brody, Elaine. (1983). "Characteristics of Middle-Aged Daughters and Help to Their Elderly Mothers." *Journal of Marriage and the Family* 45(1): 193–202.

Langman, Lauren. (1987). "Social Stratification." In Marvin B. Sussman and Suzanne K. Steinmetz (eds.), *Handbook of Marriage and the Family* (pp. 211–247). New York: Plenum Press.

Lawton, Leora, Silverstein, Merril, and Bengtson, Vern L. (1994). "Solidarity Between Generations in Families." In Vern L. Bengtson and Robert A. Harootyan (eds.), *Intergenerational Linkages: Hidden Connections in American Society* (pp. 19–42). New York: Springer Publishing.

Lawton, M. Powell, Rajagopal, Doris, Brody, Elaine, and Kleban, Morton. (1992). "The Dynamics of Caregiving for a Demented Elder Among Black and White Families." *The Journals of Gerontology: Social Sciences* 47: S156–S164.

Lee, Gary R. (1992). "Gender Differences in Parent Care: A Fact in Search of a Theory." In Jeffrey W. Dwyer and Raymond T. Coward (eds.), *Gender, Families, and Elder Care* (pp. 120–131). Newbury Park, CA: Sage Publications.

Lee, Gary R., Dwyer, Jeffrey W., and Coward, Raymond T. (1993). "Gender Differences in Parent Care: Demographic Factors and Same-Gender Differences." *The Journals of Gerontology: Social Sciences* 48(1): S9–S16.

Lee, Gary R., Netzer, Julie, and Coward, Raymond. (1994). "Filial Responsibility Expectations and Patterns of Intergenerational Assistance." *Journal of Marriage and the Family* 56: 559–565.

Lerner, Melvin J., Somers, Darryl G., Reid, David, Chiriboga, David, and Tierney, Mary. (1991). "Adult Children as Caregivers: Egocentric Biases in Judgments of Sibling Contributions." *The Gerontologist* 31(6): 746–755.

Levesque, Louise, Cossette, Sylvie, and Laurin, Liane. (1995). "A Multi-dimensional Examination of the Psychological and Social Well-Being of Caregivers of a Demented Relative." *Research on Aging* 17(3): 332–360.

Lewis, J. (1987). "Daughters Caring for Mothers." Technical Report to the Rockefeller Foundation, London School of Economics.

Lieberman, Morton, and Fisher, Lawrence. (1995). "The Impact of Chronic Illness on the Health and Well-being of Family Members." *The Gerontologist* 35(1): 94–102.

Lin, Ge, and Rogerson, Peter A. (1995). "Elderly Parents and the Geographical Availability of Their Adult Children." *Research on Aging* 17(3): 303–331.

Linn, Margaret W., Linn, Bernard S., and Stein, Shayna. (1989). "Effect of Nursing Home Staff Training on Quality of Patient Survival." *International Journal of Aging and Human Development* 28(4): 305–315.

Linsk, Nathan L., Keigher, Sharon M., England, Suzanne E., and Simon-Rusinowitz, Lori. (1995). In Rosalie A. Kane and Joan D. Penrod (eds.), *Family Caregiving in an Aging Society: Policy Perspectives* (pp. 64–91). Thousand Oaks, CA: Sage Publications.

Lowenthal, Marjorie F., Thurnher, Majda, and Chiriboga, David. (1975). *Four Stages of Life*. San Francisco, CA: Jossey-Bass.

Magnus, M. (1988). "Eldercare: Corporate Awareness, But Little Action." *Personnel Journal* 67: 19–23.

Markides, Kyriakos S. (1995). "Aging and Ethnicity." *The Gerontologist* 35(2): 276–277.

Markides, Kyriakos S., and Mindel, Charles H. (1987). *Aging and Ethnicity*. Newbury Park, CA: Sage Publications.

Mattessich, Paul, and Hill, Reuben. (1987). "Life Cycle and Family Development." In Marvin B. Sussman and Suzanne K. Steinmetz (eds.), *Handbook of Marriage and the Family* (pp. 437–469). New York: Plenum Press.

Matthews, Sarah H. (1995). "Gender and the Division of Filial Responsibility Between Lone Sisters and Their Brothers." *The Journals of Gerontology: Social Sciences* 50B(5): S312–S320.

Matthews, Sarah H., and Rosner, Tena Tarler. (1988). "Shared Filial Responsibility: The Family as the Primary Caregiver." *Journal of Marriage and the Family* 50: 185–195.

Matthews, Sarah H., Werkner, Janet, and Delaney, Paula. (1989). "Relative Contributions of Help by Employed and Non-Employed Sisters to Their Elderly Parents." *The Journals of Gerontology: Social Sciences* 44(1): S36–44.

Maugans, Jayne E. (1994). *Aging Parents, Ambivalent Baby Boomers: A Critical Approach to Gerontology*. Dix Hills, NY: General Hall.

McAdoo, Harriet Pipes. (1993). *Family Ethnicity: Strength in Diversity*. Newbury Park, CA: Sage.

Merrill, Deborah M. (1990). "The Tradeoff Between Caregiving and Employment for Familial Caregivers of the Disabled Elderly." Unpublished doctoral dissertation, Brown University.

Merrill, Deborah M. (1993). "Daughters-in-Law as Caregivers to the Elderly." *Research on Aging* 15(1): 70–91.

Merrill, Deborah M. (1996). "Conflict and Cooperation Among Adult Siblings During the Transition to the Role of Filial Caregiver." *Journal of Social and Personal Relationships* 13(3): 399–413.

Miller, Baila, Campbell, Richard, Farran, Carol, Kaufman, Julie, and Davis, Lucille. (1995). "Race, Control, Mastery, and Caregiver Stress." *The Journals of Gerontology: Social Sciences* 50B(6): S374–S382.

Miller, Baila, McFall, Stephanie, and Campbell, Richard T. (1994). "Changes in Sources of Community Long Term Care Among African American and White Frail Older Persons." *The Journals of Gerontology: Social Sciences* 49(1): S14–S24.

Moen, Phyllis. (1992). *Women's Two Roles: A Contemporary Dilemma.* New York: Auburn House.

Moen, Phyllis. (1994). "Women, Work, and Family: A Sociological Perspective on Changing Roles." In Matilda White Riley, Robert L. Kahn, and Anne Foner (eds.), *Age and Structural Lag* (pp. 151–170). New York: John Wiley and Sons.

Moen, Phyllis, Robison, Julie, and Dempster-McClain, Donna. (1995). "Caregiving and Women's Well-Being: A Life Course Approach." *Journal of Health and Social Behavior* 36: 259–273.

Montgomery, Rhonda J. V. (1992). "Gender Differences in Patterns of Child-Parent Caregiving Relationships." In Jeffrey W. Dwyer and Raymond T. Coward (eds.), *Gender, Families, and Elder Care* (pp. 65–83). Newbury Park, CA: Sage Publications.

Montgomery, Rhonda J. V. (1995). "Examining Respite Care: Promises and Limitations." In Rosalie A. Kane and Joan D. Penrod (eds.), *Caregiving in an Aging Society: Policy Perspectives* (pp. 29–45). Thousand Oaks, CA: Sage Publications.

Montgomery, Rhonda J. V., Gonyea, J. G. and Hooyman, N. R. (1985). "Caregiving and the Experience of Subjective and Objective Burden." *Family Relations* 34: 19–26.

Montgomery, Rhonda J. V., and Kamo, Y. (1989). "Parent Care by Sons and Daughters." In J. A. Mancini (ed.), *Aging Parents and Adult Children* (pp. 213–230). Lexington, MA: Lexington Books.

Mor, V., Stalker, M. Z., Gralla, R., Scher, H. I., Cimma, C., Park, D., Flaherty, A. M., Kiss, M., Nelson, P., Laliberte, L., Schwartz, R., Marks, P. A., and Oettgen, H. F. (1988). "Day Hospital as an Alternative to Inpatient Care for Cancer Patients: A Random Assignment Trial." *Journal of Clinical Epidemiology* 41(8): 771–785.

Morris, Robert. (1983). "Caring for Vulnerable Family Members: Alternative Policy Options." In Robert Perlman (ed.), *Family Home Care: Critical Issues for Services and Policies* (pp. 244–263). New York: Haworth Press.

Mui, Ada. (1995). "Caring for Frail Elderly Parents: A Comparison of Adult Sons and Daughters." *The Gerontologist* 35(1): 86–93.

Murrell, Stanley A., and Norris, Fran H. (1991). "Differential Social Support and Life Change as Contributors to the Social Class-Distress Relationship in Older Adults." *Psychology and Aging* 6: 223–231.

Mutran, Elizabeth. (1985). "Intergenerational Family Support Among Blacks and Whites: Response to Culture or to Socioeconomic Differences." *The Journals of Gerontology: Social Sciences* 40: 382–389.

Mutschler, Phyllis M. (1994). "From Executive Suite to Production Line: How Employees in Different Occupations Manage Elder Care Responsibilities." *Research on Aging* 16(1): 7–26.

Myers, D. R., and Dickerson, B. E. (1990). "Intragenerational Interdependence Among Older, Low-Income African American, Mexican American, and Anglo Siblings." *Family Perspective* 24: 217–243.

Neal, Margaret B., Chapman, Nancy J., Ingersoll-Dayton, Berit, and Emlen, Arthur. (1993). *Balancing Work and Caregiving for Children, Adults, and Elders.* Newbury Park, CA: Sage Publications.

Newman, Katherine S. (1993). *Declining Fortunes.* New York: Basic Books.

Noelker, Linda S., and Poulshock, S. Walter. (1982). *The Effects on Families of Caring for Impaired Elderly in Residence.* Final report of AoA grant number 90–AR–2112. Cleveland, OH: Benjamin Rose Institute.

Noelker, Linda S., and Townsend, Aloen L. (1987). "Perceived Caregiving Effectiveness: The Impact of Parental Impairment, Community Resources, and Caregiver Characteristics." In Timothy H. Brubaker (ed.), *Aging, Health, and Family: Long Term Care* (pp. 58–79). Newbury Park, CA: Sage Publications.

Olson, Miriam Meltzer. (1989). "Family Participation in Posthospital Care: Women's Work." *Journal of Psychosocial Oncology* 7(1/2): 77–93.

Oppenheimer, Valerie Kincade. (1981). "The Changing Nature of Life Cycle Squeezes: Implications for the Socioeconomic Position of the Elderly." In James March (ed.), *Aging Stability and Change in the Family* (pp. 47–81). New York: Academic Press.

Patton, Michael Quinn. (1990). *Qualitative Evaluation and Research Methods* (2nd ed.). Newbury Park, CA: Sage Publications.

Pearlin, Leonard I. (1992). "The Careers of Caregivers." *The Gerontologist* 32: 647.

Penrod, Joan D., Kane, Rosalie A., Kane, Robert L., and Finch, Michael D. (1995). "Who Cares: The Size, Scope, and Composition of the Caregiver Support System." *The Gerontologist* 35(4): 489–497.

Perlman, Robert (ed.). (1983). *Family Home Care: Critical Issues for Services and Policies.* New York: Haworth Press.

Pratt, Clara, Schmall, Vicki, and Wright, Scott. (1987). "Ethical Concerns of Family Caregivers to Dementia Patients." *The Gerontologist* 27(5): 632–638.

Pruchno, Rachel, and Resch, Nancy. (1989). "Husbands and Wives as Caregivers: Antecedents of Depression and Burden." *The Gerontologist* 29(2): 159–165.

Pyke, Karen D., and Bengtson, Vern L. (1996). "Caring More or Less: Individualistic and Collectivist Systems of Family Eldercare." *Journal of Marriage and the Family* 58: 379–392.

Quadagno, Jill, Sims, Cebra, Squier, D. Ann, and Walker, Georgia. (1987). "Long-Term Care Community Services and Family Caregiving." In Timothy H. Brubaker (ed.), *Aging, Health, and Family: Long-Term Care* (pp. 116–128). Newbury Park, CA: Sage Publications.

Qureshi, Hazel, and Walker, Alan. (1989). *The Caring Relationship: Elderly People and Their Families*. London: Macmillan.

Reinharz, Shulamit. (1992). "Feminist Interview Research." In *Feminist Methods in Social Research* (pp. 18–45). Oxford: Oxford University Press.

Reiss, David. (1981). *The Family's Construction of Reality*. Cambridge, MA: Harvard University Press.

Riley, Matilda White, Kahn, Robert L., and Foner, Anne. (1994). *Age and Structural Lag*. New York: John Wiley and Sons.

Riley, Matilda White, and Riley, John W., Jr. (1993a). "Age and Opportunity Structures." Presented to the Eastern Sociological Society, Boston, MA, March.

Riley, Matilda White, and Riley, John W., Jr. (1993b). "Connections: Kin and Cohort." In Vern L. Bengtson and W. Andrew Achenbaum (eds.), *The Changing Contract Across Generations* (pp. 169–189). New York: Aldine de Gruyter.

Rivlin, Alice M., and Wiener, Joshua M. (1988). *Caring for the Disabled Elderly: Who Will Pay?* Washington, DC: Brookings Institution.

Robison, Julie, Moen, Phyllis, and Dempster-McClain, Donna. (1995). "Women's Caregiving: Changing Profiles and Pathways." *The Journals of Gerontology: Social Sciences* 50B(6): S362–S373.

Rosenthal, Carolyn. (1986). "Family Supports in Later Life: Does Ethnicity Make a Difference?" *The Gerontologist* 26(1): 19–24.

Rosenthal, Carolyn J., and Dawson, Peter. (1992). "Families and the Institutionalized Elderly." In G.M.M. Jones and B.M.L. Miessen (eds.), *Caregiving in Dementia: Research and Applications* (pp. 398–418). New York: Tavistock/Routledge.

Rosenthal, Carolyn J., Matthews, Sarah H., and Marshall, Victor W. (1991). "Is Parent Care Normative? The Experiences of a Sample of Middle-Aged Women." In Beth B. Hess and Elizabeth W. Markson (eds.), *Growing*

Old in America (pp. 427–440). New Brunswick, NJ: Transaction Publishers.

Rosenthal, Carolyn J., Sulman, Joanne, and Marshall, Victor W. (1993). "Depressive Symptoms in Family Caregivers of Long-Stay Patients." *The Gerontologist* 33: 249–257.

Rossi, Alice S., and Rossi, Peter H. (1990). *Of Human Bonding: Parent-Child Relations Across the Life Course.* New York: Aldine de Gruyter.

Rubin, Lillian B. (1976). *Worlds of Pain: Life in the Working-Class Family.* New York: HarperCollins.

Rubin, Lillian B. (1994). *Families on the Fault Line.* New York: HarperCollins.

Ryff, Carol D., and Seltzer, Marsha Mailick. (1995). "Family Relations and Individual Development in Adulthood and Aging." In Rosemary Blieszner and Victoria Hilkevitch Bedford (eds.), *Handbook of Aging and the Family* (pp. 95–113). Westport, CT: Greenwood Press.

Scharlach, Andrew. (1994). "Caregiving and Employment: Competing or Complementary Roles?" *The Gerontologist* 34(3): 378–385.

Scharlach, Andrew, and Boyd, Sandra. (1989). "Caregiving and Employment: Results of an Employee Survey." *The Gerontologist* 29(3): 382–387.

Scharlach, Andrew, Sobel, Eugene L., and Roberts, Robert E. L. (1991). "Employment and Caregiver Strain: An Integrative Model." *The Gerontologist* 31(6): 778–787.

Schoonover, Claire, and Brody, Elaine. (1986). "Patterns of Parent Care When Adult Daughters Work and When They Do Not." *The Gerontologist* 26(4): 372–381.

Seccombe, Karen. (1992). "Employment, the Family, and Employer-Based Policies." In Jeffrey Dwyer and Raymond Coward (eds.), *Gender, Families, and Elder Care* (pp. 165–180). Newbury Park, CA: Sage Publications.

Shanas, Ethel. (1979a). "Social Myth as Hypothesis: The Case of the Family Relations of Old People." *The Gerontologist* 19: 3–9.

Shanas, Ethel. (1979b). "The Family as a Social Support System in Old Age." *The Gerontologist* 19(2): 169–174.

Shaughnessy, Peter W., and Kramer, Andrew M. (1990). "The Increased Needs of Patients in Nursing Homes and Patients Receiving Home Health Care." *New England Journal of Medicine* 322: 21–27.

Silverstein, Merril, Parrott, Tonya M., and Bengtson, Vern L. (1995). "Factors That Predispose Middle-Aged Sons and Daughters to Provide Social Support to Older Parents." *Journal of Marriage and the Family* 57: 465–475.

Smith, Gregory C., Tobin, Sheldon S., Robertson-Tchabo, Elizabeth Anne, and Power, Paul W. (eds.). (1995). *Strengthening Aging Families: Diversity in Practice and Policy.* Thousand Oaks, CA: Sage Publications.

Smith-Lovin, Lynn, and Tickamyer, Ann. (1978). "Nonrecursive Models of Labor Force Participation, Fertility Behavior, and Sex Role Attitudes." *American Sociological Review* 43: 541–556.

Smyer, Michael, Brannon, Diane, and Cohn, Margaret. (1992). "Improving Nursing Home Care Through Training and Job Redesign." *The Gerontologist* 32: 327–333.

Snyder, Barbara, and Keefe, Kathy. (1985). "The Unmet Needs of Family Caregivers for Frail and Disabled Adults." *Social Work in Health Care* 10: 1–14.

Sokolovsky, Jay. (1990). "Bringing Culture Back Home: Ethnicity, Aging, and Family Support." In *The Cultural Context of Aging: Worldwide Perspectives*. New York: Bergin and Garvey.

Sokolovsky, Jay, and Cohen, C. I. (1981). "Measuring Social Interaction of the Urban Elderly: A Methodological Synthesis." *International Journal of Aging and Human Development* 13: 233–244.

Soldo, Beth J., Agree, Emily M., and Wolfe, Douglas A. (1989). "The Balance Between Formal and Informal Care." In Marcia G. Ory and Kathleen Bond (eds.), *Aging and Health Care: Social Science and Policy Perspectives*. New York: Routledge.

Soldo, Beth, and Myllyluoma, Jaana. (1983). "Caregivers Who Live with Dependent Elderly." *The Gerontologist* 23(6): 605–611.

Spitze, Glenna, and Logan, John. (1990). "Sons, Daughters, and Intergenerational Social Support." *Journal of Marriage and the Family* 52: 420–430.

Squier, D. Ann, and Quadagno, Jill. (1988). "The Italian American Family." In C. H. Mindel, R. W. Haberstein, and W. Roosevelt, Jr. (eds.), *Ethnic Families in America* (pp. 109–137). New York: Elsevier.

Starkman, Elaine Marcus. (1993). *Learning to Sit in the Silence: A Journal of Caretaking*. Watsonville, CA: Papier-Mache Press.

Starrels, Marjorie E., Ingersoll-Dayton, Berit, Neal, Margaret, and Yamada, Hiroko. (1995). "Intergenerational Solidarity and the Workplace: Employees' Caregiving for their Parents." *Journal of Marriage and the Family* 57: 751–762.

Stern, Steven. (1996). "Measuring Child Work and Residence Adjustments to Parents' Long-Term Care Needs." *The Gerontologist* 36(1): 76–87.

Stoller, Eleanor Palo. (1983). "Parental Caregiving by Adult Children." *Journal of Marriage and the Family* 45: 851–858.

Stoller, Eleanor Palo. (1989). "Formal Services and Informal Helping: The Myth of Service Substitution." *Journal of Applied Gerontology* 8: 37–52.

Stoller, Eleano Palo. (1990). "Males as Helpers: The Roles of Sons, Relatives, and Friends." *The Gerontologist* 30: 228–235.

Stoller, Eleanor Palo, Forster, Lorna Earl, and Duniho, Tamara Sutin. (1992). "Systems of Parent Care Within Siblings Networks." *Research on Aging* 14(1): 28–49.

Stoller, Eleanor Palo, and Gibson, Rose Campbell. (1994). *Worlds of Difference: Inequality in the Aging Experience*. Thousand Oaks, CA: Pine Forge Press.

Stoller, Eleanor Palo, and Pugliesi, Karen. (1989). "Other Roles of Caregivers: Competing Responsibilities or Supportive Services." *The Journals of Gerontology: Social Sciences* 44(6): S231–S238.

Stolzenberg, Ross, and Waite, Linda. (1977). "Age, Fertility Expectations and Plans for Employment." *American Sociological Review* 42: 769–783.

Stommel, Manfred, Given, Barbara A., Given, Charles W., and Collins, Clare. (1995). "The Impact of the Frequency of Care Activities on the Division of Labor Between Primary Caregivers and Other Care Providers." *Research on Aging* 17(4): 412–433.

Stone, Robyn, Cafferata, Gail Lee, and Sangl, Judith. (1987). "Caregivers of the Frail Elderly: A National Profile." *The Gerontologist* 27(5): 616–626.

Stone, Robyn, and Short, Pamela Farley. (1990). "The Competing Demands of Employment and Informal Caregiving to Disabled Elders." *Medical Care* 28(6): 513–526.

Strawbridge, William J., and Wallhagen, Margaret I. (1991). "Impact of Family Conflict on Adult Child Caregivers." *The Gerontologist* 31(6): 770–777.

Stueve, Ann, and O'Donnell, Lydia. (1989). "Interactions Between Women and Their Elderly Parents: Constraints of Daughters Employment." *Research on Aging* 11(3): 331–353.

Stull, Donald E. (1993). "Ethnic Seniors' Preferences for Long-Term Care Services and Financing: A Case for an Informed Choice." In Charles M. Barresi and Donald E. Stull (eds.), *Ethnic Elderly and Long-Term Care* (pp. 264–278). New York: Springer Publishing Co.

Suitor, J. Jill, and Pillemer, Karl. (1994). "Family Caregiving and Marital Satisfaction: Findings from a One Year Panel Study of Women Caring for Parents with Dementia." *Journal of Marriage and the Family* 56: 681–690.

Suitor, J. Jill, Pillemer, Karl, Keeton, Shirley, and Robison, Julie. (1995). "Aged Parents and Aging Children: Determinants of Relationship Quality." In Rosemary Blieszner and Victoria Hilkevitch Bedford (eds.), *Handbook of Aging and the Family* (pp. 223–242). Westport, CT: Greenwood Press.

Sussman, Marvin B. (1988). "The Isolated Nuclear Family: Fact or Fiction." In Suzanne K. Steinmetz (ed.), *Family and Support Systems Across the Life Span* (pp. 1–30). New York: Plenum Press.

Talbott, Maria M. (1990). "The Negative Side of the Relationship Between Older Widows and Their Adult Children: The Mothers' Perspective." *The Gerontologist* 30(5): 595–603.

Tennstedt, Sharon L., Crawford, S. L., and McKinlay, John B. (1993). "Is Family Care on the Decline? A Longitudinal Investigation of the Substitution of

Formal Long-term Care Services for Informal Care." *The Milbank Quarterly* 71: 601–624.

Tennstedt, Sharon L., McKinlay, John, and Sullivan, Lisa. (1989). "Informal Care for Frail Elders: The Role of Secondary Caregiver." *The Gerontologist* 29: 677–683.

Thompson, Edward H., Futterman, Andrew M., Gallagher-Thompson, Dolores, Rose, Jonathon M., and Lovett, Steven B. (1993). "Social Support and Caregiving Burden in Family Caregivers of Frail Elders." *The Journals of Gerontology: Social Sciences* 48(5): S245–S254.

Toseland, Ronald W., Smith, Gregory, and McCallion, Phillip. (1995). "Supporting the Family in Elder Care." In Gregory C. Smith, Sheldon S. Tobin, Elizabeth Anne Robertson-Tchabo, and Paul W. Power (eds.), *Strengthening Aging Families: Diversity in Practice and Policy* (pp. 3–24). Thousand Oaks, CA: Sage Publications.

Townsend, Aloen L., and Noelker, Linda S. (1987). "The Impact of Family Relationships on Perceived Caregiving Effectiveness." In Timothy H. Brubaker (ed.), *Aging, Health, and Family* (pp. 80–99). Newbury Park, CA: Sage Publications.

Townsend, Aloen L., Noelker, Linda S., Deimling, Gary, and Bass, David. (1989). "Longitudinal Impact of Interhousehold Caregiving on Adult Children's Mental Health." *Psychology and Aging* 4: 393–401.

The Travelers Companies. (1985). *The Travelers Employee Caregiver Survey: A Survey on Caregiving Responsibilities of Travelers Employees for Older Americans.* Hartford, CT: The Travelers.

Treas, Judith. (1977). "Family Support Systems for the Aged." *The Gerontologist* 17(6): 486–491.

Turner, R. Jay, and Marino, Franco. (1994). "Social Support and Social Structure: A Descriptive Epidemiology." *Journal of Health and Social Behavior* 35(3): 193–212.

Uchino, Bert N., Kiecolt-Glaser, Janice K., and Cacioppo, John T. (1992). "Age-Related Changes in Cardiovascular Response as a Function of a Chronic Stressor and Social Support." *Journal of Personality and Social Psychology* 54: 1063–1070.

Uhlenberg, Peter, and Cooney, Teresa M. (1990). "Family Size and Mother-Child Relations in Later Life." *The Gerontologist* 30(5): 618–625.

Verbrugge, Lois M. (1982). "Work Satisfaction and Physical Health." *Journal of Community Health* 7: 262–283.

Voydanoff, Patricia. (1987). *Work and Family Life.* Newbury Park, CA: Sage Publications.

Wagner, Donna L. (1991). "Eldercare: A Workplace Issue." In Beth B. Hess and Elizabeth W. Markson (eds.), *Growing Old in America* (pp. 377–387). New Brunswick, NJ: Transaction Publishers.

Wagner, Donna L., Creedon, M. A., Sasala, J. M., and Neal, M. B. (1989). *Employees and Eldercare: Designing Effective Responses for the Workplace*. Bridgeport, CT: University of Bridgeport, Center for the Study of Aging.

Waite, Linda, and Stolzenberg, Ross. (1976). "Intended Childbearing and Labor Force Participation of Young Women: Insights from Nonrecursive Models." *American Sociological Review* 41: 235–252.

Walker, A. (1983). "Care for Elderly People: A Conflict Between Women and the State." In J. Finch and D. Groves (eds.), *A Labour of Love: Women, Work, and Caring* (pp. 106–128). London: Routledge and Kegan Paul.

Walker, Alan. (1996). "The Relationship Between the Family and the State in the Care of Older People." In Jill Quadagno and Debra Street (eds.), *Aging for the Twenty-First Century* (pp. 269–285). New York: St. Martin's Press.

Walker, Alexis J., and Allen, Katherine R. (1991). "Relationships Between Caregiving Daughters and Their Elderly Mothers." *The Gerontologist* 31(3): 389–396.

Walker, Alexis J., Martin, Sally S. K., and Jones, Laura L. (1992). "The Benefits and Costs of Caregiving and Care Receiving for Daughters and Mothers." *The Journals of Gerontology: Social Sciences* 47(3): S130–S139.

Walker, Alexis J., and Pratt, Clara C. (1991). "Daughters' Help to Mothers: Intergenerational Aid Versus Caregiving." *Journal of Marriage and the Family* 53: 3–12.

Wallace, Steven P., and Estes, Carroll L. (1989). "Health Policy for the Elderly: Federal Policy and Institutional Change." In R. C. Rist (ed.), *Policy Issues for the 1990's: Policy Studies Review Annual*, Vol. 9 (pp. 591–613). New Brunswick, NJ: Transaction Books.

Webster, Pamela, and Herzog, Regula. (1995). "Effects of Parental Divorce and Memories of Family Problems on Relationships Between Adult Children and Their Parents." *The Journals of Gerontology: Social Sciences* 50B(1): S24–S34.

Weeks, J., and Cuellar, J. (1981). "The Role of Family Members in the Helping Networks of Older People." *The Gerontologist* 21: 338–394.

Whitbeck, Les, Hoyt, Danny R., and Huck, Shirley M. (1994). "Early Family Relationships, Intergenerational Solidarity, and Support Provided to Parents by Their Adult Children." *The Journals of Gerontology: Social Sciences* 49(2): S85–S94.

White, Lynn. (1994). "Growing Up with Single Parents and Stepparents: Long Term Effects on Family Solidarity." *Journal of Marriage and the Family* 56: 935–948.

Whitfield, S. and Krompholz, B. (1981). *The Family Support Demonstration Project*. Annapolis: State of Maryland, Office on Aging.

Wilson, H. S. (1989). "Family Caregiving for a Relative with Alzheimer's Dementia: Coping with Negative Choices." *Nursing Research* 38: 94–98.

Winton, Chester A. (1995). *Frameworks for Studying Families*. Guilford, CT: Dushkin Publishing Group.

Woolfson, Peter. (1996). "Cross-Cultural Families: The Franco Americans." In Jill Quadagno and Debra Street (eds.), *Aging for the Twenty-First Century: Readings in Social Gerontology* (pp. 119–127). New York: St. Martin's Press.

Wright, F. (1983). "Single Careers: Employment, Housework, and Caring." In J. Finch and D. Groves (eds.), *A Labour of Love: Women, Working, and Caring* (pp. 89–105). London: Routledge and Kegan Paul.

Zarit, S. H., Todd, P. A., and Zarit, J. M. (1986). "Subjective Burden of Husbands and Wives as Caregivers: A Longitudinal Study," *The Gerontologist* 26: 260–266.

Index

About the Author

DEBORAH M. MERRILL is Assistant Professor of Sociology at Clark University. Over the past several years she has published articles in both gerontology and family studies.

ISBN 0-86569-269-6

LAKE COUNTY PUBLIC LIBRARY
INDIANA

AD	FF	MU
AV	GR	NC
BO	HI	SJ
CL	HO	CN L JUL 2 0 98
DS	LS	

THIS BOOK IS RENEWABLE BY PHONE OR IN PERSON IF THERE IS NO RESERVE
WAITING OR FINE DUE.

LCP #0390